Personal Knowledge and Beyond

Personal Knowledge and Beyond

Reshaping the Ethnography of Religion

EDITED BY

James V. Spickard, J. Shawn Landres, and Meredith B. McGuire

New York University Press

NEW YORK AND LONDON

NEW YORK UNIVERSITY PRESS
New York and London

Library of Congress Cataloging-in Publication Data
Personal knowledge and beyond : reshaping the ethnography of religion /
edited by James V. Spickard, J. Shawn Landres, Meredith B. McGuire.
p. cm.
Includes bibliographical references and index.
ISBN 0–8147–9802–0 (alk. paper) —
ISBN 0–8147–9803–9 (pbk. : alk. paper)
1. Religion—Methodology.   2. Ethnology—Methodology.
3. Ethnology—Religious aspects.   I. Spickard, James V.
II. Landres, J. Shawn   III. McGuire, Meredith B.
BL41 .P468 2002
306.6'07'2—dc21   2001004688

New York University Press books are printed on acid-free paper,
and their binding materials are chosen for strength and durability.

Manufactured in the United States of America
10 9 8 7 6 5 4 3 2 1

For Otto Maduro

Contents

Introduction: Whither Ethnography? Transforming the
Social-Scientific Study of Religion   1
    James V. Spickard and J. Shawn Landres

PART I   Being an Ethnographer

1   Truth, Subjectivity, and Ethnographic Research   17
    Lynn Davidman

2   From the Heart of My Laptop: Personal Passion and
    Research on Violence against Women   27
    Nancy Nason-Clark

3   Walking between the Worlds: Permeable Boundaries,
    Ambiguous Identities   33
    Mary Jo Neitz

4   Dancing on the Fence: Researching Lesbian, Gay,
    Bisexual, and Transgender Christians   47
    Melissa M. Wilcox

PART II   Doing Ethnography

5   Between the Living and the Dead: Fieldwork, History,
    and the Interpreter's Position   63
    Thomas A. Tweed

6   "But Are They Really Christian?" Contesting
    Knowledge and Identity in and out of the Field   75
    Simon Coleman

7   Transitional Identities: Self, Other, and the
    Ethnographic Process   88
    Janet L. Jacobs

8   Being (in) the Field: Defining Ethnography in
     Southern California and Central Slovakia   100
     J. Shawn Landres

9   Encountering Latina Mobilization: Field Research on the
     U.S./Mexico Border   113
     Milagros Peña

PART III   Writing and Reading Ethnography

10   Writing about "the Other," Revisited   127
     Karen McCarthy Brown

11   "There's Power in the Blood": Writing Serpent Handling
     as Everyday Life   134
     Jim Birckhead

12   Voicing Spiritualities: Anchored Composites as an
     Approach to Understanding Religious Commitment   146
     Marion S. Goldman

13   Against Univocality: Re-reading Ethnographies of
     Conservative Protestant Women   162
     Julie Ingersoll

14   A Conscious Connection to All That Is: *The Color Purple*
     as Subversive and Critical Ethnography   175
     Cheryl Townsend Gilkes

PART IV   Beyond Personal Knowledge

15   New-Old Directions in the Social Scientific Study
     of Religion: Ethnography, Phenomenology, and
     the Human Body   195
     Meredith B. McGuire

16   Greening Ethnography and the Study of Religion   212
     Laurel Kearns

17   As the Other Sees Us: On Reciprocity and Mutual
     Reflection in the Study of Native American Religions   225
     Armin W. Geertz

18 On the Epistemology of Post-Colonial Ethnography 237
        James V. Spickard

    References 253
    Contributors 275
    Index 281

Introduction

Whither Ethnography? Transforming the Social-Scientific Study of Religion

James V. Spickard and J. Shawn Landres

> The choice is not between regretting the past and em-
> bracing the future. Nor is it between the anthropologist
> as hero and as the very model of a postmodern major
> general. It is between, on the one hand, sustaining a re-
> search tradition upon which a discipline, "soft" and
> half-formed perhaps but morally essential, has been
> built and, on the other, "displacing," "reworking," "rene-
> gotiating," "reimagining," or "reinventing" that tradi-
> tion, in favor of a more "multiply centered," "pluralis-
> tic," "dialogical" approach, one which sees poking into
> the lives of people who are not in a position to poke into
> yours as something of a colonial relic.
>
> —Clifford Geertz (1998, 72)

Locating Ethnography

There has long been a methodological divide in the social-scientific study of religion. On one side, there have been "the generalizers": those who use polling data and membership lists to present the overall trends of religious life. On the other side, there have been "the particularizers": those who show us the minute details of specific religions, letting us see their concrete effects on small numbers of people. The former tell us what kind of people are religious and how they are religious, and let us know what accompanies their religious behavior. The latter explore what religion means to the individuals they interview, how they make sense of it, and how they use it to make sense of their world. As Jürgen Habermas (1968) showed over thirty years ago, these two styles are each valuable, though for different ends. They arise out of complementary human interests. The first comes from a desire to find lawlike regularities in human life; the second stems from a wish to understand how particular people see the world.

Generalizing inquiry seeks the rules of social life, the laws of social motion, to paraphrase Marx, by which we can better understand human life in general. Its prime focus is on "How?": How do religions form? How do they change over time? How do they attract members? How do they lose them? Such questions are best posed comparatively, so scholars using this approach look for the patterns behind disparate cases. Statistical researchers, for example, try to generalize from persons to populations. Anthropological ethnologists, to take a second example, catalog traits from many cultures to see if they can find the rules that govern such combinations. Each treats individual cases only to the extent that they illustrate wider trends. Generalizing social science believes that truth is found in such patterns, not details.

Particularizers do not look for such general social laws but seek to understand specific communities of people. They focus on people's intentions: Why do these people say they do what they do? What are they intending when they pray? What do they mean when they say they are serving "God" or "the gods"? Such questions help them to understand individuals and communities rather than explaining whole societies. They may even have wider significance—indeed, many contemporary particularizers connect the patterns they find in their local sites to society at large. Nevertheless, particularizers keep their informants front and center. They remain focused on a specific time and place; their findings are set in history rather than transcending it. These scholars do not tell us what people-in-general do, but tell us what some people do in the particular community that they have observed. Only afterward do they consider how these details relate to the whole. This is a different intellectual product—one that focuses on human meaning, not laws and patterns.

Ethnographers are good examples of such particularizers, for they choose a specific research locale, which they spend several years getting to know. It might be a New York synagogue (Davidman 1991), a Chicago Catholic parish (Neitz 1987), a Japanese healing cult (Spickard 1991a), or a particular practitioner of Haitian Vodou (K. Brown 1991). Or ethnographers might study networks of Appalachian snake handlers (Birckhead 1997), Cuban-exile visitors to a Miami shrine (Tweed 1997a), or professional women who joined the Rajneesh movement (Goldman 1999). They listen and watch, question, think, and listen again—always trying to make sense of their informants' lives. Whether their topic is a foreign pilgrimage site or the church next door, whether the resulting prose is academic or popular, the ethnographer has "been there." Their research succeeds when they can portray the natives as if from the inside.

There are, of course, other terms that capture this "generalizing" vs. "particularizing" divide—if not exactly as we have framed it here, at least from related angles. Besides the "ethnology" vs. "ethnography" pair just mentioned, anthropologists have distinguished "nomothetic" from "ideographic" and "etic" from "emic" as basic approaches to social life (Harris 1968). Sociologists have preferred terms like "comparative" vs. "descriptive," though they have lately embraced "ethnography" as well.[1] Although these sets are not identical, the first term generally implies a wish to find society's underlying rules, while the second term implies a wish to understand a social or cultural scene in its full individuality.

Particularizers traditionally have held less status than generalizers in the social-scientific study of religion and have been outnumbered by them, though this is now changing. Quantitative sociologists and psychologists have historically ruled the field, and they get their data from surveys, not from the minutiae of religious life. These generalizers have long claimed their broad results to be more authoritative in the development of general theories of religion. Academic anthropology has been the ethnographers' haunt, but few anthropologists attend the meetings of such groups as the Association for the Sociology of Religion, the Society for the Scientific Study of Religion, and the Religious Research Association (to name just the three most prominent in North America). Few anthropologists write for their journals, and religion-specific groups of anthropologists have been slow to form. The fact that the American Anthropological Association usually meets at the same time of year as the American Academy of Religion—and in a different city—does not help matters. Such institutional barriers have slowed ethnography's growth among scholars of the religious life.

On the other hand, a number of non-anthropologists who came of intellectual age during the 1970s and 1980s have come to value the ethnographic way. Seeing how different religions are from each other, they distrust premature generalization. The rapid growth of religious options in this period—from the flowering of new religions to the rise of the Christian Right—made ethnographic research all the more necessary, for too many standard survey questions were not relevant to these new faiths. For example, questions about "belief in God" are irrelevant to Buddhists, whose religion is orthopractical rather than orthodox. Surveys framed to fit traditional Christians not only missed much that mattered to other groups, but increasingly misunderstood new Christian groups as well. Many scholars realized that they could not write about religion-in-general without knowing more than they did about religion-in-particular. They found a need to understand meanings as well as patterns. This perception changed their research careers.

Feminism, too, had an impact. As Neitz (2000) notes, a commitment to putting women at the center of social analysis showed quite clearly how the world is experienced differently by women and men. Exploring this experience requires ethnography; it is not an accident that many—not all—of the most prominent contemporary ethnographers of religion are also feminist women. Not only have these new ethnographers—women and men—published widely, but they have also gained notice and position in the major professional groups. They have won important grants for research, charting the new religious landscape. Generalizers have come to rely on this work to enrich their questionnaires and statistical analyses. Ethnography's second-class status in the study of religion seems fated to end.

Criticizing Ethnography

Given this sea change, it is ironic that scholars of religion have started to adopt what they understand to be "standard" ethnographic practices, just when those practices have come under attack from anthropologists. If ethnography's rationale is "being there" and "knowing the natives," recent anthropological critics point out that these activities are rather problematic. Not only does mere presence not ensure insight (though no one ever thought it did), but also the very possibility of understanding others seems to have been lost. How much can one really know another people? How completely can one see the world through their eyes? Even if one can, how does one report such knowledge to readers, for whom ethnography's appeal may be a prurient exoticism rather than a sincere wish to encounter other people's lifeways?[2] Recent academic anthropology has seen a deluge of books and articles questioning the epistemological premises of such reporting.

Several issues stand out in this critique, of which we will only highlight four. These are: the problem of subjectivity; the insider/outsider problem; the question of researcher identity; and issues of power. They are among the many topics that our contributors treat in the chapters that follow.

First, quantitative researchers have long accused ethnographers of unthinkingly mixing their own thoughts and concerns with those of the people they study. How else, they ask, could one get two such different pictures of the same Mexican town as Robert Redfield's *Tepoztlán* (1930) and Oscar Lewis's *Life in a Mexican Village* (1951)? Yes, ethnography can present people's lives and religions in full color, but does that color not often come from the glasses that researchers wear, whether rose or blue?

Ethnographers have made various replies, the most honest of which admit the problem and offer ways to combat it. Some opt for methodological rigor, routinizing data collection to avoid bias— though this effort can produce such oddities as "ethnoscience," which limits people's worldviews to lists of terms. Others work as teams, in the hopes that several perspectives will be better than one—especially if the teams include members of the group under study. Still others freely admit their subjectivity, saying that no "objective" system can replace human insight, and do not claim their work to be anything other than fiction.

The problem is especially thorny for those studying religions, as religions are—among other things—systems of ideas that orient people to the cosmos. Religions tell their members what is real, what is important, and how to live in a world that gives them few ready-made guides. In addition, most religions claim that one worldview is better than others', that one is "right" and that others are at least partly "wrong." If ethnographers accept this claim, they must limit their work to recording exactly what the natives say. If they do more than this—if they try to explain what native thought is "really" about or put it in any sort of context—they implicitly claim this "really" for a more inclusive worldview. Yet, this amounts to positing a superior religion. On what intellectual basis can this be sustained?

The chapters by Davidman, Coleman, Landres, Birckhead, Goldman, and McGuire—among others—shed various lights on this problem of how ethnographers know what we know.

Second, similar questions arise about the ethnographer's relationship with the people under study—particularly about the ways in which such ties shape knowledge. The traditional model demands that the field-worker keep a strict social and intellectual distance from his or her subjects. As a rule, this model imagines an elite, Western researcher—often White and male—reporting on nonelite subalterns; the results are written for fellow elites, not for those whose lives are probed. How does this social dynamic slant one's results? Would informant-centered research be any less (or more) scientific? What boundaries between the analyst and the analyzed can—or should—be maintained? Does this vary according to the type of religion being studied? Such interpersonal issues pervade actual fieldwork, forcing the abandonment of a naïve "been there, seen that" view.

The nature of religion makes these questions especially biting. It is much easier to change one's religion than to change one's social class, nationality, ethnicity, and whole way of life. One can join the Assemblies of God, Chabad Lubavitch, or the Church of World Messianity without leaving one's family and day job—considerations that have prevented many anthropological ethnographers from staying with "their" far-off tribes. Does joining the group one is studying make a fieldworker's knowledge less—or more—authoritative? What kind of relationship with group members is most appropriate: personally, ethically, and for the production of knowledge? One can study the Nuer without becoming Nuer, but can one study evangelical Christianity without somehow "getting inside" the faith that defines it? Such questions have long bedeviled ethnographers, but scholars of religions find them particularly apposite.

The chapters by Neitz, Tweed, Coleman, Jacobs, Peña, Brown, and Birckhead all explore this issue from several angles.

Third, a somewhat different set of issues arises from the ethnographer's real or imputed social identity. Ethnographers have long noted that women and men have access to different social spheres, though this often lies unacknowledged in accounts that treat men's worlds as central and women's worlds as sideshows. However, age, ethnicity, sexual orientation, life experience, and one's own religious identity also shape what one can learn. Does it take a gay or lesbian researcher to investigate gay or lesbian religious worlds—either because this identity opens doors or because it primes one to notice things that straight researchers would miss? Does being Jewish give one access to—and help one understand—the religious response to oppression in a way that passes non-Jews by? What happens to one's ethnography if one discounts the role of identity by hiding behind the myth of the "universal" researcher? Or if one accents that identity, so much so that it overcomes all?

We can pose these questions from the other side: What happens to the ethnographer's identity in the research process? It is not news that anthropologists are changed by their fieldwork, though traditional accounts hid the details. What happens when ethnographers acknowledge the personal changes they have undergone and even use them as part of their data? Questions like these are taken up by most of our contributors and are central to the chapters by Davidman, Neitz, Wilcox, Tweed, Coleman, Jacobs, Landres, Peña, Brown, Birckhead, and McGuire.

Fourth, there are political issues. Ethnographic anthropology arose at the end of the nineteenth century to serve the needs of Western colonialism, as American, British, French, and Russian imperial bureaucrats wanted to avoid the shoals that had sunk their Spanish and Portuguese predecessors. The better they knew their subjects, they believed, the easier would be their sway. So they hired anthropologists: from James Mooney (1965), who investigated the Sioux Ghost Dance at the turn of the last century, through Evans-Pritchard (1940), who explored Nuer politics in the Sudan in the 1930s—and incidentally led native raids on the Italians (C. Geertz 1988)—to the less well-regarded 1960s anthropologists who fed the CIA data on the Pathet Lao (Horowitz 1974).

Sociological ethnography was born in the Chicago settlement houses; it was not interested in rule but in assimilation. How could the "socially disadvantaged" be made to join the middle-class world? Sociologists from W. F. Whyte (1943) to Elliot Liebow (1967) and their journalistic successors (e.g.: Kozol 1988; Kotlowitz 1991; Lemann 1992) have been guided by the sense that the first step in helping poor people was to know them. Their descriptions of gang members, Blacks, homeless families, and other social outsiders humanized such people to mainstream readers and thus helped support social programs to improve their lot. Too often, though, such ethnographies fed the semiconscious idea that given the right support and surroundings, the "disadvantaged" would become "just like us."

Again, the ethnographic study of religion is especially challenged, as it copes with a heritage in which nonmainstream faiths need to be explained. While the religions of the marginalized are no longer seen as just an irrational response to social dislocation, there is still a tendency to think of them as problematic. Thus, there are more ethnographies of

African American Pentecostalism than of the mainstream African Methodist Episcopal Church, more studies of new religions than of Episcopalians, and so on. We play to a popular fascination with "Others"— though the best ethnographies have used this fascination to question mainstream beliefs as well.

Though few ethnographers now work for colonial offices and settlement houses, their informants often still think that they represent governments and power centers. Despite ethical qualms, many take advantage of this, for such relative social power gives them access to information that others would be denied. As elites writing about nonelites for elite readers, their authorial styles most often suppress this sociopolitical context, but they do not reduce its importance. Is such ethnography not a "colonial relic," to use Clifford Geertz's term?

The chapters by Armin Geertz and by Spickard most directly confront this issue, though others (Neitz, Birckhead) touch on it too.

Anthropological Reactions

It is hard to exaggerate the impact that such concerns for knowledge, identity, and power have had on the anthropological establishment. The list of authors is staggering, as nearly every major figure has weighed in. Among others, Talal Asad (1973) and Eric Wolf (1982) unmasked the complicity of anthropologists in the colonial process. Edwin Ardener (1972), along with Michelle Rosaldo and Louise Lamphere (1974), exposed its male bias. Clifford Geertz's *Works and Lives* (1988) showed how rhetoric as much as fact shaped several classic ethnographies. Renato Rosaldo (1989) questioned the very idea of culture, on which traditional ethnographies were based. Akhil Gupta, James Ferguson, and their collaborators (1997) explored the politics of ethnographic settings.[3]

A closer look at just two such efforts shows some of the issues involved. Both *Writing Culture* (Clifford and Marcus 1986) and *After Writing Culture* (James, Hockey, and Dawson 1997) devote themselves to the "problem of representation." The former highlights the question of how ethnographies are written, while the latter focuses on the issue of what such writing really accomplishes. Among other things, contributors to the first volume note that "ethnographic truths are . . . inherently partial"

(1986, 7) rather than complete pictures of the societies they describe. They are "cooperative and collaborative" (127) rather than the results of the ethnographer's own disinterested vision. Ethnographic "representations are social facts" (256) that tell us as much about the observer's social location as they do about the natives. The ethical dilemma here is: How can I (as an ethnographer) be sure that I am really understanding the people that I study? Clifford, Marcus, and their colleagues conclude that one cannot guarantee anything, and so recommend showing readers the conceptual scaffolding that holds up one's narrative, so that one's work can be checked. They even recommend letting one's informants erect their own scaffolding—cutting out the middleman in the interests of getting a better picture.

In the second volume, James and her colleagues extend these epistemological concerns to politics, noting that ethnographers' reports can be put to some gruesome uses. Here the ethical dilemma runs: Why should it matter that I get it right? Because what I write will affect how "people like me" see the "Others," and that in turn will affect the decisions "people like me" make about these "Others"—whether to support them, rob them, or bomb them. As the "Others" can also read, my texts will as well affect how they see "people like me" and how they see themselves, though not in any simple or predictable way. In a post–Cold War, fin de siècle, multipolar world, we have to recognize both our interconnections and our mutual estrangement. "Getting it right" thus requires new sensibilities and new narrative forms that help capture a multivocal reality; even then, success is not guaranteed.

Indeed, the situation has evolved such that some scholars no longer think it possible to give a clear picture of their chosen people. Instead, they have become travel guides, midwives, or poets: the guides entertain us with the sights, the midwives help the natives express themselves, and the poets write about the ways that fieldwork has changed their own lives. Though it often fails to satisfy our curiosity about others, the new anthropology has the merit of being honest—and it no longer speaks in the imperial mode.

This provides but a taste of the current anthropological stew. From the feminist and ethnic critiques of the 1970s to the postmodernisms of today, anthropology has had to face its epistemological and political shortcomings. For most anthropologists, this identity crisis has made traditional ethnography impossible.

Studying Religion

Until now, such issues have not fully penetrated the social-scientific study of religion. Perhaps because they have long played second fiddle to the generalizers, or because they most often teach in departments of sociology and religious studies—out of reach of anthropology's crisis of confidence—that ethnographers of religion typically operate in the old style. They choose a religious locale, spend time (often very brief) with its inhabitants, listen, watch, question, think, listen again—and then they write reports telling us what goes on there. They neither guide us, nor midwife the natives, nor poet themselves; they simple tell us "the facts" about the religions they have studied. Too seldom do they acknowledge these facts' shaky foundations. Furthermore, some of those generalizers who have lately come to realize ethnography's virtues have decided to try their hand. They imitate their particularistic brethren, not realizing that they have missed the ethnographic criticisms of the intervening years.

This volume is dedicated to overturning such simplicity, as we seek to rethink the ethnographic study of religion in a new age. Ethnographers of religion face the same issues as do their anthropological cousins. "Doing ethnography" in the traditional way suppresses the social context of the ethnographic enterprise. It pretends that ethnographers know more than they do and imagines that their knowledge is somehow "better" and "more objective" than that produced by others. Moreover, it ignores ethnographers' relative social power—or at least ignores the ways in which their power shapes the social vision that one finds in their writing. In doing so, it misrepresents the religions it claims to describe.

Our authors are among those who have taken recent ethnographic discussions to heart, even if we do not agree on the right path forward. We come from varied fields but are all experienced researchers. As we reflect on our own work, we explore the consequences for the study of religion of rejecting the old ethnographic myths, along with the risks of forging new ones. In both a dialogue and a manifesto for change, we argue that current ethnographic practices in the study of religion are neither sufficiently reflective nor reflexive. We do not seek to exclude newcomers from the growing field of ethnography of religion; rather we seek to apprise them that the rules have changed and they are joining a different game from the one that they may have expected. The time has passed when one can do ethnography without reflecting on the issues we outline here, any more than one can do survey research without having first mastered statistics. We wish to give these issues a wider audience among scholars of religion than they have heretofore received.

We have organized the volume into four related sections. This is not a strict division, as the topics interpenetrate and we could have placed many of these chapters in more than one spot. However, each section stresses a part of the whole. The first section, *Being an Ethnographer*, focuses on issues of knowledge and identity. Lynn Davidman, Nancy Nason-Clark, Mary Jo Neitz, and Melissa Wilcox present revealing essays that show the personal side of ethnographic work. Davidman explores the role of subjectivity, showing how her own psychological processes helped her understand her subjects more deeply. Nason-Clark examines the role of emotion in the life of the academic researcher, as she confronts religious responses (or nonresponses) to violence against women. Neitz reflects on her own experiences studying a variety of religious groups and movements (including Catholic Charismatics and Wiccans); she suggests that the process of doing ethnographic research forces the researcher to assume multiple identities. Wilcox explores the effect of being both inside and outside the lesbian, gay, bisexual, transgender Christian community she investigated.

We have entitled the second section *Doing Ethnography*. Its contributors—Thomas Tweed, Simon Coleman, Janet Jacobs, Shawn Landres, and Milagros Peña—each describes ambiguities arising from his or her fieldwork. Tweed notes his own internal conflict between being both an historian and an ethnographer: the former does not give you enough information; the latter disrupts your life. Coleman explores the peculiarities of investigating Swedish Evangelical Christians, who are simultaneously investigating him. Landres argues that this play of mutual representations actually enhances fieldwork and demonstrates this with examples from his recent work in Slovakia and Southern California. Jacobs charts her growing awareness of her own ethnicity as she interviewed crypto-Jews, the hidden descendants of victims of the Spanish Inquisition. Peña shows the importance of border crossings—physical, ethnic, and conceptual—not just for herself, but for the Latina women activists she interviewed in El Paso/Ciudad Juárez.

The third section raises issues of *Writing and Reading Ethnography*. Karen McCarthy Brown reflects on her path-breaking use of first-person, experimental writing in her award-winning *Mama Lola* (1991). Jim Birckhead illustrates the difficulty of writing about Appalachian snake-handling ministers, given the fact that snake handling is simultaneously a small part of their everyday lives and the key identity that defines them to outsiders. Marion Goldman defends her use of "fictional" composite characters in her recent writing on the disciples of Rajneesh. Julie Ingersoll presents a critical reading of some recent ethnographies of conservative Protestant women, arguing that the claim that female submissiveness is somehow "empowering" silences the feminist women within these traditions. Cheryl Townsend Gilkes shows us how to read Alice Walker's *The Color Purple* as an ethnography of middle-class Black women in the 1920s South.

The four essays in the final section—*Beyond Personal Knowledge*—are all more programmatic than the foregoing. Meredith McGuire describes her return to an expanded phenomenology, as a way to deal with the issues of knowledge, identity, and power noted above. Laurel Kearns advocates an ethnographic attention to the environment, an influential factor largely ignored by past and present ethnographers of religion. Armin Geertz moves from the political complexities of research on indigenous peoples to an "ethnohermeneutics" that he hopes will breathe new life into ethnography. And Jim Spickard explores the epistemological underpinnings of current ethnographic practice, arguing that "post-colonial" ethnography has solved its political malaise by advocating two regulative ideals—"truth" and "equality"—rather than one, as did ethnography in its imperial mode.

Our volume is thus critical, but not one-sided. We do not accept without question the "displacing," "reworking," "renegotiating," "reinventing," style of ethnography to which Clifford Geertz refers above. This meta-narrative asks that ethnographers rethink their relationship to their informants and to their own society—an effort we support. Yet, calling this critique a "meta-narrative" highlights the fact that it, too, is as much myth as reality. The link between anthropology's grand theories and the actual process of fieldwork is still obscure. So is the applicability of much anthropological writing to other fields—particularly to the study of religion. What can ethnographers of religion learn about fieldwork from their anthropological cousins? What special issues do we face that others do not? What have we learned on our own, from which others might profit? This volume explores these and related questions.

We believe that the ethnography of religion must recognize the personal aspects of its knowledge: the fact that ethnographic knowledge is generated in interpersonal encounters between people with specific social locations. At the same time, ethnographic knowledge is not *only* personal; it aspires to something more. Finding that balance—encompassing personal knowledge but simultaneously going beyond it—seems to us to be the chief task facing ethnographers of religion today. Out of that belief comes the title of our volume.

Why Religion?

We have three reasons for thinking that the ethnographic study of religion is an ideal spot from which to pursue this aim. First, the study of religion is an interdisciplinary enterprise. Our authors are sociologists and anthropologists, culture theorists and historians, plus a number of specialists who fit none of these academic boxes; though divided by methodological or disciplinary background, all have something to contribute to understanding religion. They approach their varied fields with great epistemological diversity: feminist, postmodernist, postcolonialist, and critical-philosophical, to note merely a few. No topic but religion can bring such a breadth of perspectives; this stew gives richer fare than would any one or two ingredients alone. We have sought authors who challenge accepted wisdom, take intellectual risks, and can imagine new ways of doing things—who seek to be provocative without insisting that they have all the answers. Our essays are designed to make thoughtful reading.

Second, religious groups provide clear examples of the pitfalls and promises of ethnographic work—examples that are needed in a volume centered on the research process rather than any social group per se. Religions are complex enough that we can see why they need ethnographic study; survey work does not penetrate people's inner lives. In the cases used here, though, people's lives are enough like those of our readers—though certainly not entirely so—that we can quickly and clearly map out the issues involved. We can thus focus more clearly on the epistemological, political, and other methodological problems that concern us. Moreover, we can do so with a specificity that conveys far more than theory alone.

Third, although discussions of ethnography are now on the rise among scholars of religion, they have so far found neither a focus nor an agenda. We believe that this is a fruitful time for our volume to appear, for our authors are drawn from—and attempt to unite—the many disparate conversations that have so far arisen. Anthropology has long been racked by strife, and sociology has increasingly come under feminist and ethnic attack. The ethnographic study of religion has been something of a backwater on such matters and urgently needs to learn from them, at the risk of further stagnation. We have designed this volume to bring these issues to our colleagues' attention while simultaneously pushing the debate forward—beyond where it has gone in other fields.

We believe that only a deep rethinking of established practices can rescue the ethnographic study of religion from its current epistemological and political naïveté. Such innocence is unacceptable in a post-colonial era. We hope that this volume will result in a deepened sense of ethnographic responsibility—a key step toward letting the ethnographic study of religion transform the social-scientific study of religion as a whole. We wish to thank Wade Clark Roof, former President of the Society for the Scientific Study of Religion, and Christel Manning, the Program Chair for the SSSR's 1997 Annual Conference, at which some of these essays received their first hearing. We also thank our editor, Jennifer Hammer, for her continued encouragement and support. Above all, we thank our contributors, without whom this volume would not be possible.

We dedicate this volume to our colleague, Otto Maduro, a scholar of great kindness and insight.

NOTES

1. Sociologists' "quantitative" vs. "qualitative" pair does not fit here, largely because both methods can support either a generalizing or particularizing intent.

2. See Parkin (1988) for a fictional example.

3. Other notable examples include: Hymes (1969); C. Geertz (1977); Haan et al. (1983); Marcus and Fischer (1986); Clifford (1988); Fox (1991).

Part I

Being an Ethnographer

Chapter 1

Truth, Subjectivity, and Ethnographic Research

Lynn Davidman

On Sunday evening, March 8, 1968, about 7:30 P.M., my father ran down the stairs of our home shouting, "Pinny! Call Dr. Korman quick!" I was sitting in the living room, around the corner from the staircase. I quickly got up and walked over. "What could be going on?" I wondered to myself. "Could Mommy have had an attack or whatever one gets with whatever it is she has?" As these thoughts confusedly raced through my mind, I heard my father shout, "Mommy's DEAD!" I screamed. At that moment, I had remembered a friend whose father had died in fifth grade. When I asked her what she had done at the moment her father died she said, "I screamed." The memory gave me some framework for reacting. My father and brother stopped and stared at me for a moment. Then there was a rush of phone calls, the police, our next door neighbor, Norman, watching for the ambulance. The house slowly filled up with people and I heard my older brother, Pinny, bravely on the phone: "It's my mother." And then a funeral the next morning. But I still did not know what my mother's illness was—what it was she had just died from! When I had guessed, early into her illness, that she had cancer, it had been (improperly) denied. This confusion and mystification, which came to a shocking climax that Sunday evening, highlighted the taboo nature of her illness and death; they were harbingers of the silences that were to follow.

Recalling this scene, literally recalling it from a dark corner of my mind and recreating it by typing it into this essay, I reinscribe my recollections of the first moments after my mother's death into my ongoing biographical narrative. Committing this story to paper makes me highly aware of the absence of this narrative in my book, *Motherloss* (2000a), which was written at least partially to break the personal and social silences that surround (maternal) death in our society. One year after completing this work, I now wonder how it came to be that there were no descriptions of the moments of my own or my respondents' mothers' deaths within the book. Certainly, these moments had been described in many interviews. In retrospect, I realized with some dismay, I had maintained and perpetuated the very silences I was hoping to break!

As I thought about this obvious omission in my book, I thought of several factors that might help explain the absence of accounts of this dramatic moment (of a mother's death) in *Motherloss*. First, the book is focused primarily upon respondents' depictions of the impact of motherloss on their subsequent lives. The accounts produced in the interviews and represented in the text highlight the ways that people sought, through the narrative construction of their identities, to repair the major biographical disruption caused by their mother's deaths and find ways to integrate it into their ongoing sense of self. This book begins not with the story of my mother's death but with my father's death and burial for an additional reason. It was in 1993, at the cemetery in Jerusalem where my dad was being buried (and to which, contrary to my wishes, my mother's remains had been transferred several years earlier), that the book had its emotional birth. It had been at this gravesite in Jerusalem where I once again saw my mother's grave and, realizing the depths of my loss of her, I finally broke down in long-delayed and intense grief. And so it was with this scene that I began *Motherloss*. It heralded the ongoing analytic process of interweaving self-reflection with analysis of others' accounts and of the social context in which they were shaped, which was the central methodological and epistemological principle of the study. By probing my own experiences, memories, and feelings, I was better able to develop a subtly nuanced, rich, and empathetic understanding of my respondents' lives. Conversely, my growing awareness of others' experiences of motherloss helped me to better understand and access my own story.

Thus, although I had perfectly sound reasons for beginning *Motherloss* with my father's death, nevertheless, I am intrigued by the complete absence of moments of maternal death in this work. This omission highlights the almost overwhelming power of the general silencing of death, and of people's reactions to it, in our culture. Maternal death, in particular, is taboo because it results in a "deviant" family structure. In our society, the idea of a family without a mother to hold it together is almost too awful for words. I now suspect that it was the sheer pain involved in reliving those moments of death that made me, despite my best intentions, keep the actual death scenes invisible. Just as I, the thirteen-year-old girl described above, could not enter my mother's room after my father's pronouncement of her death, I, as the adult author, similarly found it too painful to reinscribe that moment (and similar ones described by respondents) into my work.

My current awareness of this conspicuous absence in *Motherloss* makes me reflect on the partial nature of all ethnographic accounts. These accounts are partial not only because they are limited by the subjectivities of authors and respondents, but also because the biographical construction of identity through narrative is an ongoing process. Narratives of the self are always in flux and subject to revision with each new telling. Any given account—as created together by an ethnographer and interviewee—and its representation in textual form is shaped and limited by individuals' readiness in any given circumstances to tell certain stories, their possession of a language in which to construct the story, and the willingness of others to hear [or read] the story into being. At any given moment in time, the nature of our situation and the experiences we have had shape our ability to recall and tell different stories of our lives. For me, the completion of *Motherloss* has gone a long way toward helping me come to terms with motherloss in my own life and has resulted in my feeling an increased sense of peace with myself and with the world. From this new place, I feel ready and safe enough to add and integrate this pivotal moment of loss into my ongoing narrative of identity.

The process of researching and writing *Motherloss*, a subject in which the emotional tones and meanings are central, required of me a holistic methodology that blended emotional forms of knowing together with intellectual. I was able to understand others' experiences of motherloss through a continuous movement back and forth between my own memories, feelings, and responses and those of my respondents. The process of digging deep into my psyche in order to develop a subtly nuanced, rich, and empathetic understanding of others' lives, and simultaneously using these insights to better comprehend my own life, deepened the sociological interpretations and analysis yielded by this research. By entering into my own feelings of pain and loss, I was able to use this emotional knowledge as a pathway to understanding the feelings of others and the general issue of loss in our culture. Ethnographers are emotion workers. By acknowledging our own emotions, ethnographers find new ways to cross the bridges to others. Working in this way affords us new insights into the intersecting realms of self, subject matter, and sociological methods; our reflection on each helps us to interrogate and enliven our knowledge of the others.

Mainstream social science has privileged a more distant form of knowing in the interests of "objectivity" and rational science. Conventional sociology argues that we can only trust our knowledge when we obtain it in ways that are divorced from our selves—our bodies, attitudes, feelings, and "biases"—because the self is a contaminant in social research. Emotional reactions—those of the researcher, the respondents, and the readers—are to be avoided and transcended because they preclude objectivity, producing noise, interference, and distortion. This stance reflects and shapes a social science that searches for structure and rationality in social life and deemphasizes meaning. It rests on the assumption that social science is all about intellect, which precludes its ability to comprehend events whose impact is not intellectual or rational. In contrast, contemporary ethnographic theory argues that in order to develop emphatic, nuanced, and sensitive accounts of people's lives we must work through with and through our knowing selves. The systematic cultivation and use of the insights available to us through our senses and through self-reflection provides a method for accessing emotional truths in all their complex, contradictory, and ambivalent nature. Using these alternative sources of knowledge, such as our own emotions and feeling states, is one way of using our experiences as human beings to understand and convey the experiences of those we meet in the field. Although the product of such a process is indeed partial, it can convey a deeper sense of meaning and "truth" than a more distanced approach.

I want to emphasize that the use of one's own emotional knowledge to gain insights into others is not only a psychological process but can be part of a methodology that yields important sociological insights as well. Although in the above example I described how my own emotions got in the way of my telling certain aspects of motherloss narratives, this new awareness allowed me to deepen my sociological analysis by reflecting on the social forces that keep us silent about death and get in the way of our fully narrating our experiences of loss and grief. This essay argues that the personal can indeed become theoretical and provide knowledge of broad social processes. In the remainder of this essay, I will use examples from my two books, *Motherloss* (2000a) and *Tradition in a Rootless World: Women Turn to Orthodox Judaism* (1991), to illustrate the general sociological patterns that can emerge using reflexive methods.

*

When I did my first interviews for *Motherloss* and began to analyze my transcripts, I was surprised to find—given the reported high level of religiosity of Americans and the belief that religion is particularly helpful at moments of existential crisis—that my respondents did not feel that institutional religion offered them much comfort and guidance at the time of their mothers' deaths. Although I had felt that way myself—that the Orthodox Judaism of my upbringing had not comforted me through my mother's illness and death—my findings seemed to contradict standard sociological understandings. However, an experience I had in the course of writing helped me to see that there may be other, noninstitutional "sacred" practices by which my interviewees maintain their mothers' symbolic presence and thus are comforted about her loss. At that time, my now-husband had moved in with me in my rather small house. There is barely enough space there for one person's things, let alone two. And so little struggles for space emerged. One day I noticed that Arthur had placed a picture of his daughters on the small desk in the living room where I have photos of my mother and over which I have a wedding picture of my maternal grandparents who had filled in for her after my mother died. I removed his daughters' picture from this desk and placed it across the room, on top of a short bookcase. The next day, this scene was repeated. I asked Arthur why he kept moving the picture back when I moved it to the bookcase and he said, "Because it does not show up well in the spot you put it." I said, "Yes, but, that desk is, is, . . . [and here I struggled for the right word, finally bursting out] . . . *my shrine to my family!*" Erecting a memorial to one's dead parents/grandparents and other ancestors is a religious practice in many cultures and even in everyday life settings it is a practice that is oriented to, and embraces notions of, the sacred.

Thus, although I typically consider myself "religiously unmusical," as did Max Weber, by becoming self-reflexive about my own "sacred" spaces and practices, I was better able to see the many symbolic practices by which my respondents are comforted by keeping their mothers present in their daily lives. Sheryl, for example, told me that she regularly prays to her mom. Although it had not been part of her devout Catholic upbringing to pray to one's personal dead, by praying to her mother she created a syncretic practice, borrowing from and adapting earlier religious models to suit her current needs. She disclaims the Catholic roots of these practices, stating that her faith had been shattered upon her mother's death.

I had that feeling that there couldn't be a God because he wouldn't let my mother die, so it must not be. Throughout my teenage years going to Church felt empty for me, because I did not believe that if there was a God that such horrible things can happen. I'm totally aware of all the traditions and rituals of my faith, but I don't practice any of them. All of my prayers that I pray, I always pray to my mother. Ever since she died, I've only prayed to my mother pretty much. I have a sense of her as always with me, she's my guardian angel.

Sheryl reacquired a sense of her mother's presence in the process of therapy, through breaking the silences in which her mother's death had long been buried. She further maintains her mother's presence in her daily life by keeping in her bedroom a picture of her mother, as well as her mother's favorite skirt. She proudly showed me a scarf a friend had brought back from London as a gift for her—it was made of the identical fabric as the shirt Sheryl's mother wore in a photo she showed me.

By keeping photographs and artifacts of her mother present at all times, Sheryl keeps her mother with her in her daily life. Many other respondents, too, sought ways to break the silences surrounding motherloss and maintain their mother's symbolic presence. This was done, for example, by talking in therapy (a very commonly sought solution both by working-class and middle-class individuals) or having mental conversations with their mothers such as one interviewee described to me. This woman, who is a runner, said that whenever she has a problem for which she needs guidance, she talks to her mom when she runs. Others maintain their mother's symbolic presence by keeping photographs of their mothers out and bringing them to special occasions. One woman carried her mother's picture with her in her bridal bouquet and then placed the same picture in her son's pocket during his bar mitzvah. Another man took a piece of his mother's wedding veil and sewed it into the yarmulke he wore to his wedding. By keeping their mothers symbolically present in various ways and talking to them or using their images at particularly important moments in their lives, we can see some elements of sacred practice in the evolution of their responses to motherloss.

Within the sociology and anthropology of religion, there is an emerging trend of studying religious practices in everyday settings, outside those institutions that traditionally have been seen as the primary settings for religious expression (Hall 1997).[1] In everyday life, religious/spiritual practices involve creating a bricolage of reclaimed, reinvented, and borrowed rituals that people draw upon to create new ceremonies that meet their current needs. By seeing how I myself had developed such a sacred space in my own home, I was afforded deeper insights into my interviewees' experiences, which helped me to become aware of a newer, emerging understanding of the nature of religious practices in everyday life.

As I worked on *Motherloss*, my dreams provided another source of knowing that ultimately deepened my analysis of the social dimensions of motherloss. Within one year of working on this project, my mother began to appear in my dreams, something that had happened only rarely before. There was a pattern to my dreams about my mother: In them, she would appear after being gone (dead?) for a while and would once again be living with me and my father and brothers in my childhood home. Yet, she was somehow not properly fulfilling her old roles, especially the task of feeding us, one of the key functions of women in families. In all of these dreams, I and sometimes my older brother were quite concerned about planning meals, purchasing food, and putting it on the table. In some of these dreams, I would confront my mother or complain to my father about her failure to feed us properly. These dreams continued over a period of three years as I worked on this project. At some points, they would be repeated four or five nights a week. These dreams not only revealed to me how tough it had been for me, as a young adolescent, to take on a maternal role, but also provided insights that shaped parts of my interviews. In fact, nearly all of my respondents described the disruption in daily meals that resulted from their mother's illness and death. These conversations helped me understand the social importance of a mother's feeding her family; it is critical not only for its nutritional value but also as a symbolic manifestation of her caring. Indeed, the social organization of gender, with its assignment of the caretaking role largely to women, is the key structural and cultural factor that shapes individuals' experiences of motherloss and its consequences.

Since I began my career as a sociologist, I have always realized the impact of the personal on my choice of sociological topics, though I have not always realized their depth and, when I have, I have not always been willing to admit that depth in print. In writing my first book, *Tradition in a Rootless World: Women Turn to Orthodox Judaism* (1991), I was in a very different stance in relation to my project than I was in writing *Motherloss*. *Motherloss* involved speaking with individuals who had experienced the very same biographical disruption as I had. *Tradition*, in contrast, focused on women who made major life choices that were the opposite of mine: They had chosen to move toward Orthodoxy as adults, whereas I had gone in the opposite direction, from an Orthodox upbringing to a secular life. Here, I found that although my emotions did not provide me with access to others' similar feelings, sometimes they actually afforded me insights into how my very different stance might be impeding my full understanding.

This study of newly Orthodox Jewish women enabled me to explore the role and nature of traditional religion in a modern world, and especially its attraction to contemporary women. Since I had rebelled against and left Orthodoxy for feminist, theological, and lifestyle reasons, I sought to understand why, in the 1980s, there was a pronounced revitalization of traditional religious groups (Jewish, Christian, and Muslim) that define women largely in terms of their roles as wives and mothers in nuclear families. I and my other feminist colleagues and friends were genuinely puzzled by this phenomenon, and I decided to explore it through participant observation and in-depth interviews in two distinct institutional contexts, in which contemporary women are attracted to and resocialized into Orthodox Judaism. Early on in this project, I learned that I had to struggle to separate my own assumptions and worldview from those of the women I was meeting. Since this was a self-selected group, it became apparent that they did not have the same feminist struggles with Orthodoxy I had; otherwise, they would simply not be there. The intrusiveness of my own blinders became clear to me one Saturday morning at Beginner's Service in one community, when the rabbi (whom I had known for most of my life) looked at me, called out my Hebrew name, Layah, and shouted, "Sing!" In my mind's eye, at that moment, I could see myself pulling down a shade in front of my face to protect me from the enthusiastic rabbi's attempts to pull me into the community. It reminded me too much of the way my father forced religious observance down my throat, and I rebelled with every fiber of my being. But as I saw that shade come down, I realized that no one else in that room was pulling down such a shield and that as long as I did so, I would never be able to understand, much less make sensible to others, the meaning of this choice for the women who embraced it.

Since a central goal of this project was to convey, as best as I could, the women's attraction to Orthodox Judaism from the perspective of their life experiences and social locations and not from mine, I knew I needed some help in sorting out my personal reactions. Otherwise, these feelings would prevent me from seeing and hearing realities that differed from my own and my research project would be a failure. I worked for over a year with a therapist to separate out my memories and feelings of being forced by my father to attend services and observe Jewish law and practices, from the realities of the women who made a conscious choice to be in the synagogue every Shabbat morning. By making visible, grappling with, and doing my best to set aside my biases, I was able to more clearly hear, comprehend, and represent to readers the experiences of the women who were adopting Orthodoxy.

Although I strove to break through my own ambivalence about Orthodoxy and about the women's adopting this way of life, I was unable to reflect on this process in any depth in writing *Tradition in a Rootless World*. In my efforts as a new Ph.D. to establish myself as a legitimate sociologist, I felt I could not afford the risk of extensive self-reflection in my work. My choice to omit my personal feelings from the text reflected my uncertainty about what role my own feelings should be allowed to play in my professional understanding of what I observed, even though much of what I observed was of a highly emotional nature, both for myself and for the people I was studying. By the time I had completed that work, I knew that my next project, on premature maternal death, would have to be written in a more self-reflexive way. My social location had become secure enough—I had tenure, a house of my own—to enable me to defy some of the assumptions of mainstream, conventional sociology and to write a more honest account of the varied sources of my knowledge and sociological insights.

As an ethnographer, I have come to appreciate deeply that different kinds of knowledge come in different ways. Just as cognitive rationality helps sociologists understand some social patterns, so too subjectivity and reflexivity are pathways to knowledge that we otherwise would not have. In my work, I have tried to move beyond the rigid scientistic dichotomy between the knower and the known and have embraced, as part of my "data," the visceral knowledge that comes to me through my own senses. I bring in this information, not for the purposes of self-exposure, but rather as a way to draw deeper insights into the subject under study. Intellectual honesty, I am certain, comes from honesty with and about oneself.

Research of this kind is potentially transformative—of self, of respondents, and of our society as a whole. In my study of motherloss, I engaged with my interviewees in the process of constructing their narratives of motherloss that enabled them to locate this biographical disruption in the context of an ongoing, continuous narrative of identity. By doing so, they were able to move beyond the state of linguistic disquietude that typically results from the silencing of important life events. Articulating—and thus reexperiencing—motherloss provides a way to order and categorize this disruption and weave it into a coherent narrative of identity. Several respondents have contacted me to tell me how participating in the interviews began for them a process of exploration and healing. By speaking their accounts into being, they not only told their stories but also reshaped and reconfigured their sense of self in the process. The telling of lives always changes those lives; by telling their life stories, respondents freed themselves from the cultural and social mystification and silencing of death and its consequences.

I, too, was transformed in the process of this research. Working steadily to break my own and my respondents' silences about motherloss enabled me, for the first time, to grieve the death of my mother. In doing so, I have brought her closer to me. No longer am I simply, in relation to her, the child who has lost her mother, but rather, I currently stand as an adult who has worked hard to come to terms with her loss and to integrate it into my being. Completing this work has brought me a newfound sense of emotional closure and peace, even as I recognize that life is fluid and that narratives of self are always in flux.

By making myself vulnerable in this process, I have invited my respondents, and ultimately my readers, to become vulnerable, too, and through that voluntary step to engage in a process that may ultimately lead to transformative gains in their lives as well. The goal of a study such as this is not only to produce information about a social phenomenon but also to touch readers emotionally. Through the language I have used I not only sought to go beyond simply informing my readers of the "facts" of the experience of motherloss but also to evoke their empathic feelings. The validity of this work lies in its ability to induce in my readers the feeling that the experiences represented in it are authentic, believable, and possible and that they are useful in helping others to understand and make meaning out of their own experiences.

NOTE

1. In this vein, Karen McCarthy Brown and I organized a conference entitled, "Religion Outside the Institutions," sponsored by the Center for the Study of American Religion at Princeton University, June 1998.

Chapter 2

From the Heart of My Laptop
Personal Passion and Research on Violence against Women

Nancy Nason-Clark

Sometimes, I am a little uncomfortable with the main character of my essay, and maybe you will be too. She grew up in a small city, preferred the company of classical composers to that of the Rolling Stones (during her teenage years), and while in high school, she worked diligently to be excused from PE classes where she would be required to strip and sweat, two activities she tried to avoid. Being quite shy, the greatest fear she experienced in the academy was when a professor would ask her to discuss a personal point of view. Perhaps she felt that she was not worthy of one. Time passed.

By now, our character was a Ph.D. student at the London School of Economics in England. Along the way, she had picked up a few skills and her research involved fairly sophisticated multivariate analyses of how people's emotional reactions to the ordination of women could be reduced to numbers, regression equations, and canonical correlations. As a researcher, she was rather obsessed with impartiality: in fact, because of her desire for "neutrality" she did not join the activist Movement for the Ordination of Women, fearing that this would be an indication of her "subjectivity." She went through great pains to be "on" but "not on" their mailing list. No one knew of the mental gymnastics she had jumped through. But, she felt smug!

The 1980s had become the 1990s. Our character was now a tenured professor. She was working away quietly in her university office, together with some great graduate students, researching gender roles in contemporary

Christianity. Very few contemporary Christians knew anything about her work, but she regularly gave conference papers, wrote a few manuscripts for publication, and did the things academics are paid to do.

By the mid-1990s, two children had arrived in her life and she was trying desperately to combine her academic and family responsibilities, sometimes with more success than others. She would nurse a baby while writing down lecture notes, pack her briefcase as she packed the diaper bag. There was little separation in her life between the professional and the personal. Her research program, "Jugglers for Jesus," explored some of the tensions and contradictions, as well as joys and successes of merging motherhood, paid employment, and volunteer religious work in the lives of women.

A government department asked her to do some research for them on child sexual abuse. After reading extensively on this issue, she was working at home one day when she came across a court record of a man who had been charged for attempting to penetrate his 2-year old daughter. She too had a 2 year old. She closed the file and purged the contents of her stomach. Finding it impossible to distance herself professionally from the subject she was studying, the final report was completed but the file was closed forever. Little did she know that this was her first lesson in activism.

Time passed.

Now as a Women's Studies scholar, she was approached by a foundation interested in establishing a national center that would investigate family violence in Canada. After funding was sought and obtained (a long story in and of itself), the Center was established premised on the notion that the five "founding mothers" would each develop a research team, involving partnerships with community agencies, to investigate woman abuse and other forms of family violence. For the last six years, she and team members have been investigating the story of what happens when an abused religious woman seeks help from her faith community in the aftermath of crises. We have been trying to tell that story from a variety of perspectives—that of the abused woman, the pastor, the congregation, and church women (and men) who attempt to help.[1]

The year has become 1998. Our sociologist, Women's Studies scholar, is receiving preaching invitations. Yes, you heard it right. The road from the ivory tower to the sacred desk of the pulpit is a rather interesting journey for an academic. Here people listen, despite the fact that they will never be directly evaluated on what you have to say. Many appear interested. They want to work out the implications of the message: violence in the lives of religious women. People comment that she speaks with so much conviction. Is she a victim? No, just a field-researcher with an important sociological story to tell.

The title of my essay, "From the Heart of My Laptop," is meant to convey a number of paradoxes facing the social researcher who is out in the trenches attempting to understand, contextualize, and evaluate social relations in the contemporary world. It is meant to highlight the neglected, even despised, role of emotion in the life of the academic researcher. Central to my essay's main thesis is the argument that the research process must be flexible enough to accommodate both the rigor of the academy (and our interdisciplinary research methods and accumulated wisdom) and the passion of the activist striving to change the social milieu.

There are pitfalls and privileges associated with both data and passion. Passion without data can be misguided, even dangerous. Sometimes those with the most passion do not want their enthusiasm or their mindset to be confronted with the reality of empirical validation. There is no question that data sometimes throws a wet blanket on our ideological positions, be they religious or secular in origin. But when our passion is rooted in the voices and experiences of others in our world, it becomes quite powerful. And that power has the potential to shape not only the path of the data but also the heart of the researcher.

I wish to make five points in this regard.

1) Researching violence against women has changed the way I do my academic work, probably forever. Over the last six years, our research team has had contact with over 1000 church women, clergy, church youth, and men and women of the pew. I have read thousands of pages of transcripts, listened to countless interviews, and talked to scores of women who know first-hand of the pain and despair that abuse has wrought in their lives. Even as I speak, I can visualize women whose journey eventually brought healing and recovery and others for whom the betrayal of the past overshadowed nearly every waking moment. And when I am asked to speak about my research in a community or church context, I have also learned to see the signs of anger and disbelief in the faces of my audience: those who "know" about these things, because they have experienced it first-hand, or those who can't imagine that this happens in their nice and neat backyard. How such knowledge and ignorance can co-exist would be fascinating if it were not so frightening.

What then is my role as an academic in forging pathways between the academy and the community? To what degree is knowledge power? How can I break down those power-boundaries by sharing in a common language the realities that we see in data that we collect? What are the religious and social implications of what I find? To be sure, there are times when this task is more challenging than others: What happens when I find unpopular myths to be prevalent? Sometimes, anonymous messages on my voice mail suggest the direction of my next project. This I was never taught in graduate school. As I now experience it, data dissemination becomes a two-way street: I am told both life stories and answers to specific questions within the confines of ethically bounded research interviews. How could I be bound by anything less than to feed back to those communities the stories, the pain, and the successes, in language that has the potential to lead to action?

2) Researching violence against women has changed me as a person—wife, mother, sister, friend.

When I first started doing more work in this area, I found that I became deeply troubled by male violence: It seemed so all-pervasive, so damaging to women, to children, even to men themselves. My ears became antennae for any talk that glorified violence in sport, on TV, or in the public arena. On many occasions, my partner David would say to me that he felt personally responsible for all these men who were so unloving, so uncaring, and so damaging to their partners. After all, in a household of three women (two very little ones), he felt that he needed to constantly remind me that not all men were bad, evil, powerful, and violent! And, of course, they weren't or aren't. I have never been a victim of wife abuse, or childhood abuse, but as I became more and more involved in the issue, I began to take on the anger that is sometimes characteristic of victims. By this stage in my research, I knew quite a lot about the pain and despair, the havoc and the betrayal and, in large measure, I held men accountable. The men in my life—as friends—were not directly responsible for the behavior of other men, but sometimes I saw them guilty by association.

3) Researching violence against women has demonstrated the inadequacies of any one discipline thinking it has all the answers to the social problems faced in our world.

If there is anything that is clear to me in the research initiative in which I have been involved it is this: no one discipline can understand fully the issue of violence against women or our response to it. And no one discipline alone can solve the problem, ease the pain, or eradicate the instances of it. Thus, we must forge new links, new partnerships between the sacred and the secular: new partnerships between disciplines in arts, humanities, and the helping professions. Problems such as violence stretch our disciplinary boundaries to the limit. For example, there is more to the story of assisting an abused woman than helping her to find shelter when her mental and physical health cannot be assured at home. In part, the transition house movement was founded on the belief that once women were safe from the violent rage of their partner, and resources and support were available, they would seek to begin a new life with their children far removed from the violence of the past. While safety always needs to be our first priority, the story is far more complicated.

4) Passion alone is not enough: data and passion are a winning combination.

The relationship between the activist and the academic is not always an easy one. From the point of view of the activist, if you have been working diligently for many years in search of a political or social goal, you will not be easily dissuaded by data from social researchers; rather, you will want to hide the researchers, dismiss their presence, or better yet, say they are not truly committed to the cause. Let me offer just one example to illustrate this point. Many victimized women do not want to end their relationship with the abuser forever; they simply want to end the abuse. They look forward to a time when the violence will cease and their lives can become tranquil again or perhaps for the first time. However violent and unpleasant the relationship may look to the outsider, and for a myriad of reasons, they want to reconcile and reunite with the partner who has caused them so much pain. As women and men committed to supporting victims of abuse, who are we to demand that they sever ties forever from a violent partner? Doesn't offering empowerment and personal agency demand that a woman is offered information, choices, and support as she makes decisions about her own life, not framed by either the abusive partner, the feminist researcher, or caregivers offering support under the umbrella of one of the helping professions?

5) There is a calculated backlash in our society, and even within the academy, to gender equity; and discussions about wife abuse quickly bring the issues to the forefront.

I was giving a workshop in Boston at an evangelical seminary. As I was speaking to the assembled audience, I noticed that a series of male heads would poke one at a time through one of the rear entrance doors, have a look and a listen, and then disappear. At one point, I noticed that my host had gone to the doorway. I was told later on that these male students wanted to see what someone talking about violence against women looked like and to check out the audience: "Who from the seminary would go to a talk like that?" When my host invited them to register for the workshop, the reply from one seminarian was curt, "We know what causes abuse: it is women themselves!"

Let there be no doubt about it. The family motif is strong. Religious conservatives, and even those not so conservative, celebrate family values and family connectedness. "Strong families working together for God and the local church" is the message they proclaim. "Let no one tear the family asunder!" But let us never forget: it is the abuser, not the abused, nor the messenger, who tears apart families.

"From the Heart of My Laptop" is meant to suggest that there is a creative tension that is often prevalent in the research and writing that I do —a tension that manifests itself most clearly in a commitment both to understand as fully as possible the experiences of abused religious women, their healing journey and the faith groups from which they seek help, and an equal commitment to work together with others to augment social change in those very communities where help is sought. Church families may be considered sacred, but they are often not safe! The road from the steeple to the shelter is rather long and arduous; there are some obstacles to be diverted and hurdles to overcome. Central to paving this road, and ensuring that it be bi-directional, is the issue of language: naming the problem, charting the healing journey, searching for strength and wholeness. As an academic researcher, I am well positioned to speak from the heart of my laptop: passion grounded in empirical reality. What I sometimes lack—and maybe this is true for you too—is courage!

NOTE

1. The first product of this research was Nason-Clark (1997).

Chapter 3

Walking between the Worlds
Permeable Boundaries, Ambiguous Identities

Mary Jo Neitz

In her book *Ghostly Matters* (1997), Avery Gordon calls us to the task of unsettling:

> To be haunted and to write from that location, to take on the condition of what you study, is not a methodology of a consciousness you can simply adopt or adapt as a set of rules or an identity; it produces its own insights and blindnesses. Following the ghosts is about making a contact that changes you and refashions the social relations in which you are located. (22)

This is a chapter about my unsettling. I find when I am with the witches I study, and they are engaging in their spiritual pursuits, I sometimes feel earthly, grounded; whereas when I am doing sociology, I sometimes feel rather ghostly. In this project, I can't always experience what the witches experience, yet the categories and constructs we sociologists have "conjured" lack certainty. Realist descriptions fail to satisfy. I write to evoke. I write to provoke.

Walking between the Worlds

Like many things in my life, studying Wicca was a bit of an accident.[1] I was not a witch. It was not a part of my research agenda when I was finishing my book about Catholic Charismatics (Neitz 1987). But looking backward, I can construct a kind of trajectory.

In 1983, I taught a course called "Feminist Research and Criticism" for which I assigned Mary Daly's *Gyn-Ecology* (1978). A student complained to the dean: she said I was a man-hating feminist, a lesbian, and a witch. The dean called in the director of Women's Studies and the chair of Sociology. Did it help them that they knew I was involved in a relationship with a man at the time? Did it help them that, to their knowledge, I had nothing to do with witches at that time? They supported me. The student dropped the course.

In 1985, I became interested in comparing women who participated in what I was calling "effervescent religions." I was intrigued by the claims made by the Catholic Charismatic women I had studied. They said that, while the social norms of the movement were undeniably restrictive for women, the theology was liberating. They felt freed by having a direct relationship with God. Durkheim, one of the few social scientists to write about effervescent religion, argued that religious traditions that encourage such feelings of freedom must necessarily be accompanied by restrictive social norms. I wanted to compare the Charismatic women I studied with other groups that believed that women had unmediated access to spiritual power. For the sociology meetings that year, I wrote a paper comparing Catholic Charismatics with modern witches, nineteenth-century spiritualists, and Quakers in their founding period (Neitz 1985). It was my introduction to Wicca.

In 1987, I decided to do fieldwork on Wicca. I decided not to do it in the place where I lived. I had a sabbatical coming up, and I felt that there were ethical and political dangers in doing it locally. I worried about conservative state legislators getting wind of what one of their employees was up to. Remembering the beer cans in my front lawn when I put up the sign in my yard for Harriet Woods (the Democratic candidate running against John Danforth in Missouri for the United States Senate in 1982), I also worried about the response to Wicca from the more conservative students at the university. If someone thought I was a metaphorical witch for teaching Mary Daly, what would they think about my spending full moons participating in magical ritual with real witches? On the other hand, I also worried about the ethical problems that could result from encountering someone in a ritual context, and then meeting her again in the evaluative context of the classroom. This seemed a likely possibility, given the overlap between the neopagan community and the Women's Studies students. I decided to create distance between my life and my research by moving the research hundreds of miles away.

I believe that my decision was the right one. But for fieldworkers, the problems of distance are not so easily managed. For me, fieldwork always raises issues of identity. I find myself asking, who I am and what am I doing here? When we do fieldwork, our disciplines train us to use what we learn in the field for thinking about our worlds: as Levi-Strauss put it, "Totems are for thinking." But we also use our own experiences for trying to understand the worlds of others. In seeking to understand how other people make sense of their worlds, I interrogate myself as I interrogate them. I ask myself how are we alike? How are we different? Where do we see the world in the same way? Where do we not?

In doing research in religious groups, multiple identities are brought into play: religious identities, sexual identities, gender identities, racial identities, class identities, political and occupational identities. Complex and shifting, each of these is available to be mobilized in entering into a situation and in constructing and co-constructing the meanings that unfold there. Woman/feminist/lesbian/witch/scholar/native/other. There is no easy way to divide up "them" and "me." I found myself thinking that I always "walk between the worlds." A woman I interviewed a number of years ago told me that if you are a woman and you are aware, you are a witch.[2] As I listened to her, I tried out her definition: Am I a woman? Am I aware? Am I a witch?

The Problem of Voice

Notes from Winter Solstice 1997

This is the year I am on leave writing the book. In mid-December my partner, an avowed atheist, turns to me and says, "What do we do for winter solstice?" I look at her. In our Decembers together, we have never celebrated the winter solstice. Winter solstice had always been preempted by the encompassing family demands of the Christmas season. One year I made an attempt, but we were traveling, and there was no time for it. The next year my mother stayed with us for an extended period, and my partner took a break from us, which happened to fall on the Solstice. I sent a small gift to her—a shepherd's sundial—at the house of the friend with whom she was staying. The next year the Solstice fell on the day her mother and sister arrived at our house to spend Christmas with us. Although we always celebrate the vernal equinox by eating greens from our cold frame (and sometimes by planting peas) in the bluster of March, we had never celebrated the winter solstice. The summer solstice celebrates itself. It is nearly always on that day that the wild roses that frame our property on two sides burst into bloom. We are blessed on that day with bushes taller than I covered with the single pink blooms of the wild roses. If we are lucky, we still have the last of the spring produce—asparagus, and snow peas and lettuce, and maybe the first zucchini squash. If we open a bottle of champagne, it is only an echo of the celebration of summer that is happening all around us.

But, in the dark of winter, this year she was asking me, how do we celebrate the Solstice. It will not surprise those who know me that we ate. We ate a winter stew. Root vegetables—potatoes, turnips, rutabagas, carrots, leeks. Rich with wine and mushrooms and herbs. We drank champagne.

My religious practice is growing, preparing, and eating food. Of course, I live in the secular world, and that includes power bars stashed in my desk drawer, and maybe even an occasional visit to McDonald's. But growing, preparing, and eating food are my rituals.

When I read the epilogue to Starhawk's *Dreaming the Dark* (1982), I am drawn to the notion of hope that resides in the promise of spring, in the day succeeding the night. She writes:

> And still we have not yet lost hope.
>
> That hope sways on an edge so delicate that it is possible that the choices any one of us makes could tip the balance. If these words at moments seem to have power for you, take it as a measure of the power you will have if you reach for it, if you draw it up from the dark, if you risk it. And perhaps it is you, your reaching, your voice, your work, your joy, your love, that will make the difference. Perhaps it is up to you to reclaim the world.
>
> Or perhaps it is up to us all, to join our hands, our voices, to reach into the dark and reshape it into a clear night sky where we can walk without fear, into a well of healing from which we can all drink, into the velvet skin of life, the newly fertile ground.
>
> It is late and I am very tired. Yet, I know that I can lie down and sleep and rise up fresh each morning, as the heavy moon will rise and set. That is our magic; our power to return, as something always pushes up from the ground that can feed us.
>
> So tonight, I find myself feeling hope. I am feeling that exhilarating, scary sense of certainty, of a spell brewing, as if we were all part of a ritual that is now beginning to work. For the force that pushes us toward each other, flesh to flesh, heart to heart—that moves us to dance, to work, to birth and to weave—is a power that never stops reaching out for life. (181–182)

Her description calls to me. I practice my faith when I connect with others, when we try to change the world. I feel that I celebrate my faith when I garden, working with the ground that feeds us.

May 1996

> I attend a Priestess Gathering sponsored by the Reformed Congregation of the Goddess, an organization of Dianic witches that I have been observing since its beginnings in 1986. The first night we gather in affinity groups. After dinner we peruse the signs on the tables, and each of us chooses a table with a label designating the spiritual path upon which we saw ourselves. I choose the "earthwalker table." Entering into the experience of the conference, I want to be with other women who practice their faith through gardening. The first woman who spoke asks if any of us were having a success in getting the fairies to come into our gardens. There ensues a conversation about how the women at the table had tried this or that or read about this or that. My feeling that these women are on the same path with me wanes.

The next winter I am working on a section of my book that deals with contemporary witches' interpretations of the European witchcraft persecutions in the early modern period. The period witches call the "burning times." Reading Starhawk's epilogue to *Dreaming the Dark* (199–205), I encounter a section in which she explicates Ivan Illich's condemnation of formal education and the standardization of language. As Starhawk describes it, for her the enlightenment was indeed an "endarkenment."[3] I feel very uncomfortable. I identify with her discussion of the exclusion of women, but still feel uneasy. Given that I work in an institution of formal education, I can't help wondering which side I would have been on. The discussion pulls at my divided loyalties.

> I imagine writing something that weaves the places with which I resonate and the places where I say, no, that is not me. In the rituals of courtship, my lover once asked me what I believed in. Somewhat spontaneously, I said that I believed that the sun comes up in the morning. That spring follows winter, and summer follows spring, and autumn follows summer. Then we have winter, and spring again.

How does having these beliefs make a difference for what I write? My "faith commitment," whether I call it witchcraft or not, is a commitment to hope. My symbol is not the cross or even the pentagram, but the spiral.

I resonate with the vision of hope that I see in these witches, and with their expanded vision of what is possible.

A white male friend of mine, whom I see at meetings of social scientists who study religion, worries that we are not critical enough about the religions we study. He fears that we scholars end up endorsing the status quo. But that assumes that the religions we study constitute the status quo. Feminist researchers who study marginalized peoples operate from a different assumption. We often speak of giving voice to those who have no voice.[4] Witches are not without voice. I ask myself who has a voice and in what domain.

A Line of Fault

Dorothy Smith's essay, "A Sociology for Women," always evokes a visceral sense of recognition for me. As a woman sociologist I know the line of fault that she describes. When I started making notes for this essay, thinking about my walking between the worlds, I thought about Smith's description of the researcher's bifurcation. Smith begins her essay with the following words:

> This inquiry into the implication of a sociology for women begins from the discovery of a point of rupture in my/our consciousness—the culture or ideology of our society—in relation to the world known otherwise, the world directly felt, sensed, responded to, prior to its social expression. From this starting point, the next step locates that experience in the social relations organizing and determining precisely the disjuncture, that line of fault along which the consciousness of women must emerge. (Smith 1987, 49)

Smith's central insights about the relations of ruling and the creation of knowledge remain critical to my own attempts to create a feminist sociology. Yet, the world of feminist scholarship has grown more complex than it was when I first encountered Dorothy Smith's evocation of the line of fault over twenty years ago. I no longer perceive the world as so clearly divided into two sides. The points of connection and contention between people are not always easy to predict. Identities are fractured and multiple. As a woman writing about women, I find identities are fluid and ambiguous.

February 1998

I am involved in a study about the viability of rural churches.[5] It is the fourth panel of a study that was begun in the 1950s. I am brought into the study to work with a new ethnographic project, which will supplement the survey data with six case studies. The researchers meet with the advisory group of church leaders. The meetings start with a prayer. The co-principal investigator on the project, Director of the Center for Rural Ministry at the Missouri School of Religion, wants to build community by going around the conference table with each person telling his story. These are kind and good-hearted people. They work for social justice and believe in ecumenism. Their walk with Jesus brings them to this table where I am sitting. These men talk of their pastoring; they tell stories about their wives and children. I wait for my turn. In my head I try their format. But if I say, "My partner is a blues guitarist, who paints houses for her day job, and we have no children," I fear it will not connect me with them. It will not create a bond of trust between us. I talk about having grown up in a rural area, and my involvement in other studies of religious groups. As we talk about rural churches, we discover that we do care about some of the same things in the study: we both want to make religious meanings visible and to avoid defining viability in terms of growth. We make a connection through their mobilizing family ties and me mobilizing my scholarly identity.[6] Later, the director invites me to give a presentation at a conference for retired pastors. When he introduces me at the conference, he does not mention my research on witches. I give my talk, and then I am on a panel with an African American pastor from the Church of God who spoke the day before. The morning closes with a spontaneous communion service that grew organically out of the positive feeling generated by their time together. I share in the positive feelings. They ask me to stay. I stay. But I cannot take communion.

Reading R. Stephen Warner's *New Wine in Old Wineskins* (1988) with my sociology of religion class, I came across the passage where Warner described what he was comfortable doing as a participant observer and what he was not (74). As I read the familiar paragraph, familiar in part because I have said similar things, I remember the lines I drew in my study of Charismatic Catholics. Neither Warner nor I took communion with the people we studied. To me, taking communion signifies belonging. It also signifies believing.

I grew up a believer. Roman Catholic: A tradition that holds up virgin mothers and virgin martyrs as role models for girls. I did not "fall away" from the church. Kin to the defenestrated heretics of the Reformation, I felt pushed. Out the window. I felt there was no room for a person like me. Feeling betrayed by what I had loved, I left. I do not want to be part of a tradition that is so overwhelmingly patriarchal.

Witches too have rituals of community. The ritual circle signifies a sacred space. In some traditions, one enacts a symbolic purification before entering. It is common in Gardnerian and Neogardnerian traditions, in entering the circle, for each entrant to pass to the one following, the phrase, "[I enter this circle] in perfect love and perfect trust." I enter their circles. I say those words. I interpret my saying those words in such a way that saying them leaves intact my feelings of integrity. This is not something I can do with regard to taking communion in a Christian Church. Recently, women from another neopagan tradition joined the Reformed Congregation of the Goddess, and they brought with them this standard practice. A Saturday night ritual the new women organized at a Priestess Gathering incorporated this element. Hearing such orthodox pagan words surprised me, and yet I did not hesitate to say the words. Other Dianic witches attending, with their own boundaries to negotiate, refused to say the words. To what extent is it my distance from both Dianic and more orthodox neopagan traditions that makes those boundaries less significant for me, and allows me to participate in this ritual?

Ambiguous Identities

I have been thinking about these ambiguous identities, and how the question is complicated by the nature of Wicca itself, the very ambiguity of which frustrates my quest for the boundary: Who is in, who is out? Early in the research process, I found myself writing a paper on studying unbounded religious movements (Neitz 1994). How do I locate the researcher? When I studied Catholics, I had a better sense of where the boundaries lay.

As a comparison group, for my dissertation research I interviewed lay Catholics whose spiritual lives were at the core of their identities, but who were not part of the Charismatic Movement which was the main focus of my work. I had trouble understanding some of these women who, like me, found the Catholic Church's patriarchy exclusionary, but, unlike me, had stayed in the church. One woman I interviewed in a wealthy suburb told me how important it is to work from within the church and resist its misogyny. She said she attended Mass, and that during the group recitation of the Nicene Creed (a prayer that states the core theological beliefs, starting with "I believe in one God, Father Almighty . . .") when they came to parts she didn't accept, she just skipped those parts. She goes to communion. I did not experience the boundaries as permeable in the way that she did. In my case, not taking communion as a researcher is hardly a neutral act; it is not merely a way of drawing the line between observing and participating, although it is that as well. Clearly, my drawing that particular line has much to do with me and my history.

When I finished field research on Catholic Charismatics, it was with a sigh of relief. I turned to the witches, anticipating a greater level of comfort with people who would share more of my values, be more like me. I did not anticipate how often I would feel a gulf between "me" and "them."

On the face of it, Witchcraft requires less doctrinal commitment than the Catholic Church. The Reformed Congregation of the Goddess (RCG) asks congregants to sign an "Affirmation of Women's Spirituality," certain parts of which are controversial among the membership.[7] But in the view of the founder, the important thing is the path, not the creed. In a Priestess Training Program workbook, she explains as follows:

> The congregation is dedicated to those following a positive path of spiritual development. The philosophy of spiritual development is expressed in the Affirmation of Women's Spirituality and in the Consecration Affirmation. . . . Considering the affirmations challenges you to define your spiritual beliefs. It is not necessary for you to come to the same conclusions as those expressed on the Affirmation in order to be a member of the congregation. The Affirmation is not a test of faith. It is a statement of belief which a majority of the women in the congregation hold to be a valid expression of their experience. . . . We do not ask that you agree totally with the Affirmations. We do ask that you think about your beliefs and define them for yourself. . . . If you find, after considering the Affirmations, you are primarily in agreement with them or willing to explore your areas of uncertainty, we will welcome you into Cella Training. (Jade 9997, 9)

The definition of what it is to be a witch is not exclusive. Nor is it stated what one must believe to be in or out.

But the founders would argue that it only appears that RCG requires less of you. Fewer rules means that you have to work harder and be more conscious of your actions and intentions—you cannot just blindly follow the path. You may have to search for the path. Is that what I am doing here? What my research is about?

Woman, Native, Other

In her chapter, "The Language of Nativism: Anthropology as a Scientific Conversation of Man with Man," Trinh Minh-ha states the following:

> The *proper* anthropologist should be prevented from "going over the hill," should be trained for detachment in the field if he wishes to remain on the winning side. . . . [To become] a member of that cult has been seen as loss, a loss of objectivity, for the man changed sides and—why not say it—betrayed his own kind. (Trinh 1989, 55; italics in the original)

Going native is like having a male to female sex change in our society: People ask what is wrong with you to give up male privilege in such a radical way?

The issue in "going native" is an issue about sides: I have naively wondered why it is that other scholars wonder if I am a witch, or a Charismatic Catholic, and question the legitimacy of my work, while for the prominent white, male scholars in my field to research Protestants—and to use their considerable resources in the behalf of their kind—does not compromise them in any way. No one questions their legitimacy in speaking for "their" people, nor their authority to do so.

Studying a marginal group raises a question about taking sides. The disciplinary disciplinarians are really asking, why would you betray your own kind? Why would you give up the privileges of being on the side of the powerful? They assume that in becoming a sociologist, I, as a non-Protestant, a woman researcher, experience the world and can deploy privileged authority in the same way that they do.

The idea of "going native" also assumes that there are two sides: the side of Western science as opposed to the native side. It assumes these relations are adversarial.

Here again, the issue is one of trust. For Western science, going native breaks trust. How can they trust us anymore if we don't follow their rules? I think that it is less that they believe in objectivity—in the sense of the importance of not having an effect on the situation—than it is the case that membership in the club (and sharing the privilege) is based on following their rules. If a researcher breaks these rules, what other rules might she be breaking as well?

A Sociology of the Possible

I feel that I cannot write a "realist tale" in the form of "I, the Expert, saw this, and I am going to tell *you* about *them*." On the other hand, I do not feel that I can write a "We-are-all-in-this-together" narrative either. Judy Wittner (1998b) argues that writing from your location is the central characteristic of feminist research. How do I locate myself in relation to these shifting boundaries?

I am reminded of Anne Goldman's *Take My Word* (1996) about how marginal subjects represent themselves when denied access to more culturally central forms of publication. She counters these women's accounts of themselves to accounts of "others" written by anthropologists. Goldman writes:

> James Clifford's characterization of the nineteenth century ethnographer as attaining ethnographic authority by "undergoing a personal learning experience comparable to an initiation" is suggestive here.... The "initiation accords the ethnographer cultural mastery, identifying him as bicultural: fluent in the cultural codes of his own world and the one he is studying. The presumed subject (object) of study meanwhile, represented as ever more firmly rooted in his own world—or rather in the world the ethnographer makes for him in print—becomes by comparison far less of an authority." (177–178)

A friend of mine reviews books for "Booklist." She is a poet and a professor; she is an authority. I met her at an academic conference on women's spirituality held in Colorado in 1988. Living in Fairbanks, Alaska, she and her friends started a Dianic circle in 1974, basing their rituals on reading Robert Graves' *The White Goddess* (1948)—and their own imaginations. On our drive to another Priestess Gathering sponsored by the Reformed Congregation of the Goddess, in May of 1998, she complains to me that all the academic books about Women's Spirituality she reads are from the outside; they make her and her friends into "*Them*." She doesn't recognize herself. I think about the book I am writing.

It is not only that my friend disagrees with these writers about what is important, but it is also a matter of positioning. The writers refuse to acknowledge the possibility that the boundaries between "witches" and "writers" might be permeable. Witches in these books are locked into position as the "they" that is studied.

I cannot write a book where I, the expert, tell an audience about the curious customs of some far away *others*, in part because I cannot assume that the subjects and the audience for my book are distinct from each other. This, too, is a blurred boundary.

There is a sense that I write for and with the witches, in a conversation together, as well as about them. They write books themselves. We read each others' books. We sometimes write for different purposes. I learn from what they write. I hope that they recognize themselves in what I write—even when it is not what they would say themselves or how they would say it. Some of them tell me that they learn from me, from my reports of practices, from my interpretations.

I am trying to locate my narrative in the local and particular. Not to generalize overly about witches but to talk about Jade and Ryn and Amber and Jackie. To claim my interpretations as my interpretations. To acknowledge not only what I have learned from them but also how I have learned it, through what I have seen and heard and experienced in my encounters, and in the collaborative conversations through which I made sense of the parts of the world I came to share with them. To use the rhetoric of "we" in the places where I stand with witches in resisting the dominant culture's understandings of gender and sexuality, and to invite readers to be a part of that "we" as well. To write a text that is multivocal. To make small claims for my big ideas. To write in the language of possibility not necessity. This is key for me now: to write in the language of possibility.

This also solves a problem. Witchcraft is unrepresentable. It is too diverse and idiosyncratic. Too particular and too local to capture with generalizations. An oral tradition with no constraints against antinomianism. But the problems I face—problems of representation and location—characterize ethnography today. Some critics of social science practice believe that we can no longer do ethnography because there is no subject position (Behar and Gordon 1995; Clough 1998). We are unsettled, yet we struggle to find ways to claim what we know—know from our own located place—without an authority based on scientific imperialism. From this haunted location, where there are no clear boundaries between subjects, audiences, and tellers, I can no longer identify as simply the researcher. Yet, there are stories to be told, and we are finding the ways to write our stories.

NOTES

1. My narrative here takes an episodic form—things happened to me, I didn't plan it out, and things could have happened in a different way. I am aware that this way of telling the story is more common for women than for men, more common for working-class people than for middle-class people. For a discussion on forms of storytelling, see Passerini (1993).

2. The view that all women are witches and only need recognize it to call their power into being was given wide circulation in the "Witch Manifesto" published in Morgan (1970) among other places. According to my informant, men can become witches as well, but they must study.

3. This point is discussed at length by Trinh (1989). She argues as follows:

Consciousness here is not the result of an accumulation of knowledge and experience but the term of an ongoing unsettling process. . . . The idealized quest for knowledge and power makes it often difficult to admit that enlightenment (as exemplified by the West) often brings about endarkenment. More light, less darkness. More darkness, less light. It is a question of degrees and these are two degrees of one phenomenon. By attempting to exclude one (darkness) for the sake of the other (light), the modernist project of building universal knowledge has indulged itself in such self-gratifying oppositions as civilization/primitivism, progress/backwardness, evolution/stagnation. With the decline of the colonial idea of advancement in rationality and liberty, what becomes obvious is the necessity to reactivate that very part of the modernist project at the nascent stage: the radical calling into question, in every undertaking, of everything that one tends to take for granted. (40)

4. The notion that feminist research gives voice to women who have not been heard is present in the methodological writings of many feminist scholars. For an overview see Reinharz (1992). Oral historians have struggled with how to do this; see for example, Anderson et al. (1987). DeVault (1999) has written about the process of listening to women's voices in interview encounter. See also Krieger (1983; 1988) for discussions of authorial subjectivity in writing with women's voices.

5. "Viability in the Rural Church." Principal co-investigators: Jere Gillis and John Bennett. Funded by the Eli Lilly Foundation.

6. Patricia Williams begins her powerful essay, "The Pain of Word Bondage" (1991, 146–65), with a similar story. She and a colleague, both law professors, but he a white man and she a black woman, are looking for apartments after arriving in New York City:

We both wanted to establish enduring relationships with the people in whose houses we would be living; we both wanted to enhance trust of ourselves and to allow whatever closeness was possible. This similarity of desire, however, could not reconcile our very different relations to the tonalities of law. Peter, for example, appeared to be extremely self-conscious of his power potential (either real or imagistic) as white or male or lawyer authority figure. He therefore wanted to go to some lengths to overcome the wall that image might impose. The logical ways of establishing some measure of trust between strangers were an avoidance of power and a preference for informal processes generally.

On the other hand, I was raised to be acutely conscious of the likelihood that no matter what degree of professional I am, people will greet and dismiss my black femaleness as unreliable, untrustworthy, hostile, angry, powerless, irrational, and probably destitute. . . . So it helps me to clarify boundary; to show that I can speak the language of lease is my way of enhancing trust in me in my business affairs. . . . Unlike Peter, I am still engaged in a struggle to set up transactions at arm's length, as legitimately commercial, and to portray myself as a bargainer of separate worth, distinct power, sufficient rights to manipulate commerce. (147–148)

In these different contexts, the experience of marginality made me and Williams feel that the mechanisms for building trust that seemed obvious to the white men were not available to us.

7. Jade reports that it is the very first affirmative action, "To know that I can create my own reality," that elicits the most questioning from women who join the congregation. (Message posted to RCGI e-groups.com. July 8, 2000)

Chapter 4

Dancing on the Fence
Researching Lesbian, Gay, Bisexual, and Transgender Christians

Melissa M. Wilcox

Fences, both real and metaphorical, are nearly ubiquitous in contemporary U.S. culture. We have white picket fences, "Don't fence me in," playground fencing, and razor-wire security fences. Weathered wooden fences evoke romantic images of "the countryside" or "out West." Fly over any major metropolitan area and you will see row upon row of suburban homes, their property lines neatly divided by fences of all shapes and sizes. Travel closer to the city center and you find less friendly fences designed not just as symbolic boundary markers, but as obstacles preventing passage from one side to the other.

The theme connecting all of these fences is their binary nature. As opposed to a wall or battlement, a fence is a narrow structure upon which one cannot sit, walk, or live. It clearly delineates two sides and forces a choice (or enforces one's lack of choice) between them: "my side" and "your side," for example, or "inside" and "outside." It is nearly always possible, if not always desirable, to move from one side to the other, but it is difficult to remain between sides for long.

In light of these limitations, it is interesting that fence metaphors and strictly delineated boundaries are evident both in the communities I study and in the community of scholars to whom I report the results of my work. There are those within lesbian and gay communities, as indeed among heterosexuals, who derisively refer to bisexuals as "fence-sitters." Just as young lesbians and gay men frequently hear that their sexual orientation is "just a phase," so some gays and lesbians say of bisexual identity that it represents a phase in one's sexual development, a reluctance finally to choose between the sociocultural advantages of heterosexuality and one's "true" identity as gay or lesbian. Likewise, heterosexuals may view bisexuality as a form of sowing one's wild oats before coming to rest in one's "true" heterosexual orientation. In either case, homosexuality and heterosexuality become the two sides between which one must choose: dividing them is a narrow fence, a boundary or place of passage, and not a comfortable middle ground.

As with material fences, one must question whether this boundary serves primarily to keep its creators in or to keep their opposite numbers out. Strongly defended boundaries are often linked to fears regarding a breach of those boundaries, but is the feared breach in this case a break-out or a break-in? From the heterosexual side of the divide, the concern at first appears to center around a break-in: right-wing rhetoric, for instance, continues to insist that lesbians and gay men perpetuate their communities by drawing impressionable young heterosexuals into their fold. Steven Seidman (1997, 1998), on the other hand, has suggested that a break-out is more to be feared among heterosexuals. The increasing visibility of gays and lesbians and their growing acceptance by mainstream culture, he argues, has resulted paradoxically in a redoubling of efforts by heterosexuals to affirm that they are *not* homosexual.

The view from the other side of the fence also fails to provide clear-cut answers. On the one hand, some lesbians are reluctant to become sexually involved with bisexual women because of concerns about sexually transmitted diseases. Since many lesbians were involved with men before coming out, these concerns betray not only the common stereotype of bisexuals' promiscuity but also the underlying issue of purity that is at stake. Borrowing a concept from Mary Douglas (1966), it is possible to read bisexuals as categorical anomalies that threaten the presumed purity of the lesbian community.[1] The sexual fence would then seem to be preventing a break-in of heterosexuals into lesbian and gay space. However, the concern again goes both ways: one could argue equally cogently that anti-bisexual sentiment reflects an underlying fear that once given the opportunity to cross the border into heterosexual territory, some homosexuals might want to stay in the "straight" world.

Less intimate than sexual identity boundaries, but equally contentious, is the debate within anthropology and sociology over designations of "insider" and "outsider" (cf. McCutcheon 1999).[2] Like the paired categories of homosexual and heterosexual, these opposed terms posit a clear divide in identities with no room for middle ground. An "insider," some believe, may be hindered in her research efforts by her identification with the group she studies. Loyalty might stifle her critique, for instance, or her familiarity with the group might make it difficult for her to gain interpretive clarity. Insiders, in other words, cannot see the forest for the trees. Therefore, while researchers traditionally have relied upon insiders for (and as) fieldwork "data," many continue to frown upon analytical work conducted by insiders.

Just as a growing respect for fluid identities has resulted in greater acceptance of bisexuals in the contemporary United States, increased academic attention to issues of objectivity and subjectivity has led many ethnographers to question the structural soundness and even the existence of the fence that divides insider from outsider. Moreover, the academy enforces insider/outsider boundaries inconsistently: while Western "outsiders" are considered to have an advantage over "insiders" in studying non-Western cultures, non-Westerners are not granted the same epistemological priority in their analyses of Western cultures. In fact, the study of Western cultures by insiders has been an acceptable academic pursuit since the beginnings of sociology. The concern, then, seems to center less on insiders and outsiders than on an academic, Western "self" and its nonacademic, non-Western "other."

Especially disruptive in this case is the "self" who becomes "other" or the person who is both simultaneously: the ethnographer gone native and the native turned ethnographer. Like bisexuals, field researchers who "go native" are categorical anomalies. Once insiders to academia, and perpetually insiders to some extent, they do the unthinkable not only by crossing the fence to stand with those outside the academy, but also by blending insider and outsider status. Insiders to academia, as well as to the group they study, these border crossers are, at the same time, outsiders to both. Likewise, members of non-Western cultures or nondominant Western subcultures who engage in field research can never shed their outsider identity entirely. Cultural insiders by profession but cultural outsiders by birth, they too challenge the binary categories of ethnographic identity.

This essay centers on the experiences of an inveterate border-crosser and fence-sitter in researching the lives, beliefs, and religious practices of lesbian, gay, bisexual, and transgender (hereafter referred to as LGBT) Christians. Although I begin with my own experiences of straddling outsider-insider divides, the essay ranges over a number of issues that are pertinent not only to my own work but also, I believe, to all field research conducted in a postmodern world dominated by hybrid identities and bricolage.

Straddling the Fence

Given the preceding discussion, this section of the essay would work best if I were bisexual in addition to crossing insider-outsider boundaries as a researcher. Unfortunately for the artistic structure of the piece, both of my feet are firmly on the lesbian side of the sexual fence. In other ways, though, my own identities placed me as both outsider and insider in the communities I studied recently.

The experiences in which this essay is based were part of several years of fieldwork in member congregations of the Universal Fellowship of Metropolitan Community Churches (UFMCC; individual churches are referred to as MCCs), a Christian denomination that specifically serves lesbian, gay, bisexual, and transgender (LGBT) communities (Wilcox 2000). Over the course of my research I attended services at five different MCCs in California, sent out a lengthy questionnaire to those on the mailing lists of two of the congregations, and conducted seventy-two in-depth interviews with pastors, members, former members, and affiliates of the same two congregations. As a member myself of the LGBT community, I had a certain interpretive advantage over heterosexuals who must learn a new culture and combat culturally inculcated homophobia while they conduct their research.[3] Religiously, on the other hand, I was definitely an outsider; though I attended Protestant churches for a few years as a child, I have never identified with Christianity.

Despite the potential disadvantages of this religious difference, I believe my research also benefited from the fact that my understanding of Christianity is not that of an insider. When I first began this work, it was in part out of befuddlement: like many non-Christian LGBT people, I could not understand why members of my community would be involved in a religion whose representatives had rejected them with such force. This incomprehension led me to ask questions that might not otherwise have occurred to me: questions about the meaning of Christianity for those I interviewed, questions about why they stayed in the church, questions about how they could justify identifying as LGBT and Christian in the face of apparently anti-LGBT biblical passages, and so on. The answers to several of those inquiries formed the backbone of my ideas on the advantages of religious individualism. Had I been a committed Christian, a complete insider rather than a partial one, I might not have seen things in the same way.

Had I been a partial insider in another way—Christian but heterosexual, say—I might again have picked up on different issues or angles within my research and been hindered in still other ways. In teaching introductory Women's Studies, I frame the theme of difference in the metaphor of parallax. I suggest to my students that just as humans need two overlapping fields of vision in order for our visual depth perception to function properly, so we need the experiences and theories of a variety of women and men for the sake of our analytical depth perception: to understand the dynamics of gender, race, class, and sexuality. Likewise, I think, the many permutations of partial insider, complete insider, and complete outsider identities among researchers offer us a number of vantage points on the same phenomenon, and only by relying on these in combination do we have any hope of understanding it accurately.

Self-Representation: Construction and Communication of Identity

From the outset, fieldwork necessitates both the construction and the communication of identity on the part of all those involved. Aware that the research may reach the public domain and perhaps anxious to present themselves in the best light possible, study participants must consider how to communicate their identities, their lives, and their beliefs. Leaders, especially in a religious setting, must decide whether and how much to restrict the researcher's access to people, places, and events. Moreover, the researcher must choose how to present herself and her project, aware that such decisions have a significant effect on the participation and openness of her hosts.

These issues are only compounded by the addition of what Goffman (1963) has called "stigmatized identities." Like many non-dominant groups, LGBT people have ample reason to be suspicious of researchers' motives and findings. During the course of the twentieth century, studies of LGBT people often have made use of biased samples, started from predetermined and incorrect assumptions, and put LGBT people at increased personal or political risk. Even studies conducted by researchers sympathetic to LGBT concerns have occasionally suffered from these drawbacks (e.g.: Humphreys 1970; Bauer 1976). Yet, LGBT people often are aware that if some academic researchers can portray their communities in a negative light, others are capable of furthering accurate and positive public images of those communities. Given the right researcher, then, as well as the right setting, at least some LGBT people have a stake in participating fully in such projects.

I embarked upon my recent research project prepared for the full range of these reactions—or so I thought. In both churches, for instance, I attended the first service with my current partner. Thus, for the people who attended that service, I was identified as a member of the LGBT community before I was identified as a researcher. They knew me first as someone who presumably understood and also was vulnerable to the attacks, mistreatment, and misunderstanding of academics, public officials, media, theologians, and the like. Additionally, I chose to conduct my research at churches in which I had preexisting contacts: one my partner formerly had attended, while two close friends of mine had belonged to the other for several years.

Some members of each community were initially suspicious of me, however, and some remained suspicious throughout the project. I was in fact an outsider and would have been one even had I been Christian as well, because in the sanctuary, in the social hall, in people's homes and cafes and everywhere else I met to conduct interviews, it was the academic aspect of my identity that was foremost.

Although I understood the reasons behind it, the intensity of this suspicion took me by surprise. When I was preparing to mail out the questionnaires, the pastor of Oceanfront MCC requested that I include a letter from her endorsing the project, in addition to my own cover letter that explained it, presented my academic credentials, and provided university-based recourse for aggrieved study participants.[4] Reverend Sharon wished to have her congregation know that both the questionnaire and I had received her full support. In a way, the letter provided church members with her assurance that I was not the sort of academic who would misuse the information they provided. Although I was more than happy to accede to these requests, I found Reverend Sharon's extreme caution surprising and suspected it was unnecessary. The questionnaires from MCC Valle Rico, however, proved me wrong.

Having been asked to include a cover letter in Oceanfront's surveys, I inquired at Valle Rico whether the pastor with whom I was working would like to add a letter to his congregation's questionnaires. He declined, saying he thought the congregation at his church was generally more "out" and less concerned about such things than Oceanfront's congregation. But two days after the envelopes went out, my telephone began ringing—and at first it was not with volunteers for interviews. Four furious callers and three correspondents, all affiliated with MCC Valle Rico, demanded to know where I had gotten their addresses, how I could presume to ask about their sexual orientation (one of the demographic questions on a survey that was mainly about religion), and why the church had allowed me access to the mailing list. More than one caller insisted that I had retained a copy of the church's mailing list and had recorded which survey was sent to whom, thus enabling me to link the personal data from my ostensibly anonymous survey to the name and address of the person in question. Although these accusations were false and I had in fact taken great pains to ensure the anonymity even of my own records and fieldnotes, I was unable to assuage the fears of these callers.

Fortunately, these fiercely defensive reactions were followed in short order by completed surveys and eventually by interview participants who were in fact disappointed to learn that they would not be included by name in any publications. Nevertheless, the experience brought home to me the continuing vulnerability of LGBT people, even in these days of Vermont marriages, *Ellen*, and *Will and Grace*. It reminded me of the responsibilities that accompany field research and proved that academic credentials are not—indeed, should not be—sufficient to earn the trust of a community.

If the core of self-presentation is trust for the researcher in LGBT communities, for the LGBT people involved in such a study the concern is with the provision of accurate public images of their communities. Indeed, despite academic misunderstandings and mistreatment of LGBT people, there is a long history among white and middle-class lesbians and gay men of alliances with academics in the quest for "scientific" affirmation.[5] Before the 1970s, for example, the homophile movement focused in part on promoting research and academic commentary on homosexuals. Although its members certainly hoped for supportive findings, they were most concerned to break the stranglehold of prejudice and antiquated theories on public opinion about lesbians and gay men (cf. D'Emilio 1983; Katz 1992). In the same vein, a number of people who participated in my MCC study expressed a hope that my work would help to "get our story out," would present an academically (scientifically) certified—and of course positive—representation of their lives, their beliefs, their struggles and triumphs. Field researchers speak today of the responsibility to give back to the community that assists us with our research; for this community, the expected gift was an accurate, positive, and publicly visible portrayal by a credible academic "outsider."

Heisenberg in Church

Fieldwork has its risks, its unexpected results, as well as its responsibilities. One is the near-guarantee that field research will change the researcher. The vehement protests of traditional academics notwithstanding, none of us is a purely detached, objective observer. I, for one, never expected to become a passionate witness to the power of faith in the lives of LGBT Christians! A second risk, and a puzzling ethical dilemma, is the effect that we as researchers may have on those participating in our projects. As Heisenberg established for quantum physics, so too in fieldwork it is impossible to make fully independent observations of the "object" of one's studies. As in physics, the very definitions and assumptions that shape the research process partially predetermine the results. Moreover, the process of observation itself alters that which we observe.

Although these issues are relevant to fieldwork in a variety of contexts, I find the challenges and ethical dilemmas to be particularly sharp in research on religion and research among LGBT people. Three gay men in the MCC study—Marc, Miguel, and an anonymous respondent—illustrate these complexities particularly well.

Marc, who identifies himself as a metaphysical Christian, believes that few events happen by chance—and this included the questions I asked him during the interview. When we discussed theology, he explained his belief that humans are the result of God's wish to materialize. "I am 'I AM' in my own way," he told me. I suggested that such an outlook seemed to be an extremely powerful affirmation of LGBT identity, and that in fact it could even be pushed to imply that God is at least partially lesbian, gay, bisexual, and transgender. Marc responded hesitantly to this suggestion, but eventually concluded that although he had never before considered such an interpretation, "maybe that's what I needed to hear," because "it made perfect sense." At the close of the interview, Marc thanked me, saying that I had given him "some . . . really good things to think about." I left feeling as though I had inadvertently become, or perhaps masqueraded as, a source of spiritual enlightenment.

In the interview with Marc, I involuntarily ran afoul of ethnography's firmly engrained rules of non-intervention and was uncomfortable with my apparent lack of control over my own effects on study participants. However, I had not yet thought to question the rules themselves. As a result, when I faced a severe challenge to non-interventionist ethics, I was unprepared to grapple with the ethical dilemma facing me. That dilemma itself, though, brought me to realize that our current ethics may in fact be insufficient, because intervention in the lives of study participants can cut both ways. On the one hand, it is the height of arrogance to assume that one's own worldviews and knowledge are more useful to study participants than the tools they already possess; this is exactly why Freire (1970) held that teachers working among oppressed groups should begin not by speaking but by listening. On the other hand, it is equally arrogant to maintain the stance of a "disinterested observer" in the face of human suffering.

Miguel, a Latino in his mid-forties, was raised in the Salvation Army. When I spoke with him in August 1998, he was searching for a church that would affirm his religious background yet also support him as a gay man. With pain clearly written on his face, Miguel spoke of "a battle . . . inside of me," intensifying with age, over the meaning and purpose of his life as a gay Christian. "I'm a firm believer that God made me gay," he told me. "But yet I was just reading in the Bible last night . . . the one passage that clearly states that homosexuals don't have a place anywhere." On the other hand, he added later, "I can't believe that God would have made me this way simply to condemn me." Until he is certain of God's wishes for him, Miguel is remaining single, and he described his life as being incredibly lonely. Having come out myself only six years earlier, I identified with Miguel's struggle and agonized over his pain. I had been through similar struggles, I had experienced the self-doubt and the soul-searching, I had battled socially inculcated stereotypes of people with whom I was beginning to identify. But I had not had to contend as well with sacred texts carrying potentially damning messages. I longed to help in some way, to offer Miguel a bibliography of LGBT Christian theology, to discuss with him at length what some LGBT theologians call the biblical "clobber passages." He did not ask about books or academic arguments, maybe because his struggle was his own and maybe because I was there not as a religious studies professor but as an interviewer. Mindful of the endless accusations that LGBT people "recruit," and aware that my answers might not be the ones Miguel needed, I kept silent. To this day, I am unsure whether that was the right thing to do.

At least in Miguel's case, I could listen to and affirm his struggle. Another study participant, a Filipino man, contributed only an anonymous survey in which he wrote of his struggles as a gay Catholic. "God knows I do not like to be a homosexual," he wrote. "I thought I can change myself: I keep asking God, why me? Sometimes I'm happy, but most of the time I am depressed. Sometimes I think crazy. I wish somebody will kill me. I like to evaporate from this world." Above this passage, he wrote, "I just have to pray that I'll die very soon because I cannot kill myself. It's against God's law."

I cannot read or even think about this survey, these fourteen simple pages of questions and coded answers, without being overwhelmed by grief, despair, and rage at religious institutions whose teachings have led so many LGBT people to suicide, alcoholism, drug abuse, and forced marriages. What bothers me most, however, is the paradox of anonymity. Without a guarantee of privacy, this man might never have shared his agony with me. Yet that privacy ensures that I will never know who he is, can never reach out to him myself, or casually suggest that a pastor speak with him. It also means that I cannot even know if he is still alive.

Non-intervention ceases to make sense in these cases. How do I respond ethically to the gift this man gave me by baring his soul? The only action I can think of is to publish my research—to place his story, Miguel's story, and the many stories of self-confidence and triumph, in the public eye. For these reasons, I strive to write accessibly, to structure my work so that academic "outsiders"—pastors, church members, parents, and teachers—can learn from those who so generously contributed their stories to my research.

The Academic Is Personal Is Political

"It's academic": this is what we say to dismiss an issue as solely intellectual, theoretical, unrelated to "real," "everyday" life. Ivory towers and traditionalist protests notwithstanding, many academic pursuits are in fact closely intertwined with "real life" and deeply implicated in local, national, and international politics. Most academics will agree that personal factors play at least some role in our choice of field and our selection of research topics. So at a certain level, the academic is personal. In addition, feminists are fond of arguing that "the personal is political"—that choices made on a personal level affect the realm of politics and vice versa. If the academic is personal and the personal is political, elementary algebra tells us that the academic is also, in fact, political.

In some academic works, the political implications remain implicit or unacknowledged; in others, they are more evident or even primary. Granted the assumption of objectivity, "outsiders" to a group (usually academic and mainstream cultural "insiders") rarely are requested to discuss the political motivations and biases of their work. The one exception is those "outsiders" whose research is seen as somehow beholden to the group—funded or commissioned by it, for instance. "Insiders" to the group, as I have discussed above, face much more suspicion. They are expected to be partial to the group, their analysis and objectivity impeded by loyalty or attachment. Interestingly, rarely do we consider that an outsider to a group may be just as biased as an insider, or even more so. How can we suspect partisanship on the part of "insider" researchers without examining our "outsider" research for signs of the same racism, sexism, and homophobia that drove eugenics, founded the ethnographic myth of "primitive man," assuaged the consciences of the Tuskegee syphilis researchers, and kept homosexuality in the APA's Diagnostic and Statistical Manual until the early 1970s? One scholar who read my MCC study (Wilcox 2000) pointed out that I ought to discuss in the introduction my consciously non-objective approach to the subject. She was correct, of course, especially since as academics we tend to be presumed objective until proven subjective. But as a fence-sitter, both insider (as a lesbian) and outsider (as a non-Christian) to MCC, I found myself struggling to understand the effects of both my outsider identity and my insider identity.

It took a heterosexual scholar to point out that I was assuming LGBT identity to be ontologically real, and the reconciliation of LGBT and Christian identities to be advantageous.[6] I might have written a very different analysis of MCC had I been a heterosexual, conservative Christian, but it is worth adding that had I not made every effort to suspend my negative opinion of Christianity before beginning my research, my work might also have been quite different.

I considered continuing the previous paragraph with an affirmation of the importance of listening to our research participants—after all, we are out to study *their* understandings of themselves and the world—but instead I began pondering how I might approach a group to which I was a definite and hostile outsider. Perhaps my insider status in the LGBT community helped me to overcome the biases of my location as a religious outsider—or in other terms, perhaps my positive bias toward LGBT people outweighed my initial negative bias toward Christianity. However, what if I were to conduct fieldwork in the ex-gay movement? As a self-identified advocate of LGBT rights, how would I approach the study of a group whose very existence is entirely antithetical to my beliefs? *Would* I be capable of listening carefully to what they had to say, of rooting my analysis in their lived reality rather than in my own? And is such "objectivity" truly the most ethical approach?

My responses to Miguel and to the anonymous survey respondent add force to this question. As someone who strongly believes that the pain suffered by many LGBT Christians is due not to their sins against God but to their churches' sins against them (to borrow Christian vernacular), I would be deeply disturbed by any analysis of the ex-gay movement that did not reflect in some way the pain inflicted by anti-LGBT church teachings. Would I convince myself that this was in fact an objective analysis? In fact, as many before me have pointed out, there is no such thing as an objective analysis. There are positive analyses and negative analyses, those favorable to the group or persons in question and those unfavorable to them. There are also those analyses so far removed from the context of the people involved that they are simply irrelevant to those who originally participated in the research. So, what are to be our guidelines?

Mine are simple and perhaps easily attacked—although no more so, I believe, than any other guidelines once they are explicitly recognized rather than being disguised as "objective" analysis. They are also, I have found, extremely challenging in practice. They involve being responsible to the group under study for the accuracy of my data, citing and engaging with insider as well as outsider challenges to my analysis, and open acknowledgment of my allegiances and potential blind spots. It would be nice to recommend simply that fieldwork reflect the voices of its participants in as unadulterated a form as possible. Yet, we cannot include all of those voices, except by simply publishing the transcripts of our interviews. Even then, we are denied the "authenticity" we seek, because we determine in part what is said simply by choosing which questions to ask.

Perhaps we should not bemoan the loss of the pure datum; perhaps we should instead accept the limitations of our own humanity and turn them to the best or most ethical use possible. Given the frequency with which socially non-dominant groups have been abused, misinterpreted, and exploited by researchers, it seems only just to reverse the process. If objectivity is in fact not an option, we have a choice between advocacy, constructive criticism, destructive criticism, and irrelevant or rarified analysis. As long as we are aware of these choices and make our readers aware of them as well, I believe that each option is viable and can be engaged both responsibly and ethically. Each can also be misused, and it is part of our responsibility as "human-subjects" researchers to ensure that such misuse never occurs. Since we cannot avoid subjectivity, we must be vigilant about it and choose our loyalties wisely. Perhaps, in the end, sitting on the fence turns out to be advantageous: not only does it grant us a view of both sides, but it also prevents us from getting too comfortable.

NOTES

1. In a male-dominated society, it is quite possible that the encroachment of heterosexual men (even through their bisexual partners) into lesbian "territory" or safe space presents a greater threat than that of heterosexual women into gay male "territory."

2. James Clifford has repeatedly challenged the viability of drawing strict distinctions between cultures in a world of intercontinental travel; see Clifford (1988; 1997b).

3. Two recent studies of LGBT people in religion note such difficulties: see Primiano (1993) and Shokeid (1995).

4. Like the church names, the names of all study participants are pseudonyms. This is another ethical dilemma for field researchers, especially in LGBT studies; for this project, I resolved it by using pseudonyms for everyone involved in the study, as well as for the churches and the cities in which they are located.

5. LGBT people of color have been less likely to seek such academic affirmation, in part because communities of color also have been affected adversely by the biases of ostensibly objective academic observers. This fact, along with the tendency of LGBT communities to divide along lines of ethnicity and gender, may be part of the explanation for the under-representation of ethnic minorities in my own study—in which just over 80 percent of the survey respondents and 84 percent of the interview participants were of European descent.

6. To assert the ontological reality of LGBT identity is different, of course, from asserting its biological reality. As Judith Butler has noted (cf. 1993), the fact that identities are socially constructed does not negate their force and reality. It is this force and reality that I assume in my work, and my research seeks to understand how people interpret and grapple with such reality—including those who explain it as a temptation from Satan rather than as a biologically or culturally valid identity. My entire project would have been radically different, however, were I to believe *myself* that same-sex desire and transgender identity are simply Satanic illusions.

Part II

Doing Ethnography

Chapter 5

Between the Living and the Dead
Fieldwork, History, and the Interpreter's Position

Thomas A. Tweed

In my research, I've combined historical and ethnographic approaches. I have studied dead Buddhists and living Catholics, living Hindus and dead Methodists. And when I'm in the archives, I miss the field; when I'm in the field, I miss the archives.

That's because when I write history I'm frustrated by the muteness of the dead. As Martin Marty (1997) noted, historians are "keepers of the city of the dead." And I want to make them speak, to interrogate them: What really happened at that all-night revival in northern Kentucky? How much did you, and that first generation of Virginia slaves, retain the practices of your West African homeland? What did that image of Jesus above your bed in that South Philadelphia row house mean to you? However, when I do fieldwork, which creates messy entanglements with the living, I long to return to the dead. The dead don't inquire about my beliefs or challenge my interpretations. They don't invite me to do puja to Vishnu or to pray the rosary for the unborn. The dead almost never try to convert me.

In this essay I want to reflect on the entanglements of fieldwork and make two modest points. First, I want to suggest that fieldwork offers a useful approach to the study of U.S. religion because it allows us to consider *reception*, how devotees interpret rituals, narratives, and artifacts. But ethnography also introduces as many epistemological and moral problems as it resolves. Most important, and this is my second point, fieldwork raises vividly one issue that confronts all students of religion: What is the interpreter's position? I'll consider fieldwork's use-fulness first.

Representing Religion's Reception

One of the most interesting trends in scholarship on U.S. religion during the last ten years has been the increased use of fieldwork. Of course, cultural anthropologists, qualitative sociologists, ethnohistorians, ethnomusicologists, cultural geographers, oral historians, and folklorists have known about the rewards (and challenges) of studying the living, of using participant observation and personal interviews. And if cultural anthropologists such as Clifford Geertz and Victor Turner shaped American cultural and religious history during the 1970s and 1980s, only more recently have larger numbers of specialists in U.S. religion followed them into the field.

This ethnographic lineage stretches farther back, but several books that appeared in the late eighties and early nineties have been especially influential. Among the sociologists, Ammerman's *Bible Believers* (1987), Neitz's *Charisma and Community* (1987), Warner's *New Wine in Old Wineskins* (1988), and Davidman's *Tradition in a Rootless World* (1991) studied, respectively, a Fundamentalist congregation, a Catholic Charismatic prayer group, a small-town Protestant church, and women converts to Orthodox Judaism. Scholars from anthropology, religious studies, and folklore combined to edit *Diversities of Gifts: Field Studies in Southern Religion* (Tyson et al. 1988). Anthropologist Karen McCarthy Brown published *Mama Lola* (1991), a widely read ethnography of Haitian Vodou in New York.

Since then, a number of field studies have attracted notice. Folklorists (Patterson 1995) and anthropologists (M. Brown 1997) have written movingly of Appalachian church singing and New Age spirituality. Contributions from religious studies include Griffith's (1997) ethnography of the Women's Aglow Fellowship, Numrich's (1996) study of immigrant Theravada Buddhist temples in Chicago and Los Angeles, and McNally's (1997) research among the Minnesota Ojibwa. Other widely read studies, like Robert Orsi's *Madonna of 115th Street* (1985) and *Thank You, St. Jude* (1996), combined historical methods with observation and interviews. Even art history, which has not usually sent scholars into the field to interpret religion, has contributed a rich study of Santería practice and artifacts (D. Brown 1999). There has been—to overstate just a bit—an ethno-graphic turn in the study of U.S. religious life.[1]

Let me offer just *one* reason I've found fieldwork helpful. I presuppose an understanding of religious meaning that privileges reception and fore-grounds actors (contemporary and historical). This emphasis on recep-tion, which has been evident in many fields in the humanities and social sciences, emerges from several related convictions—that meaning is con-structed (not given), multiple (not univocal), contested (not shared), and fluid (not static). And, most important, meaning is inscribed by readers, listeners, participants, or viewers.

Literary critics have applied similar notions to the analysis of a wide range of texts, and specialists in other fields have extended reception the-ory to interpret art, music, theater, film, and television. At the same time, anthropologists and many other scholars have moved toward a more fluid understanding of "culture." Anthropologist James Peacock (1986, 75) explained this transition:

> There was a time, going back to Sir Edward Tylor, when anthropology did tend to regard culture as a thing, a static object. Culture was a collection of customs, embodied in physical artifacts brought home and exhibited in museums. . . . Such a view, is what many anthropologists regard as the old one, now modified by a stronger sense of dynamism. In the new perspec-tive, culture is seen . . . as a construction incessantly negotiated by the ac-tors and interpreted by the anthropologist.

To presuppose this understanding of culture, meaning, and interpreta-tion is to reject archeological metaphors: interpretation, in this view, does not involve *excavating* fixed meanings *imbedded* in artifacts, narratives, or practices. By extension, then, the meaning of a religious artifact is not ex-hausted by the artist's intentions; the meaning of a religious ritual is not exhausted by the clergy's prescriptions. Ordinary followers, lay elites, and religious leaders continually negotiate among themselves about the sig-nificance of gestures, stories, and things. And to ignore the viewers of re-ligious artifacts and the participants in religious rituals is to miss much.[2]

I often have felt that absence when I do historical research. I often am left with insufficient evidence to answer my questions about the meaning of things or practices for the participants themselves. This, in my judgment, is where fieldwork makes its greatest contributions. It cannot resuscitate the dead, but it allows us to turn to the living to solicit their own interpretations of their religious life. In short, for those who embrace reception theory and concomitant theories of meaning and interpretation, fieldwork opens possibilities for constructing more textured representations.

Let me elaborate by referring to *Our Lady of the Exile* (Tweed 1997a), my study of Cubans' devotion to their national patroness at her shrine in Miami. In that project I used participant observation and structured interviews, as well as archival sources and survey data, to understand the religious life of Cuban Catholic exiles at that shrine, which was dedicated in 1973. I argued that exiles struggle among themselves over the meaning of symbols, but almost all Cuban American visitors to the shrine in Miami see it as a place to express diasporic nationalism, to make sense of themselves as a displaced people. There, exiles map the landscape and history of the homeland onto the new urban environment. Through rituals and artifacts at the shrine, I suggested, the diaspora constructs its collective identity and transports itself to the Cuba of memory and desire.

Fieldwork enriched that study in several ways. For example, it allowed me to construct a richer interpretation of the shrine's architecture than if I had offered only a formal analysis of the shrine's design and considered only the architect's drawings and the building committee's explanations (see Tweed 1997a, 112–15). In the idiom of art history, the building is an example of "sculptural modernism." From the perspective of the architect and planners, it represents both the body of the Virgin and the geography of the nation. The six exterior buttresses, the shrine's founding director explained, are symbols of the six Cuban provinces, so that the exterior recreates the regional divisions of the homeland. And some visitors saw this in the building too. As one female devotee told me, "the provinces of Cuba are united on the six sides" of the exterior. The Cuban architect explained other intended meanings: it reproduces the triangular shape of the statue of Our Lady of Charity, with its flowing mantle or cloak. In that sense, the shrine director suggested, "the shrine is the symbolic expression of a short prayer Cubans say in moments of difficulty: 'Most holy Virgin cover us with your mantle.'"

Some shrine visitors echoed the clergy's interpretation. An elderly Cuban devotee who arrived in 1966 told me, "It is the mantle of the Virgin, which protects her children." But the meanings of the shrine's exterior grew more complicated for me as I listened to more and more of the Cuban pilgrims' responses to the architecture. They alerted me to other natural and historical referents. One fifty-one-year-old woman said it recalled a mountain: "It is something symbolic. Since we are not able to have the true temple [which is still on the island], it is a mountain like in

Cobre. The architecture of the shrine is like a symbol of elevation." Pilgrims' interpretations nudged me to consider other referents too. Devotees constantly talked about the Virgin as their mother (*mi madrecita*). When I juxtaposed this with the official interpretations of the building as the Virgin's body or mantle, I began to see that the dark interior space created by the conical exterior might be understood as a womb, the womb of the national patroness who protects and gives identity to the Cuban migrants. So that devotees enter as exiles, alienated from their homeland and its people, and they leave bonded (temporarily) with all on the island and in the diaspora as children of the same mother.

My hundreds of conversations with pilgrims also alerted me to other (unintended) historical referents. One exile who had arrived recently reported that the contours of the exterior were "like the history of Cuba." No other pilgrim repeated that, but the more I considered his reading, the more it illumined for me. The building's exterior, I decided, inscribed multiple meanings, intended and unintended. It recalled architectural traditions in Cuban history—not Spanish but Native and Cuban. To my surprise some devotees told me the exterior was "typically Cuban" because it "resembled the huts of Cuban Indians." I politely listened but initially dismissed this interpretation. What could Indian huts have to do with the Catholic shrine? But still I followed the lead and found representations of Taíno Indian dwellings. I was astonished: there were striking, if unintended, parallels. The *caney*, or thatched huts, were conical and had six exposed columns for support. I thought more, then, about other historical referents and noticed that an Ohori-Yoruba rondavel shrine in Benin, a cylindrical altar to Legba, also recalled the Miami shrine's exterior design. Those resonances, however, were ironic since the Catholic clergy have been preoccupied to distinguish the saints of Catholicism from the *orishas* of the Afro-Cuban religion, Santería. In this sense, these design parallels were not merely unintentional, they were oppositional, because the clergy imagine the Miami shrine as a site where they can evangelize nominal Catholics who have been influenced by Santería. So the clergy, and most visitors, would reject this decoding of historical referents, although it is interesting to note that the pilgrim who saw "the history of Cuba" in the shrine's exterior form was of African heritage.

My point here is that in these and other ways, fieldwork complicated my interpretation of the architecture. It allowed me to see more clearly the contested and diverse meanings of the symbols. The result, I think, was a less tidy but more satisfying analysis than would have been possible without my conversations with the viewers and visitors at the shrine.

On Being Between and Moving Across

But fieldwork also presents challenges. Fieldwork creates moral dilemmas and epistemological problems, which anthropologists have spent much time and energy analyzing. Still, it might be worthwhile to briefly return to one issue that most fieldworkers have pondered and my own field experience has raised: *Where* are fieldworkers when they do fieldwork? Inside, outside, or in some other social space?

During the five years I worked on my ethnographic study of Cuban devotion to Our Lady of Charity in Miami, countless encounters provoked me to wonder about my relationship with my consultants—and forced me to abandon all notions of myself as an unengaged and immutable observer. Consider a few examples.

I noticed that my position changed literally over the years of study. During the first festival mass I attended in 1991, I sat toward the top row of an outdoor stadium, scribbling notes and taking photographs in a sea of anonymity. By the 1994 festival, however, I sat five rows back from the altar, even in front of the seminarians. I had a pass marked "VIP" in the front window of my car, which allowed me to park much closer to the entrance than most of the twelve thousand participants who came to worship that humid September evening. I had moved closer to the center of things.

Yet sometimes my position inverted. Before the 1995 festival mass began, I walked near the makeshift altar on the racetrack grounds, where ten thousand local Cubans soon would say the rosary and celebrate mass. Like many others, I wore a yellow shirt because, I had learned from pilgrims at the shrine, it was Our Lady of Charity's color. At the racetrack entrance, I had bought a small Cuban flag, and that symbol protruded from my shirt pocket as I chatted with devotees and photographed the scene. Then I looked back into the crowd. Behind a two-foot metal gate, a middle-aged woman with a pressed cotton dress was gesturing toward me. I looked behind me. No, it was me she wanted. As I approached, she raised her rather ordinary camera, one you might buy at Wall Mart and asked in Spanish, "May I take one, please?" I was so surprised that I didn't answer. I was too flustered to ask what I wanted to know, what I still want to know: Why did she want my photograph? I just posed for her, with my camera dangling from my neck and that Cuban flag tilting from the pocket of my yellow shirt. But what did she see through that lens? Did she mistake me for a middle-aged Cuban devotee with affection for the Virgin and passion for the homeland, her homeland? Had we exchanged words once before a rosary or mass at the Virgin's shrine in Miami? Did a friend tell her about me? Did she read about my project in *La Voz Católica*, the Spanish language periodical that had just run a story on me and my research project? I'm not sure what she saw. But it was clear that I had become the subject of *her* curiosity. She was the interpreter.[3]

At times my position seemed so confused that I could only muster a bemused smile. One Sunday afternoon in June, for example, I traveled across Miami in a yellow school bus filled with Cuban devotees, whom the shrine director, the Most Reverend Agustín Román, had decided to take to a local Haitian mass and procession celebrating the feast of Corpus Christi. On the way over, Román, auxiliary bishop of Miami, explained the trip's purpose. It was about fostering racial harmony among Miami's Catholics. He explained that both Cubans and Haitians had suffered much, and both yearn to return to their homeland. He acknowledged the color differences—all the Cubans on the bus were white—but used a metaphor to plead for harmony: "Cuba, remember, is beans and rice, black and white." Just as Cubans love black beans and white rice, the Cuban-born bishop suggested, racial harmony among "all brothers and sisters in Christ" was possible. I was moved by his remarks, but they didn't help me locate myself any more clearly. After all, to the Haitians sitting in the pews when the forty of us walked in, I was a white, Spanish-speaking Cuban Catholic, who was visiting that day (as their Creole-speaking pastor had explained to them too) to promote unity in a city that was known for its ethnic divisiveness. To the Cubans I entered with, I was an Anglo scholar who hung out at the shrine and had been asking them questions—too many questions. Around seven o'clock that evening the procession wound its way down Little Haiti's Second Avenue in a light rain, following the Virgin Mary, the Blessed Sacrament, and rows and rows of young Haitian girls in crisp white dresses. As I walked down the glistening asphalt beside a stout Haitian woman who shielded me with her umbrella and boisterously sang hymns in Creole, I wasn't sure who I was or where I stood.[4]

Sometimes Cuban pilgrims weren't sure either. A few times, devotees at the shrine mistook me for a priest, and I quickly corrected them. Some visitors asked me if I were Cuban, as they tried to discover the origins of my interest. One exile from a town near Ft. Lauderdale pressed me on this one weekday afternoon at the Cuban shrine. After I had interviewed him, he turned the tables.

"Now that I have told you so much," he began, "may I ask why you are writing this book? Are you Cuban?"

"No," I said. Where is he going with this, I wondered.

"Are you married to a Cuban?"

"No."

That didn't make any sense to him. Why would I write about Cubans if I had no personal connection? So he pressed me further, as his extended family crowded in to gleefully eavesdrop on the interrogation. He asked again, to make sure he didn't misunderstand.

"You are not Cuban?"

I felt uncomfortable by his probing—so this is how they feel?—so I went for the clever deflection.

"No," I said in Spanish, "I am Cuban only in my heart."

To this the crowd let out a collective, "Aaaaah," as if I'd said the right thing. I meant it, but I also felt guilty because I knew my primary aim was to end the interrogation and deflect the attention.[5]

It became less clear over the five years I studied devotion at the shrine whether I was inside or outside. I lived in Miami, but I was not Cuban. I found Marian devotion familiar since my mother, and the nuns in Catholic school, had cultivated in me a respect for the veneration of Mary. But by almost all criteria, I was no longer Catholic: I no longer practiced Catholicism. Spanish also wasn't my first language. And politically, I was far to the left of most Cuban pilgrims, who loathed Fidel Castro and did not tolerate any hint of support for his socialist government. So I was outside.

But then other experiences confused that outsider status. Because I had listened to so many sad stories about exile, I had gained some sympathy for Miami's Cubans. Some of my Anglo friends and colleagues decided that I had "sided with them" (and in Miami discussions about ethnicity and religion meant taking sides). To those Anglos, I did not seem to condemn forcefully enough what they viewed as the intolerance and excesses of the reactionary exile community. On the other side of the ethnic divide, by the fourth year of study some of my Cuban friends began to tease me by suggesting that I had become "an honorary Cuban." They meant it affectionately, but I was not sure what to make of it. One thing seemed certain: I had been changed by years of interactions.

In the book (Tweed 1997a, 9), I tell another story that illustrates how the interactions shifted my position as interpreter. Several years into my fieldwork, I visited the statue of the Cuban Virgin at Washington's National Shrine of the Immaculate Conception, which includes dozens of images and chapels dedicated to the saints of American ethnic communities. As I located the Virgin's image, I found myself—spontaneously and inexplicably—praying in Spanish to Our Lady of Charity for the liberation of Cuba: "*Virgen Santísima, salva a Cuba.*" What was that? I wondered afterward. Even after considering the religious and political implications of this for some time, I'm still not sure what I did and why. Had I gone native, at least for that one moment, identifying with a political viewpoint and religious worldview I did not share? Had my abandoned childhood piety resurfaced temporarily? Was it simply an act of respect and empathy for those who had been so kind and told me so many sad stories? I still have no idea. But I find the incident useful because it reminds me of my ambivalent position as interpreter. One fieldworker (Sarsby 1984, 132) has described my experience well:

> The ethnographer will always be somewhere on the continuum between empathy and repulsion, home and strangeness, and seeing and not seeing.

But the issue is still more muddled than that. Not only was my position as interpreter confused, but sometimes those whom I studied tried to *change* my position. In the least perplexing version of this, members of the community challenged my interpretation. A few of the clergy who read drafts of the manuscript said their share of nice things, but they also expressed discomfort with some elements of my interpretation. One Cuban priest, for example, thought that I was too hard on the clergy when I pointed out their concern for evangelizing followers of Santería. It is not unusual to find that those you interpret challenge your interpretations. It bothered me, but I did not find it too difficult to resolve. I simply decided to include, word for word, the priest's criticism of my analysis. I did not grant him veto power, but I did allow him to dispute my reading, so that readers could adjudicate the disagreement between us (even if I inevitably and unintentionally privileged my version of the disagreement). I did the same with other clerical objections about my treatment of Santería.

For example, the shrine's director once asked me to speak to a group of twenty-something Cubans. Of course I agreed, since he had endured hours and hours of interviews and provided inestimable assistance. But when I mentioned Santería and the history of Cuba's unchurched population, he grew uncomfortable. As we left the shrine that day, he said only, mustering as much kindness as possible: "It takes many voices." Again, my strategy was to include his remark in the book (Tweed 1997a, 166, vii).

I also have encountered even more troubling reminders of my contested position, as when clergy or laity tried to convert me. That happened occasionally at the Miami shrine, but it was more frequent (and troubling) in recent fieldwork among Filipino Catholics. As I was interviewing and observing Filipino American devotion at a Catholic shrine in Washington, D.C., I met Maggie, who became one of my most helpful consultants. But she, like that man from Ft. Lauderdale at the Cuban shrine, could not understand why I was writing about her. She asked me about my religious views and was troubled that I am not a practicing Catholic. Her strategy, which I only deciphered slowly, was to nudge me back into the Catholic Church. One afternoon in June 1997, for instance, she asked me to meet her at her bank office for our scheduled interview. I agreed, of course. When I arrived, she hurried me out saying that we were late.[6]

"Late for what? I asked.

"Oh, I thought that you might like to see a rosary prayer group in the next door office building."

I agreed, somewhat perplexed. When we arrived a few minutes late to the small conference room, twelve Filipinas and one African American woman sat around a long table. At its center was a twelve-inch statue of Mary. To her left a crucifix and two white candles. All the women fingered rosary beads, sliding their hands down from bead to bead as they recited the formalized prayers, which were offered to ban abortion, I learned later. My Filipina friend handed me a plastic rosary they kept for visitors, and she looked at me expectantly, as if I now was supposed to join in. Momentarily dazed by the moral dilemma she posed, I mumbled a few Hail Marys, before deciding that I would only observe the rest of the lunchtime office ritual. After my initial surprise, I was grateful that she had brought me, and I said so. She then asked me for a favor, as I walked her back to the office. Would I please go across town to the Catholic center and copy down the Spanish inscription on the painting of Our Lady of Guadeloupe there? It seemed an odd request, but she had helped me so much that I could not refuse. When I arrived, I realized that it was an outreach center designed to attract new converts and revive lapsed Catholics.

Only a few days later, while I was visiting the Filipino chapel at the National Shrine, did I realize what had happened. She had tried to bring me back to the fold with that noon-hour rosary and manufactured errand. Maggie was going to get me back in the pews any way she could, even if it meant a little deception. Just then, as I recognized Maggie's missionary impulse, that longing stirred in me again. How comforting it would be, I thought, to extract myself from the entanglements of fieldwork and abandon the study of the living. I longed again for the archives, the historians' cozy graveyard. I welcomed the (now) comforting muteness of the dead.

But as I walked toward the Filipino chapel I realized there was no place of refuge. Interpreters always stand in an ambivalent position, and our interpretations always are situated, never nowhere in particular or everywhere at once. So where was I? I found myself *between*—between inside and outside, fact and value, subject and object. And, as I focused my attention alternately on the distinctive rewards of the archives and the field, I found myself between the living and dead too. Or, to be more precise, like the transnational migrants I was studying, I was actually always moving *across*. I remembered that in my study of Cubans at the shrine I had argued that their rituals and artifacts were *translocative*, propelling the Virgin's devotees back and forth between the homeland and the new land. In a similar way, Maggie helped me to see that I too was shifting constantly between here and there, inside and outside. So perhaps I should set off for the archives. But historical research has its epistemological and moral problems, too. Cavorting with the dead, I decided, could not fully or finally ease my disquietude. At that moment I clung only to my renewed commitment to a professional principle: that we are obliged in all our work, ethnographic and historical, to be as clear as possible about our confused location, to be as attentive as possible to our continually shifting position. And in that reflexivity is all the comfort available to interpreters.[7]

But as I left the Filipino chapel that evening, I thought again about Maggie. I couldn't help but decide right then: my next book will be history.

NOTES

1. Four recent collections of case studies offer some sense of the swelling interest in field studies of U.S. religion: Warner and Wittner (1998), Hall (1997), Orsi (1999), Becker and Eiesland (1997).

2. There is an enormous literature on reception theory, too large to cite here. Helpful works in literary studies, media studies, dramatic arts, art history, and cultural studies include the following: MacHor and Goldstein (2000), Holub

(1992), Allen (1987), Radway (1991), Elkins (1996), Freedberg (1988), Morgan (1996), Iser (1989), Bennett (1998).

3. Fieldnotes, festival mass, 9/9/95, Hialeah Race Track, Hialeah, Florida. The festival mass used to be held in Miami Marine Stadium, but in 1992, Hurricane Andrew destroyed that structure. Organizers have moved the ritual since then—to Bayfront Park (1992), Dinner Key Auditorium (1993), Hialeah Racetrack (1994–99), and American Airlines Arena (2000). On the 2000 festival mass, see Cantero (2000, 12–13).

4. Fieldnotes, 6/5/94, Corpus Christi festival mass and procession, Haitian Center, Miami.

5. Fieldnotes, 9/7/94, Shrine of Our Lady of Charity, Miami. I was uncomfortable in this exchange, and I recorded that in my notes and thought about that afterward. As Sherryl Kleinman and Martha A. Copp (1993) have argued, it is important for ethnographers to be self-conscious about the emotions that arise from the entangled relationships and intense experiences in the field.

6. Fieldnotes, 6/5/97, World Bank, Washington, D.C. For my analysis of the Filipino oratory and ethnicity at the National Shrine, see Tweed (2000).

7. I have discussed the "situated" character of interpretation in Tweed (1997b). See also Haraway (1991, 183–201). Emphasizing the relationship between the fieldworker and the person she is studying, and the concomitant risk involved, Robert A. Orsi (1998, 220) has noted another way in which the interpreter stands between:

> The ground upon which such a researcher stands belongs neither to herself or to the other but has come into being between them, precisely because of the meeting of the two. This is ground that would not have existed apart from the relationship between the researcher and her subject.

On diasporic religion and translocative artifacts and rituals, see Tweed (1997a, 91–133).

Chapter 6

"But Are They Really Christian?"
Contesting Knowledge and Identity in and out of the Field

Simon Coleman

The Magic of Fieldwork

A few days before I started to write this piece, I found myself reading Michael Taussig's *Mimesis and Alterity* (1993). The book is a vivid exploration of "the mimetic faculty, the nature that culture uses to create second nature, the faculty to copy, imitate, make models, explore difference, yield into and become Other" (xiii). Taussig ranges from a description of Charles Darwin standing on a beach in Tierra del Fuego, encountering local people who display remarkable prowess at mimicking their English visitor, to an analysis of the imitative powers of machines such as the phonograph and camera. He emphasizes the *politics* of imitation, its frequent involvement in hierarchical and colonial relations in the history of human encounters. He also points out that mimesis recalls Sir James Frazer's (1890) venerable notion of "sympathetic magic"—in other words, the ability to own and control an original "Other" through processes of replication and representation.

I was consulting Taussig's work for different purposes but was struck by the relevance of his ideas for an understanding of anthropological assumptions about the nature of fieldwork and subsequent production of ethnography. When I first entered "the field" some fourteen years ago, intent on gathering data for a Ph.D. on Protestant charismatics in Sweden, I had received relatively little formal training in techniques of gathering data. My teachers assumed that a year's immersion would convert me into an expert on the lives and beliefs of "my people." Although apprehensive at the thought of the trials that lay ahead, I and other fledgling doctoral candidates took comfort in the fact that we were about to engage in the Holy Grail for budding anthropologists: "participant observation." Naturally, we made some initial ritual preparations—attempting to acquire relevant language skills, obtaining visas, and so on—but the main thing was to be "there" (in the field) as opposed to remaining "here" (at home). Having arrived at our chosen site, we might conduct interviews and administer questionnaires, but our chief tool would be the gradual process of accommodating to, and becoming accepted by, our informants. Acceptance meant not standing out too much from the crowd; fitting in with what was deemed correct behavior within the culture of our choice; often, just mimicking what local people did. The knowledge to be gained was not just about facts and figures; it was also about crossing an experiential divide, learning what it felt to be one of "them."

Fieldwork, in this view, can be seen as a sophisticated form of sympathetic magic, a means of blending the Self with the Other sufficiently to allow legitimate anthropological appropriation and subsequent representation of exotic culture. Mimetic acts are implicated in the embodied actions of the fieldworker, who consciously presents a Self that is both plausible to informants and close enough to indigenous ways of life to permit privileged understanding. In her evocative and moving ethnographic memoir, *The Spirit and the Drum* (1987, 31), Edith Turner describes her involvement in the lives of Ndembu people in terms that suggest a removal of her own agency, alongside a conversion toward religious conviction and away from Marxist materialism:

> Nothing I can do can pull me away from these people into a separate shape that is supposed to be "myself." . . . So you will need to look into the story, into the very rituals to find me, because I have practically disappeared into them. The spirit which has caught me desires to be made manifest, and there's not a thing I can do about it.

This is a striking description of the imitative "magic" of fieldwork. It is probably unusual in the extent to which it claims that a blending of oneself with one's informants has been achieved but does have parallels with many other anthropological accounts. For instance, in her engaging analysis of modern witchcraft in London, Tanya Luhrmann notes (1989, 17): "Very early on in the study I realized that the new subjective experiences involved in learning to practice magic were crucial to an individual's decision to become further involved. I decided that I would understand magic best if I did what people did to become magicians." However, Luhrmann is more cautious than Turner in assessing her ability to achieve complete involvement and interpretative insight (14): "The fieldworker cannot learn what 'they' 'believe': nor can she ever really know what really occurs in the mind of any one individual." Thus, the constant conversations and mimetic practices that constitute fieldwork are necessary but incomplete: the "magic" of imitation has limited powers.[1]

Admittedly, religion is a particularly difficult subject for the fieldworker to tackle, partly because of its nonempirical nature, and partly because of the rationalist assumptions of much social scientific scholarship. Luhrmann's ethnography is a subtle analysis of the ambiguities of "belief" for her informants as well as for herself. Nonetheless, as Bowie (2000, 10) notes, it is at least plausible to assume that "disbelief" can be suspended in the name of ethnographic investigation: "It is certainly possible to remain open to another culture and its beliefs, and perhaps be profoundly affected by them, without feeling it necessary to enter into discussions of truth or falsity." At the same time, Bowie (11–13) is correct to argue that anthropologists cannot duck difficult questions of authorship, appropriation of knowledge, and the politics of representation.

In this essay, I want to deal with issues of mimesis, representation, and knowledge through shifting the conventional focus of ethnographic attention away from the idea that "we" are studying and writing about "them." As fieldworkers, we usually assume that the salient and powerful work of representation—and thus of assigning cultural identity—is carried out by us. Is this always true, however? What of the voices and actions of our informants? Do they not interpret, contest, appropriate, and perhaps re-present what we do in accordance with their own agendas? And must we continue to assume that there is a fundamental social, cultural, and analytical divide between "the field" and "home"?

The informants whom I describe in this essay are extremely "religious" according to most conventional, Western understandings of the term. They participate in the activities of an organization that has moved, since its foundation in the early 1980s, from obscurity to fame (and national notoriety) as an important player in the worldwide "Faith/Health and Wealth/Prosperity" movement (Coleman 1996; 2000).[2] The "Word of Life Foundation" (*Livets Ord*), based in an industrial zone on the outskirts of the city of Uppsala, Sweden, now runs possibly the largest Bible School in

Europe alongside a congregation, media business, self-contained schooling system, and university. Activities commonly carried out by believers
include constructing texts alongside cultivating experience; systematizing
knowledge so that it can be assimilated by themselves as well as by future
initiates; drawing up boundaries between Self and Other, home and the
(missionary) field, but also working out how to transcend such boundaries. In certain respects, their activities seem surprisingly similar to
those of secular Western anthropologists. As we shall see, they have
prompted me to wonder about the nature and direction of mimesis in my
fieldwork: Who, in other words, has been mimicking whom?

Entering "The Field"

Ethnographic accounts of arriving at fieldwork sites are often more than
just geographical descriptions of where a particular group of people happens to be located. They can be used to express the vast cultural gulf to be
traversed by the anthropologist (and, by implication, the reader) in the
course of the text. Napoleon Chagnon's (1968, 5) portrayal of his arrival
among the Yanomamö is the example that has stuck in my mind since
undergraduate days. He steps off a boat, immediately encounters some
fierce looking characters with wads of green tobacco hanging from their
mouths, and wonders how best to end his fieldwork there and then.[3] Anthropologists who study religious groups, especially those in the West, do
not necessarily have such dramatic introductions to the field. For instance, Luhrmann (1989, 17) notes that, as a white, middle-class intellectual, she could not readily be distinguished from her "people." I certainly
did not look that different from many of my charismatic friends in Sweden. Moreover, arrival in Uppsala involved an entirely familiar activity,
that of spreading my possessions around student accommodation owned
by the local university. My choice of a place to live was not intended to
keep me in an academic haven, separate from my informants: many of
them lived in the same apartment block at the edge of town. Even my
original decision as to fieldwork location had involved a particular blur-
ring of the boundaries between field site and the academy. A few months
earlier, I had paid an exploratory trip to Uppsala and talked to a member
of the local Pentecostal church who also happened to be an anthropologist. He had informed me of the Word of Life's existence and the impact it
was having in religious and wider circles. Going back earlier still, I had

first become interested in Christianity when a fellow student had tried to convert me during an undergraduate lecture, and offered to take me to a service at her local charismatic church in Cambridge, England.

I had nonetheless assumed that, once settled in Uppsala, I could negotiate access to the Word of Life and thenceforth treat it as my own, self-contained "tribe." Although I was affiliated with the city's university, I intended (with Malinowski in mind) to "get off the verandah" and immerse myself in charismatic culture. However, the academy kept coming back into view. It turned out that some of the university's theology students visited the Word of Life, and some of their lecturers were engaged in (usually highly critical) studies of the group. In addition, I was struck by an encounter I had with a local anthropologist within a day of arriving in Sweden. After we were introduced to each other, I went through the ritual of describing my proposed fieldwork, assuming that he would then make some vaguely encouraging noises. Instead, he exclaimed: "Why on earth do you want to study those nuts?" This was hardly the response I would have received if I had said I was planning a re-study of Nuer religion or Ndembu ritual. After a number of similar conversations, I came to realize that the Word of Life had hit a sensitive nerve among liberal Swedish intellectuals.

For theologians (and many journalists), the group represented an anomalous mixture of right-wing politics, business practices, and oversimplified Christian dogma (Coleman 1989). It was also something of a threat: the founder and head pastor of the Word of Life Foundation, Ulf Ekman, had gained a theology degree at Uppsala University, and a member of the Word of Life had recently started up a weekly meeting specifically aimed to attract university students. For social scientists, the Word of Life represented a different, but equally distasteful, phenomenon. At times, I began to feel that I had stumbled upon an area of study that was taboo within my own intellectual community. Everybody agreed that the Word of Life had "culture," but to some of the researchers I met in Sweden it was culture of the wrong kind, ethnographic matter that was out of place in classifications of suitable fieldwork sites. For a start, the group was clearly very Americanized—it invited preachers from the United States to preach at regular intervals—and so could hardly be considered a discrete social unit. Indeed, it actively encouraged people (from all parts of the world) to flow through its various courses and conferences without staying for more than a few months, so that they could then spread the Word to other cities and countries. More significantly, it was rather hard to think of Word of Life members as conventional ethnographic subjects, peripheral to centers of social power (cf. Borofsky 2000). Participants usually welcomed their connections with the United States and promoted strategies, borrowed from North American preachers, of aggressively seeking material resources and public influence within and beyond their local community. Many, indeed, were richer (and had better computers) than I did. Furthermore, while some of the anthropologists I met in Sweden were, like me, studying religion and ritual, they were usually conducting fieldwork over "there" rather than "here." On the one hand, the Word of Life represented a culture of global missionization that was spreading to and "polluting" many spaces occupied by fieldworkers in non-Western contexts. On the other hand, it was also very visibly located "at home," gaining unfavorable publicity in secular, Social Democratic Sweden.

I suspect that its anomalous character was one of the things that originally attracted me to the Word of Life. Raised in a home environment that combined atheism, cultural Judaism, and distant traces of Scottish Presbyterianism, I found the deeply felt commitment of its members fascinating but remote from my own experience. Despite (or perhaps because of) my decision to work in an urban, Western context, I was choosing to research a decidedly "exotic" culture. At the same time, I had the good fortune to stumble upon a group that was becoming a prime object of national discourse during the 1980s—indeed, the center of a moral panic concerning what was and was not truly Swedish. Yet, such fortune carried with it certain methodological problems. How could I actually define my field of study? The Word of Life was clearly influenced not only by its relations with people and other ministries far beyond Sweden, but also by its need to seek a legitimate place within society at large. The "field" that constituted the group as a cultural and social phenomenon included the considerable media, medical, and academic attention that was focused upon its activities. Some of its members were themselves students. Whether I liked it or not, I was going to have to bring the academy back into view. It was more than a place where I could find colleagues to discuss ideas; it would have to become part of my "ethnographic gaze."[4]

Charismatic Anthropology?

The notion of the gaze, with its Foucauldian implications, implies a certain kind of imbalance: in the classic Enlightenment image of Jeremy

Bentham's panopticon, a single person monitors the actions of a multitude of prisoners, none of whom is granted a vision of their jailer. Applied to anthropology, the gaze might present a suggestive (if depressing) vision of the ethnographer as empowered spectator, although of course we attempt to assuage our sins by overtly "participating" as well as "observing." In my own case, I soon started to attend meetings at the Word of Life and found that I blended quite well into an organization that was full of other young people. The second pastor of the group, whom I explicitly consulted, said he would have no objection to my attending meetings, but added that neither he nor other members would have time to help me in any direct way. However, as weeks passed, I found quite a few people who were willing to talk to me and accept me as part of their social networks.

Over the years, I have paid a number of visits to the Word of Life, updating my initial fieldwork period of fifteen months (from spring 1986 to summer 1987). I confess that I have never felt myself "merge" into the rituals in the way Edith Turner describes her experiences among the Ndembu. Each time I return and attend my first service—which may involve some two thousand people dancing enthusiastically, speaking in tongues, and then listening to a two-hour long sermon—I experience a sensation that comes as close as I ever can to Chagnon's initial desire to be somewhere else as fast as possible. Yet this feeling soon passes, and I find myself adjusting to a familiar fieldwork habitus, or embodied regime, reflecting an assimilation of mimetic acts built up over years of fieldwork.

Despite many obvious contrasts with the everyday routine of the academic life, certain aspects of participation in Word of Life actually seem quite familiar. Taking notes during sermons hardly marks me as the anthropologist, as many others are doing so with equal fervor. More generally, participation in the group involves numerous forms of self-objectification through a wide variety of media. Members not only are constructing testimonies of faith and conversion narratives but also are constantly taking photographs, making video films, and producing tape recordings of services or missionary visits. Newspapers and newsletters examine past events and advertise future ones. Charismatic leaders are diligent producers of books, particularly exemplary autobiographies. Word of Life members are used to the idea of representing themselves to themselves, as well as to potentially convertible and/or hostile others.

Such means of self-representation, deployed by many conservative Protestants, may be deployed to turn the tables on unsuspecting visitors.

Susan Harding (1987) describes what happened when she visited a Baptist pastor in the United States, thinking she was going to interview him. Instead, dialogue was converted into monologue, as the pastor seamlessly and unstoppably blended biblical imagery and striking personal experience in a narrative that was aimed at Harding the potential convert, not Harding the anthropology professor. She left the encounter feeling that "I had been invaded by the fundamental Baptist tongue I was investigating" (169). The pastor had proved to be extremely adept at positing and then dismantling the boundary (and hierarchy) between saved Self and unsaved Other, converting the ethnographic gaze into an evangelical one.

At the Word of Life, I have never experienced quite such a direct assault on my own anthropological assumptions, but I have become very aware of the ability of many Swedish charismatics to locate themselves in relation to a world of other, powerful discourses, such as those of academia and the media. Some Bible School and university students are specifically trained in the theory and uses of communications technology, and believers often emphasize the importance of acquiring knowledge that will be of use in "the world." I remember one occasion, in particular, when I attended a meeting of Christian Student Front, a group of Uppsala University students broadly sympathetic to Faith ideas who regularly prayed together and discussed possible careers. The head of the group, a thoughtful man who later started up a national newspaper reporting on Prosperity Ministries,[5] announced that he was going to talk about the various subjects taught at the university. From him, we learned that certain areas of study, such as law and engineering, were clearly useful to the Christian since they helped believers gain important positions within society at large. However, he noted that two subjects were to be treated with extreme caution. Anthropology was suspect because it taught that cultures around the world worshipped many gods, failing to stress that, in reality, only one, all-powerful divinity really existed. Theology, meanwhile, as currently taught at most universities, was too liberal and overintellectualized, sometimes even removing the idea of a credible God from its students' minds. I never learned whether any part of the talk was specifically directed at me, but I was left in no doubt as to the ability of my informants to reflect upon my own discipline and to put it firmly in its place.

In dealing with potentially threatening forces, one strategy of conservative Protestants—as with many interest groups—is to denigrate the Other. Such appeared to have been the case in the talk I have just described. Another strategy, however, is to mimic and appropriate the Other, thus assimilating it to group ends. The head of Christian Student Front actually published a book pointedly entitled *Biblical Prosperity Theology* (Holmström 1986). As he notes in the preface (6–7), his aim was to adopt a term originally coined by some Swedish theologians and to convert it to revivalist ends. More recently, I have noticed a striking development in the Word of Life's new syllabus for its university. Courses include not only theology, history, and political science, but also a range of social sciences, including "Cultural Anthropology." The latter is part of an International Relations Major that also includes "Major Religions of the World" and "Cross-Cultural Communications," and is said to involve the study of kinship, marriage systems, and different systems of belief. I do not recognize many of the books in the recommended bibliography, but there are a few significant inclusions: one is a book on sects written by the distinguished scholar who in fact examined my Ph.D. thesis (Wilson 1970); another, on nationalism, is by an equally renowned scholar who was my head of department during the time when I was writing up my fieldwork (Gellner 1983). There is a certain irony in the fact that two such well-known analysts of rationality should be invoked as part of a form of charismatic mimesis, an attempt to appropriate the power (and knowledge) of the academy through the sympathetic magic of imitation.

I doubt whether Swedish believers who are taking a Word of Life degree in International Relations view the purpose of their studies in exactly the same way as I did when I was a student. Yet, I would not wish to dismiss their views on anthropology as being entirely remote from what occurs in more "mainstream" contexts. As I have argued elsewhere (Coleman and Simpson 1999), anthropologists have been surprisingly slow to apply ethnographic techniques of assessment and reflexivity to practices of teaching and learning. There is at least anecdotal evidence to suggest that many students deploy their knowledge of the beliefs and customs of other cultures not only to pass exams but also to create personal meaning-systems.

Back from "The Field" or: "But Are They Really Christian?"

When I returned to England to write up my dissertation, I regularly met many of my fellow doctoral candidates in seminars and, more informally, in pubs. Some returnees looked and sounded exactly as they had done before they had left for the field, but most had incorporated subtle signs of their ethnographic experiences into their demeanor and language. A poncho here, a Nepali jacket there, signaled the expertise of the now experienced fieldworker, as did a few words in a foreign language thrown into a conversation, or a remark made during a seminar that would start something like "Among my people. . . ." No doubt I contributed my fair share of viewing the rest of the anthropological world through personalized ethnographic spectacles, but I became aware once more of certain political and epistemological implications of my choice of fieldwork site. Most of my colleagues were able to express a sense of personal and intellectual sympathy with peoples whose symbolic capital in the seminar room and pub derived in part from the fact that they were divorced from, or victims of, centers of Western economic and cultural power. In such company, I could hardly claim to identify myself with Protestant charismatics, other than to say that they were human, too. The very fact that such Christians were engaged in their own processes of contacting peoples around the world, as well as apparently choosing to annex the symbolic and material power of the United States in such interactions, rendered them anomalous in English as well as Swedish anthropological circles. If I had "merged" entirely into Faith rituals and ideology, I would have been engaging in a form of mimesis that would have betrayed much of what cultural and social anthropology claims to represent.

Theologians in the United Kingdom and the United States have also displayed broadly similar attitudes to their Scandinavian counterparts. The following example, drawn from a conference presentation I gave a few years ago at a conference in the north of England, is but one of many that I could have quoted. Having given a paper discussing the ways in which Word of Life members were deploying ideas drawn from business in their self-presentations and understandings of their global project, I expected the discussant (himself a liberal Protestant from the United States) to comment upon the parallels I had drawn between Faith ideology and broader notions of capitalism. In fact, he commented briefly that he found my paper interesting, and then added: "But Simon, the *important* question is, are they really Christian?" From the point of view of a more "mainstream" form of Western Christianity, I suspect that it is tempting to regard the Word of Life and similar religious groups as peripheral to the real work of a compassionate and tolerant religious faith. In that sense, liberal Christians and anthropologists share a desire to promote pluralism with a certain predilection to seek sources of virtue and identity in the disadvantaged (those who can be deemed to require the voice of a humane representative of a privileged class). My own reaction when asked such a question is, I admit, one of considerable frustration. Of course, I understand that different disciplines have different concerns. However, the important question, as far as I am concerned, is precisely *not* whether members of the Word of Life are "really" Christian (whatever that means), but that they have as much to tell us about culture and humanity at large as any other social phenomenon.

Concluding Remarks: But Are They Really Anthropologists?

In his historical analysis of anthropology, Johannes Fabian (1983) famously argued that ethnographers have tended to separate the "here and now" of scholarship with the "there and then" of fieldwork sites. Anthropologists have made their object by distancing it from the Self, both geographically and temporally. Mimesis of the Other, inherent within fieldwork practice as I have described it, has traditionally relied upon the assumption that anthropologists are specialists at *translating* meanings and experiences between separate cultural worlds. Of course, many examples do exist of attempts to break down hierarchical relations of power between observers and observed. Scholars have attempted to give an extended, unmediated voice to informants (e.g. Strathern 1979), cooperated with indigenous peoples in creating understandings of the past (e.g. Layton 1994), and highlighted the long history of mutually constitutive economic relations that have existed between colonial powers and so-called primitives (e.g. Wolf 1982).

My point in this essay goes beyond a recommendation that anthropologists should recognize that fieldwork entails certain forms of hierarchy. It is that fieldwork can provoke a set of powerful representations and discourses whose scope not only includes but also transcends the writings of the "secular" anthropologist.[6] I have described fieldwork relating to a religious group whose members, rather like anthropologists, regard their identity as constituted by the action of reaching out into cultural worlds beyond "the local." Such worlds can include not only foreign places visited but also powerful areas of expertise and production of knowledge, such as media communication and academia. The "field," for an ethnographer of the Word of Life, does not end with Uppsala or even Sweden, given the mobility of its members and the extension of its offices into such places as the United Kingdom and the United States. Believers are perfectly capable of employing anthropological discourse in a reflexive manner, and although I might not regard them as doing exactly "my" kind of anthropology, I would not presume to state that they are incapable, by definition, of being "real" anthropologists. Indeed, while recently writing a book on the connections between the practices of the Faith Movement and processes of globalization (Coleman 2000), I found myself reflecting upon the fact that my own conceptualization of global processes was partially based on charismatic understandings of what Ulf Ekman (1985) has called "faith which conquers the world."

Nor can I assume that my own writings are easily divorceable from the self-constitution of the Word of Life. I am aware of the fact that members of the group have read a mini-ethnography that I published in Swedish (Coleman 1991). So far as I can tell, some approved of it (not least because it did not contain biting criticism), while others were more wary of anything that did not actively promote a Faith message. Ulf Ekman certainly quoted a passage in a letter to a local newspaper, using my reference to a "network" of people hostile to the group to claim that his opponents were a mutually reinforcing, if misguided, force.

It might be stated that the Word of Life is a special case, a group that is unusual in the resources it can command, its awareness of mainstream Western discourses, and its literally evangelical zeal to enter into and control the lives of the as-yet-unconverted. All of that is undeniable. Still, we can hardly sustain the ethnographic myth that the places and peoples we study are bounded, self-contained, and incapable of their own reflexive responses to multiple discourses, including those produced by academia (Olwig and Hastrup 1997). I have also argued that anthropologists could be more aware of their own classification systems in assessing suitable objects of fieldwork. The anomalous nature of the Word of Life—both a charismatic ministry and a university[7]—helps throw into relief some of the assumptions behind these classifications. Of course, I have not discussed in any detail the anomalous character of *urban Sweden* as a place to do fieldwork. But that is another story . . .

NOTES

1. Compare Stocking's (1992, 53) discussion of Malinowski's ambiguous attempts "to grasp the native's point of view."

2. The Faith Movement is a loose network of Bible schools and congregations, diffused around the globe but with its epicenter located in the United States, and in particular the ministries of such preachers as Kenneth Hagin and Kenneth Copeland. The theology of the Movement combines post-War healing revivalism and positive thinking and stresses the right of the born-again believer to receive material blessings from God.

3. By the end of the book (135), Chagnon states that he has begun to be "emotionally close" to the Yanomamö: sitting in his hammock, he abandons the ethnographic task of collecting genealogies and begins to act like a human in Yanomamö terms. The mimetic magic has apparently worked.

4. In practice, I found that at least some anthropological colleagues were open to the idea that, as Swedish citizens as well as academics, they were playing a double role of analyst and de facto informant. Among theologians, the political stakes were higher, not least because the group presented an even more direct challenge to its academic discourses.

5. Called *Trons Värld* or "World of Faith."

6. Not all social scientists are secular in their personal beliefs. In the preface to her book on charismatic Christians, Poloma (1982) discusses her attempt to combine sociological insights with use of her own spiritual experiences.

7. Historically, of course, many educational establishments have combined religious foundations with scholarly research.

Chapter 7

Transitional Identities
Self, Other, and the Ethnographic Process

Janet L. Jacobs

Over the last two decades, writings on ethnography and culture have considered both the postmodern nature of contemporary ethnographic research and the illumination of the self through the study of the other (K. Brown 1985; Clifford and Marcus 1986). In a provocative essay on "Ethnicity and the Post-Modern Arts of Memory," Michael J. Fischer (1986) insightfully observes that for the researcher, ethnography involves analyzing and defining one's self against a backdrop of the other, a dynamic of comparison and self-reflection that is often transformative for the academician. Fischer maintains that the bifocal nature of ethnographic work can lead to life changes within the researcher, such as those experienced by Louis Massignon and Victor Turner. In this regard, Fischer writes:

> The ethnic, the ethnographer, and the cross cultural scholar in general begin with a personal empathic "dual tracking," seeking in the other clarification for processes in the self. One thinks perhaps of the great Islamic scholar and Catholic mystic Louis Massignon, who used Sufism as a proxy for his dilemmas in a post-Christian, anti-mystical world. Examples could be multiplied. Among the most sensitive and best anthropological works are those that bring personal engagements of this sort into play, albeit usually only as subtext, rarely highlighted or explicitly acknowledged. One thinks of the association between the late Victor Turner's engagement with Ndembu rituals and symbols, and his turn to Catholicism; of Stanley Tambiah's work on Buddhism in Thailand, which, unlike so many written about Buddhism by Westerners, treats it with respect as a potent political force. (199)

The interactive and dynamic view of ethnography, as described by Fischer, has its origins in feminist theory and methodology, which, since the 1970s, has challenged the assumptions of neutrality upon which the social-scientific canon of objectivity is based (Cook and Fonow 1990; Reinharz 1992). Emerging out of nineteenth-century positivism, the scientific canon fosters the belief that a rigid dichotomy between the researcher (subject) and the researched (object) can and must be sustained if "pure" science is to be achieved. According to feminist scholars, such claims to objectivity create an illusion of neutrality that ignores the presence of the self in the research setting. Over seventy years ago, the well-known theorist and psychologist, Jean Piaget (1929), questioned the plausibility of the positivist methodological approach, reminding the scientist of her or his ever present intrusion in the research process:

> Objectivity consists in so fully realizing the countless intrusions of the self in everyday thought and the countless illusions which result. . . . Realism, on the contrary, consists in ignoring the existence of the self and thence regarding one's own perspective as immediately objective and absolute. Realism is thus anthropocentric illusion, finality in short, all those illusions which teem in the history of science. So long as thought has not become conscious self, it is prey to perpetual confusions between objective and subjective, between the real and the ostensible. (22)

As feminist scientists sought to make clear the suppositions of Piaget and the interplay between the self and the scientific process, the discourse on sustainable boundaries between the researcher and the researched began to inform contemporary ethnographic thought, as evidenced by Fischer's essay on ethnography and self-transformation. Fischer's observations, and the feminist perspectives that his work exemplifies, provide a framework for interpreting my own ethnographic experience while researching the descendants of the Spanish crypto-Jews. Accordingly, this essay will address the issues of identity that became salient for me as I studied and took part in the culture of modern crypto-Judaism. The chapter will begin with a brief discussion of how I entered the research field and will then examine the identity issues that emerged for the descendants whose life changes impacted my own reclamation of a Jewish ethnic self.

Unexpected Encounters: Crypto-Jewish Remnants in the Rocky Mountains

In the spring of 1994, I came across a newspaper article in the Denver Post that was reporting on the presence of crypto-Jews in southern Colorado during the seventeenth and eighteenth centuries. Included in the article were interviews from various individuals who believed that they were descendants of Spanish and Portuguese Jews whose ancestors had been forcibly converted to Christianity during the Inquisition period. The newspaper account offered a brief history of crypto-Judaism, describing how a portion of the forced converts publicly accepted Catholicism while privately preserving Judaism in the home. As the Inquisition expanded and intensified its efforts to find and punish the crypto-Jewish adherents, a large number of crypto-Jews emigrated to the Americas, bringing with them a secret form of Jewish practice that they clandestinely maintained in the colonial territories. For the story on the contemporary crypto-Jewish phenomenon, the newspaper interviewed descendants of the original crypto-Jewish settlers, some of whom were now in the process of recovering their Sephardic (Spanish Jewish) roots. Like others who read this account of alleged Jewish secrecy and survival, I became intensely interested in the possibility of a colonial Jewish presence in Colorado, as well as in other areas of the Southwest, where reports of crypto-Judaism had begun to surface. Since the early 1990s, there had been a proliferation of media reports on crypto-Judaism. Interest in this comparatively unknown piece of Spanish Jewish history had grown in response to the 1992 commemoration of the expulsion of the Jews from Spain five hundred years earlier and Columbus's simultaneous colonizing expedition to the Americas. The newspaper, radio, and magazine accounts of crypto-Judaism created a popular culture image of this phenomenon that focused heavily on family secrecy and religious persistence. Through this imagery, women in particular were singled out as having maintained remnants of Jewish rituals and beliefs that could still be found in families throughout New Mexico, Arizona, southern Colorado, Texas, and northern Mexico. The existence of a woman-centered form of religious survivalism offered compelling possibilities for research, and I soon found myself surveying the literature on Judaism, colonization, and the West. I sought to determine the credibility of modern-day descendant claims and the evidence for a twentieth-century culture of hidden Sephardic Judaism in the southwest of the United States.

The literature review turned up little more than a handful of ethnographies on descendant populations (Hernandez 1993; Nidel 1984; Santos 1983) and a plethora of studies and monographs on the history of crypto-Judaism in Spain, Portugal, and the colonies of the Americas (Gitlitz 1996; Liebman 1970). The ethnographic work centered primarily on New Mexico and Texas and referred to proceedings of the Society for the Study of Crypto-Judaism, a group of academics, clergy, and descendants who had begun to hold conferences in 1992 to disseminate and explore the modern descendant phenomenon. As I considered whether to pursue a project that would look at the relationship among ethnicity, gender, and cultural persistence, my "research fate" was sealed unexpectedly in the spring of 1995 at a Mexican restaurant near the University of Colorado campus. The restaurant had just opened within a short walk from my office and I was attracted both by the name, Mamacita's, and the promise of "authentic" Mexican style cooking. The first things I noticed when I entered the restaurant were the original paintings that decorated the walls. Among the artistic renderings was a large mural of what appeared to be the Western Wall in Jerusalem. A small Mexican boy stood praying at the Temple wall, his body wrapped in a serape and his head covered by a traditional Jewish skull cap. Somewhat surprised by the religious theme of this work, I looked around at other paintings, observing that they too appeared to mix Jewish imagery and symbolism with a Mexican cultural milieu. As I left the restaurant that day, I took notice of the mezuzah that was attached to the doorpost of the entryway. I thought at first that perhaps the owner was an Ashkenazic (German European) Jew from Mexico, where many European refugees had gone in the early twentieth century and where, with the rise of Nazism, other Jewish émigrés had settled some twenty years later. Yet, there was something about the paintings and the deeply Mexican sensibility that they conveyed, which suggested that the painter's attachment to Mexico had very deep roots, while the Jewish imagery was suggestive of another time and place.

Within a week, I returned to the restaurant and introduced myself to the owner, a woman in her mid-fifties, who had recently moved to Boulder from the Midwest. We spoke about her transition to the Rocky Mountains and the college town where her son was now living. I explained that I was a sociologist working in the area of religion and that I was very interested in the artwork that she had chosen for the decor of her restaurant. She told me that she was the artist and that the subject of her work reflected a hidden Jewish background that her family had maintained while she was still a child in Mexico. Unsure of the meaning that coincidence seemed to play in my as yet undeveloped "study" of crypto-Judaism, I arranged to meet her the following week when, with tape recorder in hand, I made the transition from curious academic to crypto-Jewish researcher and ethnographer. With great emotion and attention to detail, the restaurant owner/artist revealed a family narrative that spoke of secrecy, fears of lingering anti-Semitism, and a rich maternal culture in which stories of a Jewish past were both remembered and retold. She described how her ancestors had once been Jews and that, although she had been raised a Catholic, her mother and grandmother retained both the knowledge of their Jewish heritage and some unique family customs that bore traces of their Jewish ancestry.

This interview, my first of what would become many over the next four years, was perhaps the most significant. With the telling of the narrative, the project began to take shape as the romanticized and popular images of crypto-Judaism gave way to a more nuanced and realistic portrait of crypto-Jewish descent. As I listened to this woman's account of a childhood in Mexico, where her attachment to Jewish ancestry had been nurtured and sustained, I became convinced of the value of the research project and the power of ethnography to reveal what had for centuries remained hidden and concealed. Through the trust, honesty, and vulnerability expressed by this first participant in the crypto-Jewish project, I began to understand the depth to which the discovery of Sephardic roots transformed the identity of descendants whose knowledge and integration of Jewish heritage had bearing on the social and religious construction of themselves as ancestral Jews. Within this changing definition of the self, the ethnography took on a decidedly postmodern character as the descendants engaged in the deconstruction of themselves as Latina/o Catholics.

Reclaiming Ancestral Origins: A Postmodern Response to Hidden Ethnicity

The postmodern paradigm, as developed by the French theorist, Jean-Francois Lyotard, seems especially useful for framing the ethnic identity shifts of the crypto-Jewish descendants. Lyotard's (1984) conceptualization of postmodern culture emphasizes the changes in art, science, and literature that have emerged in response to the late-twentieth-century questioning of scientific authority and the assumptions of the past. With regard to the study of ethnicity specifically, this theoretical approach challenges the doctrine of "pure origins" that emerged out of nineteenth- and twentieth-century social-scientific ideologies of incontestable truth and objective reality. In contrast to this positivist paradigm, postmodernism recognizes the unfixed and fluid nature of identity formation and thus provides a standpoint from which to construct and understand ethnic and racialized identities. One of the most significant aspects of postmodernism is that it allows for the self-identification of individuals whose historical and cultural dislocation have placed them on the margins of a diverse set of interrelated cultural communities. For the modern descendants of crypto-Jews, this de-centering and de-essentializing of identity is fundamental to the reclamation of ethnic/religious ancestry.

Because the descendants reside at the intersection of multiple social locations, including those of religion, ethnicity, and nationality, they are engaged in the production of narratives that recreate ethnic identity through three forms of association. These are an identification with historical oppression, the articulation of cultural memory, and the oral transmission of ancestral heritage. In weaving together these three aspects of self identification, the accounts of the crypto-Jewish descendants create what Anderson (1991) has termed an "imagined community," that is, a community that may be variously defined by bonds of history, memory, language, or ritual and custom. For many ethnic and racial groups, this imagined community exists as a challenge to the threat of cultural annihilation. Among these populations, of which the crypto-Jews are one, the creation of identity-narratives becomes the basis upon which religious ancestry and ethnic heritage is established and reclaimed. Because the survival of colonized and persecuted cultures has often relied on subterfuge and secrecy, this postmodern creation of identity becomes tied to narratives constructed out of silence and fear. Such narratives historicize the experience of the crypto-Jews as descendants seek to uncover family genealogies that legitimate their claim to Jewish ancestry.

Many of the descendants have thus spent a great deal of time researching their family's genealogy, amassing extensive documentation of their family's Sephardic origins and their subsequent persecution during the Inquisition period. The most poignant moments in the research process were often those in which a descendant would describe his or her experience with the archives of Mexico City and Madrid where the records of the Inquisition are housed. A number of respondents had visited the archives or had obtained copies of documents that recorded the arrest and trial of their ancestors. These documents, written in large medieval script, bear witness to the torture and death of the medieval crypto-Jews. Among contemporary crypto-Jewish descendants, these Inquisition records have become a visual reminder of the painful realities that lay at the core of their secret Jewish identity.

While the written records of the Spanish Inquisition situate crypto-Jewish identity in a particular historical context, the postmodern construction of contemporary crypto-Judaism is more problematic. In contemporary twentieth century culture, crypto-Jewish identity is in part created out of silence. In the self-conscious secrecy that characterizes certain aspects of family life, what becomes important for descendants is that which is remembered but remains unspoken. A woman from southern New Mexico gives this insight into her family culture:

> We were a very secretive family. It was always, "don't talk about this. We don't talk about this," would be my mother's response when I would ask her questions. When I was growing up, the stories we were always told were about the Apache side, of my grandfather, who had been kidnapped by the Indians when he was a little boy, of him running down the street carrying his baby because he feared he would be kidnapped. This was the only story we were told. But then I learned the other side. My aunt thought she was dying so she could tell me, "you do know we are Jewish don't you?" This is my secretive aunt. She would even cover her mouth when she spoke. She was dying and she wanted me to know the "other side" now . . . I was stunned and shocked to find out I was Jewish, finding that secret part of your life. Now I want to go back and find that part of my story. This generation, we are the ones putting the pieces together.

In those cases where total silence was not observed, the knowledge of Jewish ancestry was communicated through narratives which simultaneously revealed the secret Jewish ancestry of the Catholic family while reproducing the fear of discovery in the next generation of descendants. Thus, their recollections are reminiscent of the writings of the Mexican Jewish author Esther Seligson (1991). In her work, she tells the story of a young Jewish woman who is about to leave the land of her birth where Jews have been persecuted. As she is leaving, her grandfather and her uncle give her contradictory advice:

> The grandfather said to her: "When you leave here, don't forget that you are Jewish." The uncle, irate, added: "When you leave here, forget that you are Jewish." (Seligson 1991, 34; quoted in Schuvaks 1996)

This dilemma, like that of the crypto-Jews, exemplifies the tensions surrounding hidden ethnic identity. To survive individuals must simultaneously remember and forget who they are and from where their families originate. As contemporary crypto-Jews negotiate the conflicting terrain of memory and denial, the project of remembering becomes tied to the creation of new narratives of ethnic identity. Through these narratives, the descendants recall the unique customs of their mothers, grandmothers, and great grandmothers, rituals that carry with them the imprint of an ancestral faith that is found in the lighting of candles, the maintenance of dietary laws, and the observance of holidays and festivals. From a postmodern point of view, the construction of crypto-Jewish identity relies on the creation of narratives that are derived from memory, from oral history, and from the historical linkage to Inquisition oppression.

Through these narratives, the descendants sought to integrate the effects of religious persecution on their burgeoning identity as ethnic Jews. In this process of self-transformation, their feelings of loss and spiritual alienation revealed a sense of longing that increasingly informed my own awareness of Jewish ethnicity and religious privilege. In the descendants' reconstruction of themselves as ancestral Jews who had been silenced and deprived of an ethno-religious heritage, I saw my own reflection as the assimilated Jewish academic. During the course of the research, I found myself engaged in the same postmodern project of identity formation that characterized the accounts of the descendants. Through the medium of ethnography, whereby I listened to and recorded the lives of others, the definition of myself as a Jew and as a scholar began to change. The boundaries between their experiences and my own intersected in a shared cultural awareness of the meaning of Jewishness in contemporary Western society.

The Ethnographic Method and the Transformation of the Researcher/Self

Among the most significant ethnographic moments in this research project, my fieldwork in Tucson, Arizona, deeply informed my own changing Jewish consciousness. Through a contact in Tucson, I was able to meet and interview a descendant family that had recently emigrated from northern Mexico. The family lived in a trailer park on the outskirts of the city, and I arranged to meet them at their home on Saturday morning, a few hours before they held their weekly Sabbath services. I arrived at the agreed-upon time and was welcomed into a small living room where I was greeted by three adults and a young child. The family consisted of a mother and father who were in their mid-sixties, their grown daughter, and their nine-year-old grandchild. After a warm welcome (we conversed in Spanish), I looked around the comfortably furnished room and immediately caught sight of a small glass jar that contained a neon light in the shape of the Star of David. They explained that this small tube light was lit each Friday night and remained lit until Saturday at sundown. Next to the light, they had carefully placed a candelabrum, a "menorah" they told me, which belonged to another family member. With these artifacts as a backdrop, the mother in the family began her narrative of crypto-Jewish heritage that had begun in northern Mexico, where her grandmother clandestinely lit candles every Friday night and where she recounted stories of the secret Jews who refused to eat pork. At the end of this emotion-filled interview, the entire family joined in singing the Hatikveh, the Israeli national anthem, first in Spanish and then in Hebrew. As I left, the child in the family gave me a bookmark that she had made that morning while I was speaking with her grandmother. On the bookmark, she had written the word Shalom in big sprawling letters, with her name, Neomi, neatly printed at the bottom.

The interaction with this family, who had transported their unique form of crypto-Judaism from Mexico to Arizona, epitomized much of the emotional attachment that the descendants felt toward Judaism and their Jewish ancestors. Although they had been raised as Christians, they spoke with passion and yearning for a Jewish ancestral heritage, which they valued and still wished to maintain. Throughout the ethnographic research, I continued to feel a deep sense of admiration for the descendants. Here were individuals who were longing to practice their Judaism openly, who were hungry for information on rituals, beliefs, and customs, and who frequently looked to me as "an expert" on Jewishness, someone who would affirm their identity and offer insight on how to be a good Jew as they embraced this shift in their ethnic/religious identity. In their accounts of family secrecy and burgeoning Jewish consciousness, I could not help but see my own reflection as an assimilated Jew in the United States, one who sporadically and casually lit the Sabbath candles and who had access to a tradition that I had the luxury to reject or accept at will.

Through the descendants' experiences and openness, I came to see myself through an assimilationist lens, which had a profound impact both on the sense of myself as a religious Jew and as a scholar. Religiously, I could hear the sermons of my Conservative Jewish childhood, in which the rabbis spoke of religious observance as both respect for a culture that was constantly under siege and as a moral obligation to Jewish teachings. As I listened to the crypto-Jewish narratives of Inquisition history and cultural persistence, the rabbinic message now appeared less trite and more meaningful, and I soon found myself lighting candles every Friday night, as I had not done since my own children were young. I even brought candles with me when I traveled, reminding myself that I had taken for granted the customs that the descendants and their ancestors had painstakingly sought to preserve. Candle lighting in particular took on a power of its own, as the accounts of the descendants reinforced images of both the medieval and postmodern secret Jews huddled behind drawn curtains and in basement spaces where they whispered Jewish prayers to no one but themselves. At this point in my re-emerging Jewish consciousness, I was keenly aware that, like so many of the media reports, I too was romanticizing the past and the memory of a secret Jewish culture. As I performed the Sabbath ritual each week in my kitchen, I sometimes imagined my own Sephardic ancestors who, according to family lore, had once been crypto-Jews in Portugal. Unlike the descendants, however, my medieval family eventually left the Iberian peninsula, taking refuge in the Ottoman empire, where they returned to the open practice of Judaism, a religion that they sustained with orthodoxy through later immigrations to Eastern Europe and the United States.

At the height of my engagement in the crypto-Jewish project, I had what one might consider a mystical experience. For years, long before I had begun the crypto-Jewish research, I would light candles in churches all over Europe, believing that sacred space was sacred space, regardless of the structural context. As was my custom, which I have now handed down to my children, I would silently pray to my own spiritual source in the magnificent sanctuaries in France and Italy and in the beautiful island chapels of Greece. In the United States, I repeated the ritual in the Sanctuary of Chimayo and in the Church of Saint Francis of Assisi in Santa Fe, both of which are located in New Mexico, an area of the Southwest that is believed to be a centuries-old home of crypto-Jewish settlers. When my empathic bonds with the descendants were strongest, I visited the large church in Santa Fe while doing fieldwork in the region. Lighting my candle in the exquisite side chapel where the statute of the Conquistadora stands, I suddenly had this image, or perhaps vision, of my Spanish Jewish ancestors: a woman lighting candles before the statue of the Virgin Mary while reciting prayers to God, asking forgiveness for the charade that the Spanish Jews had been forced to play out. In that moment, I felt both the pain and spiritual longing that the medieval crypto-Jews must have experienced, and I wondered whether my church custom had not in fact been a re-enactment of a previous ancestral past.

Whether or not the experience in the Santa Fe church was truly a mystical revelation, the "reliving" of religious secrecy led to a clearer understanding of the creative ways in which oppressed groups respond to political and social hegemony, how they find, within the dominant culture, ways of expressing prohibited forms of the sacred. At the same time, I also gained a greater appreciation for the sense of estrangement that the crypto-Jews experienced, as a colonized people who were neither Jew nor Christian, but existed on the margins of both cultural and religious traditions. As religious outsiders, I resonated with the descendants' narratives of alienation that reminded me of my own isolation and longing for a spiritual anchor in a culture in which I had always felt marginalized by my religious heritage. As issues of ethnicity and loss framed the ethnographic research, my scholarship and teaching began to reflect my newly revitalized Jewish self. In response to this self-reflexive dynamic, I started to identify not only as a feminist but also as a Jewish scholar.

This shift represented a change in the curriculum I chose for my classes and in my willingness to speak more openly about issues on which I had remained silent in the university community where I have spent most of my academic life. This is an environment where, for the better part of the last twenty years, Jewish holidays went unacknowledged on school calendars and in institutional planning, and where issues of anti-Semitism were rarely addressed. Having been a voice for feminism on the campus, I now found myself wondering why I had so tacitly ignored my ethnic background in my efforts to create a more just and diverse university culture. In my own academic home of Women's Studies, discussions of anti-Semitism were largely absent from the discourse on gender, race, and class, an absence to which I contributed by my own silence and denial. This was especially obvious at the beginning of every fall semester when I wrestled with my internalized anti-Semitism. Although I religiously canceled classes for Rosh Hashonah and Yom Kippur each year, I never explicitly gave the reason for the cancellations either on the syllabus or during class time. The Jewish students always knew, however, because the dates corresponded with the high holidays, and a few would quietly thank me for providing an opportunity for religious observance without penalty. I thus came to the crypto-Jewish project with my own sense of loss that slowly made itself known as I began to understand the depth to which a "hidden" ethnic identity informed both my life and that of the descendants.

My identification with the crypto-Jewish participants was strongly influenced by a family history that bore certain similarities to the descendants' experience. It was only in the last year of my father's life that he spoke openly of his mother's Spanish Jewish heritage and thus of his own ethnicity as a Sephardic Jew. Steeped in the culture of German Judaism that dominated his up-bringing, my father's silence around this aspect of his Jewishness seemed to bring me even closer to the crypto-Jewish descendants, who, like me, were grappling with the discovery and meaning of a recently recovered ancestry. While this immersion in the research setting facilitated an empathic bond between myself and those I was studying, I feared that this closeness might result in a self-centered interpretation of the crypto-Jewish experience that would privilege my voice over that of the descendants'. Thus, as I reflected on the similarities between the participants and myself, I tried to remain strongly aware of the differences that informed each of our lives. While the descendants and I were both Spanish-origin Jews whose forebears had suffered through periods of religious persecution, our ancestors had taken very different paths in the centuries following the forced conversions and the Spanish Inquisition.

Judging from my own experience with the crypto-Jewish project, I have come to see ethnography as a rich area of social scientific endeavor, one in which both the researcher and the researched, the self and other, are transformed and influenced by the dynamics of data gathering and participant observation. As researchers, we enter a world that is different from our own. We seek there to find common ground through an intertwining of experiences and perspectives that may have a life-changing impact both on ourselves and on those we study. Within this dynamic of change and transformation, my work with the descendants of the crypto-Jews has had a profound effect on my identity as a Jew and as a feminist. Through this research project, I have strengthened my attachment to a Jewish cultural heritage, having seen in others a longing for connection that I deeply desire for myself. Finally, I have gained a greater awareness of my own ethnic and religious consciousness and of an alienation that I have only just begun to understand.

Chapter 8

Being (in) the Field

Defining Ethnography in Southern California and Central Slovakia

J. Shawn Landres

In *Ethnography Through Thick and Thin*, George Marcus (1998:192–198) suggests that the difference between sociological and anthropological reflexivity lies in their attitude toward difference—and social distance—between the fieldworker and the field. For sociologists, Marcus argues, reflexivity obtains in the acknowledgment that there is an irreconcilable, irreducible difference between the ethnographer and the subject of study. For anthropologists, however, reflexivity is found through locating the diffuse and diverse relationships that link the observer with the observed. I am a graduate student with training in two disciplines, religious studies (where my focus is in the sociology of religion) and social anthropology.[1] The experience of being an academic dual citizen makes me somewhat sensitive to the social manifestations of ideology, religious and otherwise. As a doctoral student in the Department of Religious Studies at the University of California, Santa Barbara, I have been concerned with what we might call "religion-on-the-ground": empirically observable expressions of religious belief and practice. Simultaneously, I am also a research student in Oxford's Institute of Social and Cultural Anthropology, where I have been schooled to look behind social practices for underlying beliefs and ideologies. My fieldwork experiences have touched on the link between ideology and practice, and I believe that the social anthropological study of that link highlights the importance of the ethnographer's position and self-analysis and the relationship between the fieldworker and the field.

On a summer's day in Oxford in 1998, I found myself trying to win over two rather skeptical reviewers of my proposal for extended fieldwork in Banská Bystrica, Slovakia. I had proposed to study European identity among members of two local groups, the Rotary Club and the Jewish community. One of the reviewers asked me, "And just how is it that an American studying in England can ask Slovaks whether or not they feel European?" My hasty reply—the graduate student's stock answer—was that of course I would acknowledge this in my interviews and in my write-up.

During fourteen months' fieldwork in Banská Bystrica, however, I realized that this question was far more crucial than perhaps even my bemused reviewers had intended. I wanted to find out how local élites construct and deploy transnational identities in order to win membership in the so-called European club. Because I was interested in how Slovaks make their case for being European, who I was mattered a great deal. As all ethnographers do, I consciously shaped my self-presentation in order to elicit the most useful possible responses to my interventions and inquiries. On the one hand, I was an American; on the other hand, my mother and grandfather had been born in Slovakia. On the one hand, I was a near-native son, returned "home"; on the other hand, I was a Western interloper, come to pass judgment on a struggling new country. Furthermore, I was a credentialed academic researcher (albeit a very junior one) with ties to a world-renowned university. To complicate matters further, I was Jewish, and during the Holocaust various members of my maternal family had been deported by the Slovak wartime regime; my grandparents had fled the country with my mother in 1939. Each of these identities—American, repatriated Slovak, Westerner, academic, Jew—shifted in importance throughout my research, sometimes because of, other times in spite of, my best intentions.

The ambiguity of my identities became very apparent both to others and to me during the NATO campaign in Serbia and Kosovo. Although Slovak public opinion was divided deeply over the abstract justification for the war, there was strong opposition to the intervention itself, and as a Westerner—worse, an American with ties to Britain—I was suspect. Despite all efforts to reassure my friends and colleagues, I was unable to convince anyone to consent to an interview. As a result, I did not conduct my first formal interview until nearly two months after the end of the bombing. The NATO campaign, however, did provide me many opportunities to learn about Slovakia's precarious position as a Slavic country seeking entry into the European Union. Radio and television programs, newspapers, and magazines all resounded with impassioned arguments about Slovakia's ethnic and political obligations. My own ambiguous status provoked a variety of reactions, both silent and vocal.

My Oxford University reviewers might well have asked a similar question about my blurred identity three years earlier, when I embarked upon a rather different fieldwork project in Southern California, this time working out of the Department of Religious Studies at UCSB. Under the auspices of a bicoastal grant project, entitled "Religion and Generational Cultures," I set out to study the success of New Song Church, a Los Angeles-area evangelical Protestant congregation targeting the 18 to 35-year-old age group more commonly known as "Generation X." This time, my reviewers might have asked, "And just how is it that a liberally minded Jewish academic can ask conservative Christians why their church works?"

At New Song Church, I encountered a different kind of engagement with my identity. At the conclusion of my research project, the associate pastor and I were sitting in his office discussing my findings. "Do you have any questions you never got around to asking?" he inquired. "Not really," I replied. "I'll bet you're wondering why we never tried to convert you," he prompted. "Yes, actually I was," I answered, somewhat startled by his directness. He told me that the staff members preferred to be good models rather than good persuaders and that while he hoped I would one day become a Christian, it could only happen when I was ready. Evangelism at New Song is primarily concerned with setting a Christian example through personal witness—but not so much through verbal testimony as through behavioral modeling. However, in retrospect, I am not certain that I could have documented this as straightforwardly if I had been an "insider," already "a Christian."

Beyond Reflexive Ethnography

I want to propose a model of ethnographic reflexivity that resists making distinctions between the ethnographer and the subject of study. This model is concerned less with reducing the social distance between the observer and the observed than it is with rethinking the context within which the ethnographer understands his or her encounter with the "Other." The first step in being "reflexive" in this proposed model is acknowledging that "the field" includes the ethnographer himself or herself.

This is the import of the recent "reflexive turn" in cultural anthropology. Both *Writing Culture* (Clifford and Marcus 1986) and *After Writing Culture* (James et al. 1997) devote extensive consideration to the challenges of "representation" and the relationship between ethnographic texts and their subject matter. Although *Writing Culture* asks more about the structure of representations, while *After Writing Culture* asks more about the meaning of representations, both collections focus on representations as scholars produce them.

Both texts, like others in their genre, call into question long-held assumptions about the motives and consequences of ethnographic research. From *Writing Culture* onward, the myth of the impartial anthropologist mastering all he surveys finally is put to rest. Instead, ethnographers can produce knowledge that is at best "inherently partial —committed and incomplete" (Clifford 1986:7). No single field researcher can hope to capture an entire culture; still less can he or she claim "authority" to speak for silent (or silenced) "Others." In *After Writing Culture*, Allison James, Jenny Hockey, and Andrew Dawson (1997) argue that anthropologists must "pay closer attention to the epistemological grounds of their representations and, furthermore, . . . consider the practical import of that process of reflection" (3). "Whose representations are they?" ask the authors; they note the impossibility of representing "whole cultures" and the difficulties in conveying "the ways our informants succeed in representing to themselves the unfolding events that go to make up their everyday experience" (7, 9–10). The authors also argue that the political dimensions implicit in ethnographic representation require that "we . . . no longer distance ourselves from responsibility for our texts" and that "[we] consider carefully . . . the political fall-out of our representational practices" (12–13).

However, neither book asks how the process of representation is managed by the people we study, and how those representations inevitably affect the outcome of our field research. Thus, the so-called reflexive moment in ethnography is restricted to the person of the researcher and his or her work-product. As such, the three major arguments of "reflexive anthropologists" are self-limiting and do not achieve the full potential inherent in the notion of reflexivity.

Firstly, reflexive anthropologists observe that the so-called field itself exists, if at all, only because the ethnographer says it does. Each scholar defines the "field" in each given project, and in some cases the "field" only exists because the scholar sees a coherence visible perhaps only to him- or herself. However, conventional reflexivists do not consider the often extensive negotiation that takes place before and during fieldwork, negotiation over the definition and boundaries of "the field." Fellow academics, whether colleagues or reviewers of grant proposals, may try to assert or impose their own assumptions about the field. Similarly, once in the field (however defined), researchers must often contend with local suggestions to reshape the scope of the inquiry. For example, Lynn Davidman (2000b) has recently observed that "a deeply held bias towards institutional religious forms" of American Jewry has dominated the academy; "unaffiliated Jews," she claims have become "a residual category in studies of contemporary Jewish life." Her response is to propose research that moves these "marginal Jews" from the periphery to the center (430). While I was conducting field research, I interviewed a member of the Banská Bystrica Rotary Club who suggested that there was not enough of a "community" in the club to justify studying it as such. As a result, I took a more critical approach to my assumptions that the Rotary Club was a coherent network. In both of these instances, the "field" is revealed to be a product of complex negotiations among a variety of groups, the nexus of which is the ethnographer.

Secondly, reflexive field researchers point out that all encounters between the ethnographer and his or her informants take place in and through the ethnographer's own construct. Indeed, the terms "informant," "consultant," or "interviewee" are inherently relational; they have meaning only because they refer to interaction with the fieldworker. However, the nature of that interaction has a profound effect, albeit one not often acknowledged, on the outcome of the research and its presentation in textual form. In his recent study of the controversial International Church of Christ, Gregory Stanczak (2000) reveals himself in the text only long enough to tell us that once he "sat cowering in [his] seat as disciples called out their encouragement" during a particularly fiery sermon (116). Given the aggressive evangelization techniques for which the ICC has become well known, the nature of the interaction between the fieldworker and his informants deserves greater attention than it receives in Stanczak's study.

Thirdly, reflexive ethnographers contend that, through the writing of the ethnography itself, the "field" is visible to the reader only through the mediated vision and analysis of the ethnographer-author. Moreover, to some extent, the success of the ethnography depends on the ability of the author to persuade the reader that the field is both valid and meaningful.

In her study of a synagogue service for single Generation X Jews in Los Angeles, J. Liora Gubkin (2000) begins an important paragraph in a reflexive way: "As a Generation X Jew myself, I was a participant as well. Thus, I too was privileged to partake in the fine art of flirting." Yet her description trivializes the importance of the courtship encounters during and after the service by focusing almost exclusively on her own negative and positive experiences in such a flippant tone that she even mocks a congregant who attempted to make a connection. By the end of the paragraph, she is "happy to report that I even secured a date. We met while watching Israeli dancing. My mother is ecstatic" (208). In short, this crucial element of Gubkin's analysis is trapped in its own narcissistic vision—not only was the ethnographer gazing at her own navel, but she also delights in suggesting that others were, too. The effect is to trivialize the entire field encounter.

Sheba George's (1998) insightful study of an Indian Orthodox church began as a congregational study but was published as a study of "the negotiation of gendered space" as a result of her very similar, though longer-term, involvement as an attendee at the church. Indeed, George reports that it was her initial innocent query—why only the men went caroling at Christmastime—that set the stage for her study of gender relations at the church (265–266). She further describes how her involvement in organizing a coed youth caroling group made her "the object of some sanctions that gave [her] insight into the manner in which boundaries were drawn around male participation" (281–283). Like Gubkin, George reports on a variety of uncomfortable situations in which she found herself, encounters that highlighted her liminal status as an unmarried female researcher, but George makes effective use of those situations to establish herself as inextricably implicated in a clear field of contested gender relations as an object of sustained study. She persuades us that her position was a vantage point.

All this is very useful and good, but reflexivity need not limit itself to standpoint analysis. There is a second step that anthropologists have seldom taken, which goes beyond the insight that ethnographer's *construct* "the field." More fundamentally, I shall argue that the ethnographer *is* "the field"—and quite literally. That is, ethnographers do not just *represent* and *define* "the field"; they *become* it.

To reach this conclusion, we must look more closely at the representational process: not just while the ethnographer writes up her or his research, but while she carries it out. As much as we may hate to admit it,

ethnographers actively manipulate their identities in order to get what
they want in the field setting. Informants, in turn, manipulate both their
own and the ethnographer's identities for their own ends. Thus, the fieldwork situation and its aftermath involve at least eight different representational moments:

1. "I the Anthropologist" represent myself and people like me (i.e., anthropologists and ethnographers, even academic scholars as a
   group) to the "Others."
2. The "Others" represent me to themselves. They decide for themselves who I really am and why I am among them.

These first two moments of representation take place not only at the beginning of fieldwork, when we first enter a community and attempt to locate ourselves within it, but also as fieldwork progresses and our role and
purpose change. The sociologist William Shaffir describes his initial foray
into the world of Chassidic Jewry:

> A Lubavitcher asked me: "Exactly why are you so interested in Chassidim?
> Is it just for the university or are you yourself interested?" I instinctively
> recognized the advantage of including a personal motivation in my reply,
> which was not entirely untrue, and before I had a chance to formulate a
> reply the man explained: "You see, if it is just for school then I can answer
> your questions one way. But if I know that as a Jew you are also interested
> in this, then I will answer your questions differently." . . . By projecting both
> personal and academic interests, I was attempting to display a particular
> image that I suspected would be received favorably. (Shaffir 1991:78)

In my own case in Slovakia, I found that if I amplified one part of my
background, if I told people that my mother was born in Slovakia, then
very few people asked other questions of me and were more willing to
share of themselves. I had any number of ethnic identities that I could
have chosen—Moravian, Ukrainian, Belarusian, and even Egyptian. I
consciously chose to give people the piece that I thought would make
them open up to me, or that I thought would make them relate to me in a
way that I wanted them to do. To a certain extent, both then in Slovakia
and three years earlier at New Song Church in Southern California, I presented myself in ways that skirted the issue of my own religious identity.
While some people knew I was Jewish, others did not, and I actively
avoided the subject because I did not want my Jewishness to become a
complicating factor in my research relationships. Inevitably, though,

one's identity always creeps in to shape the field and its web of relationships, and I now regret, for example, that I allowed the staff at New Song
(who knew I was Jewish) to steer me away from a "Jews for Jesus" family
active in the congregation.

Regardless of the ethnographer's efforts, however, members of the
community under study inevitably come to their own conclusions. The
anthropologist Susan Harding (1987) experienced such a questioning of
her motives when she began interviewing fundamentalist Baptists in
Lynchburg, Virginia. "I was naïve enough to think I could be detached,"
she writes. "My story about what I was doing there, instead of protecting
me from going native (a kind of ethnographer's verbal fetish) located me
in their world: I was a lost soul on the brink of salvation. And Reverend
Cantrell spoke to me accordingly." In both instances, as Harding puts it,
the exchanges were strategies to "locate [the ethnographer-outsider] in
their world." They helped the Chassidim—or the Baptists—to figure out
how to understand the ethnographer's presence in their own internal
terms. In my own experience, my closest friend in Banská Bystrica, a
member of the Rotary Club, often introduced me to friends and colleagues by highlighting my Slovak heritage. Once I moved to Banská
Bystrica on a longer-term basis, he successfully proposed my election to
membership (which also proved immeasurably helpful to my fieldwork).
In his case, he chose to resolve the ambiguity by making me (more formally) a Rotarian and (less formally) a Slovak. It was his way of resolving
the "category error" (see Wilcox, this volume) that my initially ambivalent status created.

3. The "Others" represent themselves within their own groups.
4. The "Others" represent themselves to me and to people like me.

In many respects, this is what reflexive anthropologists study—the way
people represent themselves. To be sure, much of what we see has very little to do with our presence. Nevertheless, a great deal of it is aimed directly at us. Indeed, the members of the communities we study may recognize their performed identities as such, that is, as part of an unre-
solved—perhaps irresolvable—discourse about multiple meanings of
those identities. In this respect, the fieldworker becomes what Neil Jarman calls a "watched watcher" (1997:10), the spectator who is the object
of their performance and thus a part of it. Often, they are quite consciously using all the techniques they know to stage a brilliant performance of the identity they wish to claim.

During a visit to Slovakia, I attended a reception in the Banská Bystrica Jewish community at which among other cold cuts and desserts appeared sliced ham. When I asked about this, no one seemed particularly concerned. Indeed, the members of the Jewish community did not seem particularly bothered about seeming Jewish at all. They say, for example, that they are well aware that I (a Euro-Atlantic Jew and again a "watched watcher") neither expect (nor particularly want) to see pork served at Jewish community functions. Nevertheless, they serve it and eat it anyway. In fact, there are probably any number of ways that the members of the Jewish community go about proving actively (and passively) that they are no different from anyone else. They are trying to convince themselves of this; they are trying to convince non-Jewish Slovaks of this. They do not seem particularly to care about what Euro-Atlantic and Israeli Jews think about this. Again, what is my responsibility as an anthropologist? Do I accept their performance and, as in the theatre, willingly suspend any disbelief? Do I push harder and harder to find out what (other than genealogy) separates them from their non-Jewish neighbors? Again, what if the Jews think they are just like other Slovaks but the Slovaks disagree? What if the Slovaks think the Jews are just like other Slovaks but the Jews disagree? What if the Slovak Jews think they are just like other Jews but the other Jews disagree? What if Slovak Jews disagree among themselves? What is a Jew? What is a Slovak? According to whose definition?

When I asked again, some time later about the ham at the reception, the president of the Jewish community replied briefly that of course it was "poultry ham," that they never would have served pork products. What to make of this: a Jewish community reception, with both Jews and non-Jews present, some of whom cognizant and others unaware of the nature of Jewish dietary laws, featuring what appeared to be the most non-kosher meat possible, when it was really only a simulacrum, but only the organizers of the reception knew this (or claimed this after the fact)? Who is representing what (and whom) to whom?

5. The "Others" represent me to myself.

No matter whom we say we are, the people we study and live with nonetheless come up with their own impressions and interpretations. Sometimes they share them with us, and often they do not. Susan Harding (1987; 2000) has described how during her fieldwork among fundamentalist Baptists, congregants told her outright that she was not merely an academic researcher, but that she was a "seeker" led by God to them for conversion and redemption. To a certain extent, both for William Shaffir's Lubavitcher Chassid, and for Harding's fundamentalist Baptist, this act of representation was a proselytic strategy, intended to change the researcher's self-image en route to conversion. Indeed, a reader might reasonably have expected that Gregory Stanczak (2000) would have had a similar experience while studying the International Church of Christ in Los Angeles, but he does not report it in his text.

In my case in Slovakia, my tenuous family ties provoked a variety of reactions, and while some people asked me if I felt Slovak, others simply told me that I was. At the beginning of my field stay, I found it both necessary and advantageous to apply for a "Foreign Slovak Pass," which would provide me with unrestricted residence and work authorizations based on my partially ethnic Slovak roots. When I finally received the pass, I showed it to some friends in a Jewish youth group. They looked at it and one said, "Why do you want this? What are you, nuts?" I said, "No, this is how I can work here." They could not understand why somebody who already had an American passport would want or would even need any kind of documentation in Slovakia. Even more baffling to them was why an American Jew whose mother had fled Slovakia in 1939 would want any kind of formal affiliation with that country, given its active participation in the Holocaust. These twenty-something Slovak Jews, many of whom openly admit that they would rather live somewhere else, were astonished to see an American pleased to establish ties with Slovakia: "You know, we're trying to get out—why are you trying to get in?"

6. "I the Anthropologist" represent the "Other" to fellow anthropologists, as well as to the public.
7. "I the Anthropologist" represent the "Other" to themselves.

The first of these two moments is the one to which Marcus, Fischer, and other reflexive anthropologists devote the most attention, because it is the essence of anthropological writing: an ethnography is nothing if not the representation of the "Other." The second moment of representation occurs when our written work becomes accessible to our informants and they react to their portrayal. The apocryphal story often is repeated about the contemporary anthropologist who traveled to study the Tikopia people in the South Pacific. When he asked about the meaning of a particular custom, his informant asked him to wait a moment so that he could look up the answer in his copy of Sir Raymond Firth's anthropological classic, *We, the Tikopia* (1936). This problem is particularly acute for scholars of religion encountering groups who believe they have been "burned" already and do not want to repeat the experience. Shortly before I began my project at New Song, the *Los Angeles Times* printed a story about the church and its outreach to Generation Xers. Ironically, it had been this story that first had interested me in the church. However, the staff members at New Song were very disappointed by the article. They felt that they had been misrepresented, and they were concerned that they should not be defined by the portrayal in the *Times*. My access to the church was conditioned on my taking a more detailed and certainly more academic approach to my study of the church. At the end of the project, they read my research report and compared it to other published accounts of the congregation, and they expressed their "approval" of my work.

8. Finally: "I the Anthropologist" represent "the Ethnographer" not only to the public, but also to my fellow anthropologists.

Although often the least overt of the representational moments outlined here, it is perhaps the most important to the development of the discipline of ethnography. Every new ethnography implicitly presents a prescriptive model for how ethnography ought—or ought not—to be "done." Texts such as *Writing Culture, After Writing Culture, Women Writing Culture,* and even this volume are contributions to a larger ongoing discussion about what it has meant, what it means, and what it should mean to be an ethnographer in the contemporary world. In *Gatherings in Diaspora* (Warner and Wittner 1998), Judith G. Wittner concludes her afterword—and the book itself—with an extended analysis of the impact of the relationships in the field on the published ethnographies. "All of these stories," she writes, "are necessarily partial stories. They tell readers about religious worlds as they are illuminated through the lived relationships between scholars and members of communities" (Wittner 1998a: 382). This is both a reminder and an appeal, recalling the first moment of ethnographic representation at the outset of fieldwork, that researchers consciously locate themselves and their projects in the nexus of the academy, the field, and the ethnographer.

Implicated (in) Representation

Taken separately, each of the representations outlined here has been the subject of extensive reflection among anthropologists. These moments of representation occur and re-occur throughout the research, writing, and publication process. The representations may overlap and conflict. Some representations may be purposeful, others happenstance or apparently unintended. Sometimes there are self-conscious expressions of idealized representations. For example, I have translated into English promotional materials for a Banská Bystrica trade-show firm whose owner/director is a close friend. In doing so, I have had to discuss with him the content of his materials and why he wishes to present them the way he does. Furthermore, he and others with whom I worked had—in my presence—to articulate their idealized and actual identities in a communicable way. At the same time, however, I had to ask myself how much of what I saw and heard was performed with an eye to influencing my findings about the presence or absence of European identity. Similarly, at New Song I had to ask myself how much of what was done or said in my presence had to do with my being a non-Christian or an academic.

What are the implications of studying and writing about a group that seems already to know how it wishes to be represented? If I am a "watched watcher," part of the representational process, then in certain ways I am part of the stage on which the phenomena I wish to study will play out. Moreover, insofar as I take part in the events that I study, then my own activities ought to come under the anthropological gaze. I am not only the writer, director, and producer of my ethnography—I am also an actor in it. Finally, if I am active in separate, but interrelated networks in a larger setting, then my behavior in one arena will inevitably affect my identity in the others. In light of the increasing difficulty of determining when the ethnographer is "in the field" and when off site, one can easily argue that the field is wherever the fieldworker happens to be, and from there it is a short step to the conclusion that the field *is also* the anthropologist himself. The field simply cannot exist without the relationship between the ethnographer and the object of study.

My claims need not lead to radical conclusions about ethnographic fiction or even solipsism. In his groundbreaking article on ethnographic holism, Robert Thornton (1988) argues that the purpose of ethnography is in large part "to convince the reader of the existence of an initially unperceived coherence" (292). Elsewhere, he claims that "apparent boundaries, . . . such as those that define nations, ethnic groups, age-grades, or classes, are seen to be relative in time, the observer, or to each other, and thus not 'really' there at all" (299). This previously "unperceived coherence," these "apparent boundaries," come into existence through the closure of the ethnographic text. Other discussions have focused on the production of the text itself, but that is not my aim here. I do not seek to reduce the field to fiction, but rather to call attention to the way that we as anthropologists attempt to create knowledge about what is actually "out there." The transformation begins not when we write the text, but earlier, when we define the field. In that moment, we bind ourselves to a particular slice of reality in a way that should not, indeed cannot, be undone—nor ignored.

NOTE

1. I presented an earlier version of this essay at the July 2000 meeting of the European Association of Social Anthropologists in Kraków, Poland. Conversations with Mary Jo Neitz in November 1999 and January 2000 helped me to clarify many of the ideas expressed here, as did a presentation to the American Religions Group at the University of California, Santa Barbara. My thanks are also due to Jonathan Webber, Jon Mitchell, and especially Jim Spickard. Funding for the research described here was provided by the Lilly Endowment (UCSB) and by the Keith Murray Scholarship Trust (Oxford). This chapter is dedicated to my wife, Zuzana Riemer Landres, whose patience and good humor endured both rainy days in Kraków and pent-up weekends in Los Angeles.

Chapter 9

Encountering Latina Mobilization
Field Research on the U.S./Mexico Border

Milagros Peña

Some time ago, a friend shared a story about an experience that she had at a feminist forum. The meeting brought together diverse groups of Salvadoran women from different socioeconomic and educational backgrounds to discuss a host of women's issues and some plans for action. At the meeting, the word feminism was thrown around by women who were active in feminist circles. The last day of the meeting a woman stood up and asked if someone could clarify for her the exact meaning of the word "*feminismo*" (the Spanish word for feminism). She asked if the word meant "*fe-en-mi-mismo*," which literally translates to "faith in myself" as the woman asking the question had pronounced the word. The woman added that if "*feminismo*" meant "*fe-en-mi-mismo*" then she believed in that.

My friend's story left a lasting impression on me, because, for many Latinas, the struggle with what feminism means to us touches a nerve, given some of our reservations with mainstream U.S. feminism. Many of our experiences center on the fact that others have defined feminism for us, and few of us see ourselves reflected in its articulations. There is the sense that feminism means something radical, separatist, and different from many Latinas' sense of an inclusive liberation of the oppressed in our society. Feminism is seen as excluding and bashing men. For the Latinas I interviewed as part of my study of grassroots women's activism in the El Paso/Ciudad Juárez area, feminism carries no real meaning in their day-to-day lived experiences. I learned that women there would rather talk about a "women's" movement than a "feminist" movement, because the former implies a broader coalition of politically mobilized women, concerned about class, race, and labor issues. It also asserts that poor or marginalized men stand to gain from women's liberation.

Among those I met and interviewed was Imelda Garcia, a Chicana and co-founder of *Bienestar Familiar* and an activist in *El Centro Mujeres de la Esperanza* in El Paso, Texas. Imelda's interview illustrates this point. In telling her story about the impact of the Chicano Movement on her, Imelda shared how she came to the women's movement.

> I got involved with a women's group at the university [Sul Ross State University in Alpine, Texas]. And, I struggled with it, because we had a lot of differences. I think being right out of the *Movimiento Chicano*, I could see a lot of differences in the way that we saw issues, because in the *Movimiento Chicano*, even though we women were pushing and pushing ahead, we saw *esos hermanos* [those brothers]. We were both being treated wrongfully. You know, treated badly. And, so it was very difficult, because we didn't consider them the enemy and for the women's movement a lot of times, the men were the enemy.

In fact, Chicana feminist writer Martha Cotera (1977, 36) charges that "all White women 'herstory' publications have been severely criticized for being blatant in their disregard for the pluralistic aspects of our society." My research on social movements in Peru (Peña 1995), in Michoacán, Mexico, and in the El Paso/Ciudad Juárez area has sought, among other things, to uncover what Latina women's activism looks like and what type of feminist vision we Latinas can bring to the women's movement in the United States.

Beginnings

I came to my research on the U.S./Mexico border with two potential handicaps.

First, unlike many contributors to this volume, I was not trained as an ethnographer. With a Master's of Divinity from Union Theological Seminary and a Ph.D. in Sociology from the State University of New York at Stony Brook, I had received considerable methodological training, but much of it was in the old positivist tradition, which emphasized surveys, structured interviews, and the like. My work with Mexican and Chicana women's activists was thus an education in research methods, as well as in a new social scene.

Second, I am a Latina, but not a Latina of Mexican descent. I am Dominican American, raised in urban New York. How well could I carry out research on Latina activism focused on women of Mexican descent—and in a region still influenced by rural life, in which immigration means something quite different than it does in the urban Northeast?

Fortunately, my social background did not prove to be a handicap. I quickly learned that despite our many differences, my Chicana informants and I share a common cultural heritage. Not only do we share language, though differently accented, but also the immigrants among them have life stories with many themes common to mine. We show pictures of grandparents, aunts, uncles, and cousins whom we barely know, who were left behind in our families' home countries. We often tell each other about members of our families who fled dictatorships, economic hardship, and so on, often with promises to return. We share our minority status in a nation that honors inclusion more in word than in deed. The Latina reality, despite our diversity, has more in common than not.

But the first handicap remained. I knew that preplanned surveys or interviews would not tell me about border women's activism—at least not in meaningful terms. Wanting to bring forth the broader narratives of the history, goals, objectives, and experiences of women in local non-government organizations (NGOs), I chose an oral history approach, primarily conversational. In confronting how to approach the study and develop questions for interviewing, I felt that an important component of the interview process meant letting the women speak for themselves. As Cotera (1977) and a number of us doing research on Latina activism argue, to do otherwise would only contribute to the disconnect with a feminism that seems to be only for "White" and educated women; too often, our Latina voices are marginalized if not completely ignored.

With this issue in mind, I felt it was important to develop my own open-ended list of questions, with the intention of allowing my interviews to take unforeseen directions. I wanted to make every effort to let the women I would interview develop a voice of their own. Influenced by readings in feminist research methods, I developed this interview strategy precisely because it underscores letting those interviewed speak for themselves (Behar and Gordon 1995; Reinharz 1992). Such a strategy can also let study participants reflect on their experiences; it can help them better grasp what they believe and see how those beliefs affect theirs and others' everyday lives. Latina theologian/ethicist Ana María Isasi-Díaz (1993) argues that such interviews become part of a liberative praxis for all of us.

They can be a consciousness-raising experience for us, in particular, not only because they give us an opportunity for reflection, but also because they are often vehicles for us to develop our own voices. This interview strategy broadens our narratives. A semi-directed interview approach also allowed me to develop trust and ask questions that often an outsider could not, without raising suspicions about her intentions. In my case, as a Latina, being an insider was important. Because of our common cultural heritage, and the fact that so much of our history as Latinas in this society is so similar, we felt comfortable talking, particularly when conversation became critical of U.S. feminism.

However, because I was born and grew up in New York City and not on the U.S./Mexico border, there was a lot I had to learn about the border reality. Gaining knowledge of the economic and political reality of the U.S./Mexico border would speak not just to understanding Mexican Americans' marginal status within the United States, but would also lead me to understand why ultimately Mexicana/Chicana/Mexican American women came to articulate their border experiences with a vision toward global feminism.

Bridges across the Border

Many Chicana experiences are rooted in the overall Chicana/o U.S. historical reality that has shaped the identity of people of Mexican descent on the border. An understanding of the colonial heritage of Texas and El Paso, in particular, is necessary to understand the obstacles Chicanas face in this region. Michael Omi and Howard Winant (1994) link Chicano and Mexican American racial formation to the evolution of hegemony, the way in which U.S. society is organized and ruled. They note that how it touches the lives of Mexican people has a direct bearing on their current status. Understanding these dynamics pushed me toward a greater understanding as to why Latina women's NGOs form in response to both sexism and racism, not just the former. But it was the transnational discourse articulated in the border NGOs that intrigued me, precisely because in the struggle to define our own Latina feminist identities, that border reality would mark how we organized. I got a better sense of the pattern of Latina border activism from women like activist Patricia Monreal Molina of *Organización Popular Independiente* (*OPI*—the Independent Popular Organization) in Juárez. Responding to a question on how she saw women's NGO networking, she said: *"Coincidimos mucho en el trabajo de base, o sea en la problematica que logramos."* [We coincide a lot in our grassroots work, in other words, in the challenges we bring or seek]. In fact, it is parallel and more often intersecting community work that characterizes activism on the U.S./Mexico border. Patricia Monreal Molina's insight proved crucial, because as the research developed I uncovered a networking pattern that crossed ethnic, class, and civic-religious, as well as national boundaries. Without expecting it, interviews with activists like her led to the discovery that in the greater El Paso/Ciudad Juárez area, the Latina/Chicana/Mexican mobilization networks included a network pattern highly linked to several women's religious organizations, particularly Catholic women's groups. Many of them included *"anglas"* (White women). These linkages, I discovered, emerged out of the sociopolitical contexts in which these women's NGOs work.

I came to appreciate this dynamic both because I was doing research on the border and because I was teaching at New Mexico State University in Las Cruces, New Mexico, only 50 miles north of El Paso. A number of my students were products of the border community in which I was living, working, and doing research. They told me that the border context requires alliances among and across NGOs, if they are to be effective in promoting border issues. Women's NGOs in greater El Paso would prove to be no different. Women activists there need to be focused on "being together" around women's issues than being divided by nationality, ethnicity, or concerned about the involvement of religious organizations in their mobilization processes. The NGOs are effective in their community work, because their networks provide support for and help in their overlapping missions to mobilize border women. That is why working with non-Latinas is framed as building alliances with people who share their concerns.

Still curious to learn what would bring non-Latinas to ally themselves with border women's concerns, I interviewed several non-Latina leaders active in the NGOs identified by the Latinas I was interviewing as being in their network. One of these was Sister Kathleen Erickson of the Women's Intercultural Center in Anthony, Texas/New Mexico. She traced her feeling for "a kind of women's movement" to her role as "a Sister of Mercy . . . one of the aspects of our direction statement is working with women and children." This formal commitment created the context for her support for and encouragement of activism in border communities. In fact, such activism was the spark for creating the Women's Intercultural Center. The center began in 1991, after three

Sisters of Mercy came to Anthony, New Mexico (a town, which is partly in the outskirts of El Paso, Texas and partly in New Mexico). According to Kathleen Erickson:

> We were here for at least six or eight months before we invited women to come to our women's group. The first women's group, I think, probably met in, maybe April, or so, of '92. . . . [After continuing to meet and spreading the word about the Women's Intercultural Center] we bought this property. We formed a 501c3 Nonprofit Corporation.

The Women's Intercultural Center was also responsible for the creation of a spin-off organization known as *Mujeres Unidas*, a cooperative created for job training and developing business skills.

A connection with religiously inspired organizations appeared elsewhere in my informant's stories of border women's activism. Patricia Monreal Molina noted an important characteristic in the profiles of the people who came to work in *OPI*. She and several other *OPI* founders started organizing on border issues through the base Christian communities that exist on the edge of Ciudad Juárez. In answering a question on how it is that she came to do work with women in *OPI*, an organization that defines itself more broadly than focused on just women's issues, she noted:

> Well, the thing is that since I was young I had the experience of working with women's groups in the sphere of my doing pastoral work. I worked with *colonia*[1] women as part of doing parish work in what was then known as the base Christian community movement. And it was there that I had for a number of years the opportunity to work with women as part of more a pastoral process. Later that work with women within the parish context provided other opportunities to work within the *colonia* context.

Clearly, the crossing of religious and civic boundaries is taking place on the border. But crossing boundaries between secular and religious organizations is not new, particularly if you consider internationally the number of religious "Base Communities [that] have been a force behind a range of movements" (Eckstein 1999, 8).

Here Catholic sisters and other non-Latina women's groups brought organizational skills, information, and other resources that were integral to locally based Latinas. In fact, these women's groups often created the organizational space and provided the expertise, gained from previous organizing, that helped Latinas mobilize across networks.

What the case study of the greater El Paso area shows is the ways in which collective action can be, in Alberto Melucci's words, "the result of purposes, resources, and limits, with a purposive orientation constructed by means of social relationships within a system of opportunities and constraints" (1995, 43). Within these social relationships, individuals "define in cognitive terms the field of possibilities and limits they perceive while at the same time activating their relationships so as to give sense to their 'being together' and to the goals they pursue."

Those fields of opportunities are, I argue, the basis for Latinas maximizing our participation and contribution to women's NGOs. Base Christian groups, women's religious groups, and nonreligious groups have joined us on the border and elsewhere. My own decision to undertake this research was part of the mobilization of individuals who feel vested in the community work that is taking place on the border. My own intention for this project was to contribute to mobilizing around issues that affect border women and to increase our collective potential for bringing about social change.

Transforming Borders

By the end of my interviews, it became clear to me that what we were doing in the greater El Paso area was transforming the boundary or border often set between religion, politics, ethnicity; this transformation proved to be important in the political mobilization of women in the region. The bridges that Latinas and non-Latinas, whether connected to a church or not, have built and continue to build in the greater El Paso area around women's issues are maximizing women's ability to network and to mobilize. For a great majority of the women in the NGOs I studied, as for myself, the basic connection for coming together in organizations was local political reality. This sociopolitical reality creates the social context for women to organize across race, ethnic, class, and gender lines. To understand this dynamic is to understand how Latinas are coming to shape our own way of being political, while at the same time shaping our own feminist discourse.

I found the right vocabulary for talking about this border mobilization in the work of political scientist Carol Hardy-Fanta (1993). She refers to the "gendered way" in which Latinas become active politically. Harda-Fanta notes:

A key issue within the debate about gender differences is whether there is an essential divide between the public and private dimensions of politics. For Latina women, much more than the men, the boundary between these supposedly distinct spheres of life is blurred or indistinct. With their emphasis on grassroots politics, survival politics, the politics of everyday life, and the development of a political consciousness, Latina women see connections between the problems they face personally and community issues stemming from government policies. (1993, 18–19)

Conceptualizing this gendered way of doing politics helped me understand how an NGO that did job training and another that focused on empowerment and women's spirituality were connected. It is because both respond politically to border issues.

In this context, Latinas' emphasis on grassroots politics, survival politics, and the politics of everyday life is expanded when religious organizations lend themselves to grassroots organizing. Religious groups on the border, many of them influenced by an array of feminist visions themselves, have joined Latinas in our common concerns over women's rights as human rights. I and others who lived and worked on the border were constantly aware of the plight of migrant women—including reports estimating between 100 and 200 cases of women murdered in Juárez since 1993. This reality serves as a rallying point for issues relating to violence against women, and it also brings attention to other issues affecting women and their families, no matter where they live. Those of us living on the border facing these realities saw that there was no "right" or "wrong" side of the border. Consequently, for Latinas and the non-Latinas on the border, violence against migrant women is not the migrant women's personal matter, nor just a Mexican issue, but a matter for all women.

My interviews provided the basis for understanding that the question of human rights and women's rights need to be linked if violence against women is to be dealt with in any meaningful way. Articulating the problem facing border women within the larger context of human rights' violations serves to link Latina issues to larger community issues. This point is reflected in the mission statement of *El Centro Mujeres de la Esperanza*, mentioned above. The *Centro's* mission statement is quite clear in its position.

El Centro Mujeres de la Esperanza has become a mutually culturally based community of women in the El Paso/Ciudad Juárez region. As women on the U.S./Mexico border, we stand in solidarity with women throughout the world who actively seek peace with justice for the earth and for people. The prophetic role of the center is shaped and guided by women who gather to express our realities and to share these truths at local, national, and international levels.

This more global perspective is the basis for Latina and non-Latina mobilization, as women of *El Centro* say, "to work together and to transform structures that oppress women or limit their progress." The center's vision is focused on women's concerns, but their vision is activated in broader community work. This vision is a central theme in global feminism. Global feminists challenge the notion that social life can be divided into public and private realms.

It is this global feminist perspective that I see being articulated on the border. Included here is the questioning of oppressive social structures that focus on economic and political marginalization, and of other social institutions that have historically oppressed us and our communities. It is the questioning of such oppressive social structures that drives border women to connect the personal and the spiritual with the political, and to maximize their efforts by networking with other women's NGOs in the region.

My own work with the Colonias Development Council (CDC), an NGO in Las Cruces, New Mexico, led me to appreciate the political potential of the greater El Paso/Juárez NGOs. I was invited to join CDC shortly after I arrived to take a faculty position at New Mexico State University, in 1996. I became friends with Diana Bustamante, the Executive Director of CDC, who has a long history of doing community work. In CDC, I learned firsthand from border residents and watched border women empower themselves both at home and in the community through their activism in community work.[2] Diana gave me some insight into the localized pattern of organizing, particularly for the greater El Paso region:

> That's one of the phenomena of the Southwest that they are so localized. And even when you think in terms of local politics, I'm talking about earlier [meaning in the 60s and 70s], [the feeling was] that those issues [meaning local issues] are in the forefront. National politics are kinda like "yeah we'll get involved with national politics, but that's not our concern," we're immediate—working on a day to day survival basis.

Surviving and struggling to survive with limited resources can limit social activists. Yet, even local strategizing does not take away from the fact that border women, despite putting much of their energy into local activism, see their local activism as part of a larger effort that can effect social change. Engaging political activism at the national level can be daunting and seemingly slow in producing results. I remember a plaque that hung on the wall of one of the women's NGOs I visited. It read: "Think globally, act locally." Borrowed from the international environmental movement, the slogan reflects some of border women's thinking—no matter how small the effort, we are fighting for women's rights globally when we engage in our own local concerns. It is a view voiced at meetings and articulated in a number of the NGOs mission statements. Another Chicana activist, Francisca Montoya, like Diana has a long history of community work in the Southwest. She said that she believed that the lack of proximity to really big cities is what makes border cities like El Paso and Las Cruces more likely to keep organizing almost exclusively at the local level. In addition to those already stated, I offer other explanations for the localized strategies.

After extensive interviews, I discovered that the focus on local organizing, especially in El Paso, involved a community rejection in one way or another of earlier political movements. The two movements I noted were the larger U.S. women's movement and the Chicano Movement, which through La Raza Unida Party marked a particular type of politics in El Paso and Texas. Local organizational networks developed in part in response to these movements and in part in opposition to them. I leave that discussion for another day; suffice it to say that my relationships and conversations with local activists in Las Cruces, New Mexico heightened my knowledge of the political nuances of the region. Without them, I would have missed some of the insights I gained both about Latina women's NGO activism and about the type, as well as the level, of political commitment that poor people's movements in this region of the country maintain.

Ending

Diana Bustamante, Francisca Montoya, Imelda Garcia, Patricia Monreal Molina, and others I interviewed for this project, convinced me that the insights and knowledge I gained in this research could not have been done with survey research. Each interview experience corrected preconceived notions of what I thought I would hear or "find," but confirmed others on the question of what the women's movement means for Latinas. Also, every aspect of completing an interview was important and continues to inform my interpretations of the interview narratives, further enriching the analysis. I still have vivid images of crossing the Santa Fe Bridge that connects El Paso to Juárez to go interview the women who participated in my study. The bridge is symbolic for other reasons. It represents the history of the region and served to make me vividly aware of how the lives of those whose stories are embedded in the NGOs I was studying were in one way or another touched by this history. Each time I crossed the bridge or drove to El Paso and could see the *colonias* on both sides of the border, I would play back in my mind interviews I had conducted and see how they connected to the overall border reality. These reflective moments served to push me to think about the questions I was asking, the responses that were given, and often pushed me to think about how the information I was getting fit together. Why the NGOs existed, who their members were, what were their objectives, goals, and tasks. Crossing the bridge put it all in front of me.

As researchers, taking the time to do this type of reflection and taking note of them is very important. As several of the articles that appear in *Women Writing Culture* (Behar and Gordon 1995) suggest, an important issue we have to confront in ethnographic research is the question of whose reality is being presented in the interpretation of interviews. In my view, oral and life histories and ethnographic methodology in general provide rich analysis because they engage the social researcher in discovery of new meanings and definitions. In this case, I discovered new meanings for feminism along with unexpected patterns of group alliances.

This approach to research also forces us to confront the question: For whom are we speaking and whose stories and struggles do we interpret as we do our analyses, write our results, and theorize about what it all means? The Salvadoran woman's question posed earlier in this discussion brings a different lens to feminist visions. Forcing the researcher to confront these issues makes for more sensitized social research. It forced me to engage in a more critical way in coming to understand Latina activism and our contribution to feminist paradigms.

In summary, living and doing fieldwork for four years on the U.S./Mexico border and interviewing women with whom I share similar cultural and social contexts have convinced me of the richness of the ethnographic approach. This approach pushes us to allow communities we study to speak for themselves. The communities tell us which questions are relevant, missing, need elaboration, or emphasis.

For students of social movements, the border region is a dynamic place for learning about new forms of mobilization, networks, coalitions, and alliances. My informants taught me how borders of all kinds—national, ethnic, religious, and other status boundaries—are often blurred in a sociopolitical environment, where the personal and political are viewed as one. On a more personal note, I found I reconnected with a community of women who now form part of my community; I came away with a sense that we are blazing new paths in feminist discourse. Taking a stand against women's oppression from any source, I believe, was and continues to be the first step toward a political life for many Latinas. Latinas and the work they do in NGOs, create a forum for the chispa—the spark—the passion necessary for women's politics to flower into new feminist visions.

NOTES

1. The term *colonia* refers to rural and unincorporated subdivisions of U.S. cities located along the U.S./Mexico international boundary. *Colonias* are characterized by substandard housing, inadequate plumbing and sewage disposal systems, and inadequate access to clean water. They are highly concentrated poverty pockets that are physically and legally isolated from neighboring cities.

2. It was watching and working with the women in CDC that first convinced me to do the research project on border women. I actually started my study on Latina activism in 1994/5 in Michoacán, Mexico (helped by a Fulbright-Hayes/Garcia Robles Research award), then decided to do a cross-cultural comparison with the work the women were doing in greater El Paso/Juárez.

Part III

Writing and Reading Ethnography

Chapter 10

Writing about "The Other," Revisited

Karen McCarthy Brown

Writing about "The Other" April 1992

I see now, more clearly than I did during 12 years' of labor on it, that my book *Mama Lola: A Vodou Priestess in Brooklyn* (1991) is the product of unconventional methods of anthropological research and writing.[1] The book weaves stories of Mama Lola's ancestors together with ethnographic narratives that are woven, in turn, from my own scholarly and personal voices, and from several of Mama Lola's voices, including those of six Vodou spirits who routinely possess her.

I did not set out to do experimental fieldwork, nor, when I was writing, did I see myself as jumping into the middle of a postmodernist debate on ethnography. Yet now that the book is done, I can afford the luxury of sticking my head up and surveying the wider terrain. I see that I did flout some of the conventions of anthropological fieldwork. I also have become involved, willy-nilly, in the current spirited debate about what we anthropologists—mostly white Euro-Americans—are doing when we write about those whom scholars sometimes label "the Other." Contemporary critics argue that the greater social power of the researcher overwhelms the subject and that ethnographic texts are, by default, little more than fictions, revealing more about the culture and the preoccupations of the writer than about those of the people being studied. *Mama Lola* enters this debate in two ways: First, by deliberate attention to the power issues, between Mama Lola and me, and second, by an implicit claim that more extended, intimate, and committed contact between researcher and subject can undercut the colonial mindset of much anthropological writing.

I met Alourdes (the name that I usually use to address Mama Lola) in the summer of 1978. She was then in her mid-40s and had immigrated from Haiti in 1963. I was 10 years younger and the great-granddaughter of European immigrants. On the surface we were very different. By the time I reached my mid-20s, I had my first college teaching job; at the same age Alourdes was living in the squalor of Port-au-Prince, raising two children on her own and, when there was no other way to feed them, resorting to prostitution. Yet, ironically, when we met, we shared a sense of upward mobility. A member of the first college-educated generation in my family, I had recently received my Ph.D. and had taken a position on the faculty of Drew University. Alourdes by that time owned her home and was firmly ensconced as the head of a lively, three-generational household.

She also was working full-time as a Vodou priestess, a vocation requiring the combined skills of priest, social worker, herbalist, and psychotherapist. Three generations of healers in her family had preceded her, but she was the first family member to muster the financial resources needed to pay for the elaborate initiation rituals that make the role official.

When we were introduced, I was living in a loft in SoHo, an artists' district in lower Manhattan. Alourdes's home, where she also held regular Vodou ceremonies and consulted daily with individual clients, was a small row house in the Fort Greene section of Brooklyn. The social distance between us was great, but the geographic distance small. Her house and the Vodou world she inhabited were a mere 20 minutes by car from my front door. Something clicked between Alourdes and me, although I cannot say that we liked or trusted one another right away. Perhaps it was just that each of us sensed in the other someone who could extend and challenge our world. She seemed a formidable person, strong and moody. One moment she was electric, filled with charm, the next, dour and withdrawn. I, no doubt, appeared overly polite and overly white.

For a while, we engaged in a formal little dance. I stopped by her house to visit frequently and brought her small gifts; she usually offered me coffee and took the time to sit and talk with me. Sometimes she invited me to ceremonies. I was utterly fascinated by her charismatic priestcraft and by the intimate and familial style of ritualizing that was so different from what I had seen during the years I worked on Vodou in large, urban temples in Haiti. Despite my fascination, I mostly hovered on the edge of the crowd at Alourdes's "birthday parties" for the spirits. Sometimes when she went into a trance, the Vodou spirit "riding" her would seek me out to give advice or blessing. Later I found out that one or two regulars at these events objected to my white presence and suggested that I was a spy from the immigration office. Alourdes reportedly answered that no one could tell her how to choose her friends.

After a few months, I offered to help Alourdes with ritual preparations. I ran errands, helped to cook the ritual meal, and lent a hand constructing the altar that is the focal point of each Vodou ceremony. Our friendship grew through intimacies shared in the midst of routine work, as well as through stronger bonds forged in the midst of life crises. Her son got in trouble with the law, and she turned to me for help; I went through a divorce and felt grateful for her support, which often took the form of offers of ritual healing. Soon a friendship developed that blurred and confused our previous roles of academic researcher and representative Vodou priestess. These days she calls me her "daughter," and, when I am not able to spend holidays with my biological family, I am more likely to celebrate them at her house than anywhere else.

As our friendship grew, participating in her religion felt like a natural step. I did not tumble into it in reaction to a life crisis. I chose to participate in Vodou for a mix of professional and personal reasons that I will never untangle. The single clear feeling was a powerful need to understand what Vodou was about, what it had to offer those who turned to it in times of trouble. My own attitude was very much like Alourdes's when she offered to let me *kouche* (literally, lie down or sleep)—in other words, to participate in healing ceremonies that also function as rites of initiation into Vodou. "Try it," she said, "see if it work for you."

And it did work. Vodou gave me a rich, unblinkingly honest view of life that has been one of several resources that I have drawn on in the last decade or so to sort out life's problems. Participating in rituals and deciding to offer myself a candidate for healing have given me valuable insights into how Vodou works, insights that strengthened my book considerably.

Yet my academic colleagues have raised questions. Have I lost my objectivity? Has my friendship with Alourdes biased my account of her family history, her daily life, and her spirituality? Has my participation in Vodou colored the way in which I present the religion? The answer to all these questions is a qualified Yes, although that doesn't disturb me as much as some of my colleagues wish that it did.

The analogy commonly drawn between anthropology and the natural sciences has ceased to be helpful to me. While I still care about factuality and freedom from bias, those standards are no longer the most demanding ones for my work. Over the years I have come to understand anthropological fieldwork as something closer to a social art form than a social science. It involves a particular type of human relationship, yet one that is subject to all the complexities and ambiguities of any other kind of human interaction. This conception of fieldwork does not mean that no standards are applicable; they simply are different from the traditional ones. Truth telling and justice, for example, seem to be more fitting criteria than the canons of scientific research.

In relation to *Mama Lola*, truth telling not only required enough care and persistence to get the facts straight, but also enough self-awareness and self-disclosure to allow readers to see my point of view (another term for bias) and make their own judgments about it. Because I believe that a writer's perspective is more than a collection of facts that can be listed in an introduction and then forgotten, I chose to present myself as a character in the story, interacting with Alourdes. The challenge was to do this enough to reveal the way in which I relate to her without turning the book into a story about me. A standard of truthfulness also demanded that I tell as complete a story as possible, including all the complexities, without boring or confusing readers. In other words, telling the truth required me to perform an intellectual balancing act, in which the order and clarity of abstraction were placed in tension with the dense tangle of lived experience.

Justice, which like truth telling can never be fully achieved, was an even more challenging criterion of scholarship in this case. I felt compelled to do justice to Alourdes and to her world in my writing. Both moral and aesthetic judgments came into play, for example, in choosing the telling detail or the revelatory incident designed to capture definitive aspects of her life.

Justice as a goal in my relationship with Alourdes has, meant, among other things, that I could not exploit her, misrepresent my intentions, or turn away from her once I had what I needed. Financial obligations, like those of time and energy, could not be limited to what was necessary to grease the flow of information for the book. A true friendship is not over just because a writing project is done. So she will share the profits from the book with me, and, when she cannot meet a mortgage payment or raise the money for a trip to Haiti, I expect to continue to contribute.

It has not always been easy for me to negotiate the responsibilities that I have accepted as a result of Alourdes's gift of friendship, but I would not have it any other way. Despite her limited reading and writing skills, Alourdes helped to keep me truthful and just while writing *Mama Lola*. When I was tempted to soft-pedal information that I feared might embarrass her (for example, her prostitution), she pushed me: "You got to put that in the book. Because that's the truth. Right? Woman got to do all kinda thing. Right? I do that to feed my children. I'm not ashame." The nature of anthropological fieldwork changes in situations of cultural mixing, where the subject has her own vision of the project and her own views on the standards to which it should be held accountable.

I could not have written *Mama Lola* if Alourdes had not challenged me, trusted me, and become my friend. Through our friendship, we have served scholarship's end of deepened understanding, in this case by showing Vodou at work in the intimate details of one person's life. We both hope that our risk taking will help to counter the distorted image of this ancient religion.

Revisited—March 2001

In the decade since the publication of "Writing about 'the Other,'" the field of anthropology has shifted. These days there is little agreement among anthropologists about the meaning of culture, a foundational concept of the discipline. Yet there is market interest in the cultural hybridity that characterizes borderlands and urban crossroads. Doing ethnographic research in religiously and ethnically pluralistic situations adjusts the classic concept of culture in the direction of something more porous and labile than classic definitions allow. These days, anthropologists working in cities get a fresh take on cultural issues by tracking them in the midst of dense multicultural interaction. In religious studies, urban field research opens up new dimensions of religion. For example, cities reveal a wealth of traditional and new-age religious practices that augment the spiritual lives of secular humanists and disaffected African Americans, as well as good Presbyterians from places as different as Ghana and Korea.

Anthropologists used to be heroic travelers. Now some work in local urban areas where the world comes to them in the form of immigrants. This relatively new venue raises questions about the participation of those the ethnographer studies. In the classic version of anthropological research, the anthropologist is the one who crosses cultural boundaries, learns the local language, and makes sense of local practices. I do those things when I visit Mama Lola. The difference in my research situation is that Mama Lola does much the same things. I call what I do field research. She might call what she does developing New York survival skills. Traditionally, field researchers depicted their subjects as far removed from the ethnographic writing process (something the ethnographer did "back home"). Yet, when immigrants learn about their new local culture, they develop skills that allow them agency in the ethnographic project. Mama Lola, who lived less than 30 minutes away when I was writing *Mama Lola*, was never passive in relation to the book. Furthermore, she envisioned what she wanted it to accomplish. In the hybrid contexts typical of new ethnography, a researcher's subjects have their own ideas about the ethnographic enterprise and make use of it for their own ends. I suggest that ethnographic research in multicultural urban centers is increasingly fashioned out of two-way relationships, but I do so without denying the significant and often distorting power difference between researcher and subject.

The issue of the author's presence in the text remains important because of this disequilibrium. Once the general power issues involved in ethnographic representation were uncovered, the problem of the absent author also appeared. Omniscient but invisible ethnographers leave their readers with little idea of authorial authority or how the authors interacted with the people they represented. In response to (and in some cases anticipating) these concerns, ethnographers (and particularly women ethnographers) began to include themselves in their writing. This practice was almost immediately characterized as dangerously self-indulgent. Now, many critics think the presence of the researcher in an ethnography can demystify the authority of the text, but there is little agreement about how that should be done.

I had a fairly clear strategy about my place in *Mama Lola*, yet it was often misinterpreted. Some people who read *Mama Lola* assumed that my presence in the book put us on intimate terms. They thought they could ask me anything they wanted to. I configured my presence in the text differently. I assumed that those who read the book would be more like me than Mama Lola and so I decided to use myself as a bridge between late twentieth-century American and Haitian immigrant life. Anyone who looks closely will notice that I appear in the text only when there is some difference or misunderstanding that needs explaining. In a way, my presence is what makes it possible to raise these issues of difference.

The stories in which I appear are often about my mistakes and occasionally they are funny. I reveal things about myself only when I think they will be useful to the reader in understanding Mama Lola and her world, including how I interact with her. I still think this is a reasonable strategy for acknowledging the trenchant critiques of ethnographic representation coming out of post-colonial and cultural studies. My strategy demands that wizards come out from behind curtains, not that they come out naked. Deciding the right type and amount of self-revelation and getting it in the right places requires juggling scholarly, aesthetic, and moral agendas, something that can never be done formulaically.

Ethics is a central component of responsible and worthwhile field research, yet I think that no researcher can manage to handle all ethical, that is to say human relational, issues perfectly. Doing field research is like learning a language. Mistakes are unavoidable. At times, mistakes open the way to new and deeper understanding, and that is all well and good, but ethnographers deal routinely with sensitive issues such as race and sexuality. In these days of identity politics, it is not easy to come to terms with the inevitability of making social mistakes in the field, even small ones. My students crave more discussion of ethics in the ethnographic methods seminar I offer each year. They appear to need it to deal with their anxiety. What they want from me is to "get it right" beforehand, so they can "do it right" once in the field. I tell them I have no Ten Commandments of field research to offer them. I welcome their interest in research ethics, but I remind them that ethnographic research is a social art form and therefore subject to all the complexities and confusions of human relationships in general. In research sites, as well as every other life arena, narratives are contextual and so slippery, practices are easily misapprehended—sometimes with intention—and shared meaning is always approximate. "Don't become an ethnographer," I tell my students, "if you cannot tolerate a bit of moral (as well as intellectual) ambiguity."

NOTE

1. The first part of this chapter originally appeared in *The Chronicle of Higher Education*, April 15, 1992, page A56. Reprinted by permission.

Chapter 11

"There's Power in the Blood"
Writing Serpent Handling as Everyday Life

Jim Birckhead

Would you be free from the world and of sin?
There's power in the blood, power in the blood,
There's wonderful power in the blood.
Oh now, there's power, power, wonder working power
In the blood of the lamb,
There's power, power, wonder working power
In the precious blood of the lamb . . .

—Holiness gospel song

Lord, There's power in the blood of the lamb, amen.
Amen, Jesus said, I've got all power in heaven and on
earth, amen. So, amen, let's everybody that's here, amen,
everybody just feel free to obey God, amen. Whatever
God, amen, puts on your minds and hearts to do, you
do it, amen, Praise God. If you got a song to sing, we
want you to sing it, amen. Alleluya to God. If you got a
word you want to testify or preach, you obey God,
amen. Praise the Lord, amen. Ilia, ma, ma, ma, ma, ma!
Ilia ma, ma, ma, ma! E sha ma, ma, ma, ma he! E sha,
ma, ma, ma, ma, he!

Somebody said the other day, he said, a "Brother
Pack, you preach just a little old fashioned, amen." I believe, glory to God we need to preach just a little old
fashioned, amen. And if we do, thank God, we'll show
which side we're on, amen. Alleluya to God. I believe
there's many people, amen, there's preachers, amen, in
the world, amen, you can't tell them, thank God, amen,

from the world, amen, glory to God. What we need to do is to get a perfect will of God and walk right in.

Amen, we appreciate all of you here. Amen, if we have any visitors that's never seen the serpents took up and if God anoints we gonna move, amen, we gonna take 'em up. Amen, by, in the anointing power of God, amen, it can, glory to God, amen, be done. Glory to God, amen. This is a church where you can bring your car, carbide lantern in, or your deadly, you can bring your poison, amen, or you can come in and speak in tongues, amen, a, we will never say a word to you. Glory to God, amen, you're at liberty here to do what you can. Amen! All brothers and sisters to obey God if you can, amen.

Ain't nobody holding you down, thank God.

Now we've got some rattlesnakes and copperheads here, deadly serpents. If you want to handle them, just come right on, amen. It can be done in the name of the Lord, amen. It's made, amen, for the believers, alleluia to God, amen. . . . So, we want, amen, to just move right on along with the service, amen, and amen, we appreciate everyone that's come out, amen, to lend us a helping hand in anyway, amen.

So, amen, after while we got Brother Shorty Painter and the Gospel Bullets from Spartinburg, South Carolina with us, amen, to sing. They sing for the Lord and they've got a good deliverance about their singing, amen.

—Rev. Liston Pack, Holiness Church of God In Jesus
Name annual homecoming service, August 20, 1972,
Carson Springs, Tennessee

July 1, 1995, "Snake Hollow"

Standing in the ashes of the Holiness Church of God In Jesus Name with my serpent-handling brother and friend of some 24 years, Rev. Alfred Ball, I could almost hear and feel the echoes of Liston's spirit-filled message from the annual homecoming service of 1972, the strains and refrains of the pounding gospel songs as they merged one into another, the base drums, tambourines, electric guitars, foot stomping and hand clapping, punctuated by spirit-filled screams, speaking in tongues, and serpent handling. "There's Power in the Blood." "God's Not Dead, He Is Still Alive." "Holy, Holy, Holy" ("They call us serpent handlers, but it's all right!!!!, Ilia ma, ma, ma, ma"). "There Ain't no Grave Gonna Keep This Body Down." "And I Can't Feel At Home In This World Anymore."

We stood there beneath the tall trees in the cool morning air, the eternal gurgling stream in the background, hands in pockets, shuffling our feet, lamenting the lost dreams of this spirit-filled community of saints of the early 1970s. This place, now being reclaimed by the forest and kudzu, once dubbed by *Hustler* "the snake handling capital of the world" (Fortunato 1980, 52), was now nothing but vine-covered cinders and ash, broken glass, burnt twisted nails, and a decrepit rusted out 1940s house trailer. What once looked like the inevitable triumph of God's people now lay in a pile of ashes and junk, grown over with jungle vines.

Jimmy Ray Williams' grave on the hillside looked forlorn and out of place without the "little church house" where he drank strychnine, along with Buford Pack during the Saturday night service of April 9, 1973, and died near midnight, writhing in pain in Brother Doyle's pickup truck. Brother Buford died earlier the same evening, lying in his car in the church parking lot, under the tall trees, and next to the same gurgling English Mountain stream.

Where were the other saints now? Some, like Jimmy Ray and Buford, had died in the faith, and others of natural causes. The children of some of the people from the old "hollow" church continue to "follow the signs" at Morristown, Tennessee, Marshall, North Carolina, and in churches in Alabama and Kentucky. Two or three people who died of serpent bite have been much in the media; the deaths of Melinda and John Wayne "Punkin" Brown and the custody battle over their five children are a case in point (F. Brown and McDonald 2000). Indeed, Punkin's brother, Mark, now has a web site and will answer questions about the faith from around the virtual world.

Others now attend nonserpent-handling churches. Still others have moved off to who knows where, or have lapsed into lives of sin and anomie, hanging out in Cocke County beer and whisky joints, living the bad "honky-tonk" life so bemoaned in country songs. A couple of former members drive big rigs to the West Coast, and only make it to church occasionally when they happen to be in town for a few days.

We stopped in to see Allan David Williams (the deceased strychnine drinker's son), whom Alfred hadn't seen since his divorce a number of years earlier from Allan's sister, Joyce. Allan invited me to his church, the House of Prayer at Morristown. My heart quickened at this prospect, as I hadn't had an opportunity to return to a hard-core serpent-handling church since Alfred had drifted away from serpent handling and formed another church in the late 1970s. On short trips back, I moved in Alfred's world, whatever one might call it.

My fingertips tingled in anticipation and I was in a heightened and agitated state as I made my way to the church at the edge of Morristown, Tennessee. I got lost and couldn't find the turnoff to the church, feeling panicked and frustrated. After some time, I found the rutted gravel road that snaked behind an industrial dump of rusted machinery, and my rented car bounced up the road, past shacks with washing machines on their front porches and junked-out cars in front, to the cabin church house up the hill at the end of this dead-end road.

The amplified music was deafening; the singing shrill and discordant. Saints, many of whom I knew as children, welcomed me. One gospel song slid into the next. I just sat there, clapping my hands and foot-stomping to the beat, feeling waves of sound, light, heat, and motion flowing around and through me, as if time traveling through space Billy Pilgrim-style (Vonnegut 1969) on this hot Tennessee July night. I tilted my head back and grinned, staring off into nowhere in particular, watching my life pass before me, and not believing that this was actually happening again, as in the old days. This was a moment of epiphany, of transcendence.

Though there were boxes of serpents up front, they were not taken up. Perhaps the recent serpent-bite death of Punkin Williams (Allan's brother, Jimmy's son) had made people wary. (I sadly remembered going to Punkin's birthday party in 1987, up a hollow in western North Carolina, and joking with Liston, Allan David, Alfred, Joyce, and Punkin.) After the service, I looked at the snakes, answered questions about Australian reptiles, talked about the book that I was reviewing, in which some of these saints were unfavorably mentioned (Covington 1995), and listened to the brothers and sisters casually plan a church picnic in the Smokies. Yes, this was the "community of saints" I had "imagined" in my doctoral thesis (Birckhead 1976). I drove back down the windy road with a smile stuck on my face and a flush of well-being. That old time religion still existed and the feeling was still there. Amen!

The next night at Alfred's church, I was excited to hear again his style of down-home, spirited preaching about love and helping the poor. It was good catching up with members of his congregation, many of whom I have known for years. But I felt embarrassed at being acknowledged so vociferously by Alfred from the pulpit as a returning celebrity ("all the way from Australia"). After church we went for a midnight snack to a local truck stop with Brother Joe, a long distance trucker in town for a few days on a roundabout Morristown-LA turnaround. (This might bring him back in a few weeks via Vancouver, Edmonton, Toronto, and New York). Alfred and I then sat up awhile in his home beneath the church, viewing old serpent-handling videos, reading excerpts from the two new books on serpent handling I was reviewing (Birckhead 1996), and plumbing the depths of his recent domestic entanglements and custody worries.

Over the next few days, I accompanied Alfred on pastoral visits to the sick and disabled, old and infirm in the hospital or living in welfare housing, and learned of his prison ministry, as we moved through Newport's underside in this cultural fracture zone, a hard edge to life. On a lighter side, we also went to flea markets and ate barbecue, pinto beans, cornbread, and drank gallons of iced tea, at a local dinner, where Alfred knew the waitresses and other patrons, with their laconic humor and wry chat. I thoroughly reveled in this east Tennessee ambiance and in talking with Alfred over a number of days, filled in lots of gaps in my understanding of the religion. This is what doing "fieldwork" is about.

The afterglow of this trip lingered back in Australia as I looked at my photos with fondness and good memories and was pleased with Alfred's response to the article that I had sent him:

> I think you did a "bang up" job on the review of the book. In case you have forgotten your hillbilly, that means a great job, Ha, Ha. I know you didn't forget. Just kidding. I was wondering how you would handle that as I could see from reading the book that it was not going to be so easy to do. I agree with the editor it deserved to be more than just a review. The article idea was much better and it was very well written.

I learned from his letter that he was now being allowed to spend more time with his two-year-old son, Josh, and felt that things would work out for him and the church.

Time Passed

I wasn't prepared for the 6 A.M., Monday morning phone call that shattered my deep sleep and put me in a fugue state for a week. The strong east Tennessee accent, "Is this Jim Birckhead?" It was Allan David. "Have you seen Alfred? Are he and Josh in Australia with you? Man, he's in trouble big time. He took Josh for the weekend and didn't come back. The TBI and FBI are looking for them. He has been accused of sexually molesting his daughters over a number of years in the basement of the church where they lived. They didn't tell anyone until now because of repressed memory. They are suing him for two million dollars. Montell Williams is coming to town. Maybe "Hard Copy" too. He is in trouble Big Time!"

Newspaper clippings that Joyce sent me sketched in the sad tale: "Daughters accuse preacher father of sexual assault—Rev. Alfred Ball responds to claims in local court documents as 'lies'" (*Newport Plain Talk*, 8-16-96); "Preacher accused of sexually assaulting 2 daughters—$1.5 million lawsuit filed in Cocke County Circuit Court" (*Knoxville News-Sentinel* 8-16-96); "Search on for Newport Preacher accused of rape" (*Knoxville News-Sentinel*, 10-5-96); Cocke County Sheriff's Department Detective Robert Caldwell noted that "Ball has a son living in New Mexico and a friend in Australia and that both the FBI and U.S. Customs officials have been notified of his disappearance." "Newport preacher, teen bride arrested in Kansas" (*Knoxville News-Sentinel*, 10-10-96); "Preacher jailed; bond $100,000" (*Newport Plain Talk*, 10-14-96); and "Secret tape recording offered to support charges" (*Newport Plain Talk* 11-22-96).

There it was in lurid journalistic detail. I paced the floor and tried to find an answer, to reconcile these allegations with the man I have known so well, I thought, since 1971, my Holiness brother and mentor. My thinking fell into free fall. Do I really know anything about anyone? Has all of my work on serpent handling been a mirage, a hoax, a nightmare? Alfred, articulate and rational, with a critical philosophical turn of thought, not the glassy eyed fanatic serpent-handling "Jesus man" of popular portrayal. He and I often deconstructed micro-scenes on videotapes and films on serpent handling (many of which he appeared in), providing a unique critical reading of this fleeting scene. I watched his faith shift over the years from serpent handler to ex-serpent handler, owing in part to the impact of media presentation on his consciousness, and because God told him to do so. I had always stayed with him and his family in the basement of the church where they lived, and where the alleged misdeeds had taken place. I knew his daughters well (since they were babies), but at this time, did not know the "teenage bride" who was apprehended with him in Sedan, Kansas. As I at first was not able to contact Alfred as he was on the run, and then in jail, I wrote a long letter to him and received in return a typed, four-page single-spaced letter, in which he explained himself. He accounted for each allegation and thanked me for not assuming his guilt. I then phoned him and we talked for an hour. Many of his congregation stood by him; others abandoned him as they were convinced of his guilt. He had been threatened physically. Now that he had sold the church, he and the remaining faithful met a number of times a week at members' homes in the area. He was on probation, had moved to a remote part of the county, and was driving a shuttle train at Dollywood in nearby Sevierville.

So, it was with some anxiety and trepidation that I contemplated my visit with Alfred in 1998. I had ostensibly come to present a paper on indigenous people and the environment at an international anthropology conference in Williamsburg, Virginia, and to visit friends in New York and relatives in St. Louis, Arkansas, and Texas. My time in Shushan, New York, with my old friend, Jim, whom I have known since 1955, was idyllic. The warm, sunlit summer days, lunch and wine at Simon Pearce's mill house restaurant at Quechee, Vermont, a chamber music performance at Saratoga, and a party at Jim's with a number of ex-NYC types whom I had met on previous trips back from Australia contributed to the ambiance. Several of us had been born in the same year and we reminisced about our respective childhoods in different parts of the United States. The feeling was easy and I was secure in my long-standing self of being with my old friend and age mates, not the tenuous fieldwork self of my work with Aborigines in Australia or the self whom I anticipated I would become in just a couple of days in east Tennessee. The cool night air flowed in from the Batten Kill River through this nineteenth-century house, and I did not want to leave this moment in time and descend into a Tennessee heart of darkness, to an uncertain world of summer heat and social chaos and conflict in "the South."

The early morning drive from Shushan to JFK did not go well. Jim's car overheated, lost oil, and sustained damage. We were stuck in Chatham, N.Y. for hours, causing me to miss my flight to Knoxville via Washington, D.C., giving me an unanticipated night in Manhattan to "enjoy" the city on a July night. The only flight I could get on my ticket was via O'Hare, and I arrived in Chicago as the airport was being closed down due to thunderstorms. It was a nightmare. Thousands of people were stranded, no aircraft were arriving. My flight to Knoxville was delayed longer and longer. Near midnight, a plane came in from New Orleans, and Knoxville passengers were quickly herded aboard. Arriving in

Knoxville near 2:00 A.M., with no place to stay, with Alfred's new place more than an hour away and me not knowing how to get there, I picked up the rented car, got confused on which side of the road to drive (as I am now used to Australia), and got hopelessly lost in Knoxville, a city I once knew well. I finally checked into a motel at 3:30 A.M. I phoned Alfred in the morning and we arranged to meet at a gas station/fast food place off a turnoff from I-81. My stomach was leaden as I longed for my true self of New York and Vermont with old friends who lived stable professional lives and were not the subject of news headlines and reality TV commentary.

Alfred failed to recognize me at first, as I had grown a beard since my last trip three years earlier, and I was in a rented car with Texas plates, which threw him off. We hugged warmly (in the Holiness way), and he introduced me to Cyndy (the "teenage bride" of the news stories). We had a round of iced tea and I followed them up crooked back roads to their very old house trailer up a hollow out of Bybee, Tennessee. I snapped back into that old feeling. Listening to a local country station as I followed Alfred up the narrow roads, sipping iced tea as I drove, a big smile on my face, I was in the flow again, moving into this 3-D movie, and it felt good. I had snapped back, after considerable anxiety, to my old Tennessee Holiness self. Shushan, New York, Vermont, the anthropology conference at Williamsburg, and my Australian life and self with the Githabul Tribal Nation all receded to the back regions of consciousness. At their trailer, Alfred and Cyndy recalled the ordeal of their lives as fugitives, of being arrested at gunpoint in Kansas, of being handcuffed and transported back to Tennessee, of their time in jail, of the court hearing that deprived Alfred contact with his son for five years, all the while trying to understand how the whole dismal series of events had come about. Alfred brought me up to date on former "snake hollow" saints. Liston had been quite ill, living in a trailer somewhere and driving a gravel truck. He and Alfred were still estranged and not in contact. We caught up with Alfred's mother and a few other brothers and sisters who stood by him; I learned of those who hadn't, and we avoided places where they might be. His daughters who had made the allegations, their mother, and their assorted partners who had tried to "whup" Alfred were still out there somewhere and we certainly avoided them.

Talking late into the night, I succumbed to the quietness of this rural place in the mountains. My sleep was deep and contented, almost otherworldly. In the morning we drove Cyndy to her job as a motel cleaner in

Pidgeon Forge, and Alfred and I spent the day at Dollywood, catching the country and gospel singing, with Alfred reminiscing about his days in revival with Dolly's "old time preacher man" grandfather, Jake Owen, and aspects of Alfred's Holiness ministry over the years, before, during, and after serpent handling. It was surreal, Alfred and I shuffling along with the throngs of families on vacation, doing Dollywood, ensconced in some strange ethnographic space of our own; Alfred pointing out or introducing me to this or that Parton family relative or workmate along the way. It was being "there," without being there, but in some Holiness part reality.

We continued in this mode the next day at Allan Jackson Showcar Café in Pidgeon Forge, filled with tourists and Allan Jackson video clips projected all over the wall, but still in an ethnographic-Holiness mode; still there, but not there in consciousness. A country dinner in Bybee with the usual eggs, cornbread, and grits, served as another venue for catching up. On my last day, we had lunch at the gas station/fast food place where we had first met on this trip, and I lingered too long, with Alfred saying how my support had brought him back from depression and despair. I found this moving, but was conscious of time, and because of bridge work on the interstate, was delayed by 45 minutes, leaving me time only to drop the rental car in front of the terminal and run aboard the flight to St. Louis via O'Hare, out of breath and sweating, feeling very much of east Tennessee.

The door to my serpent-handling self shut abruptly on arriving in St. Louis and being met by my brother. This was again a different reality as no one in my family would or could share my Holiness reality and experience. I did not have the words to bridge this gap, and past the point of "their" exoticism, serpent handling is inexplicable to "normal" people.

"The Word Is Still the Word"—Writing Serpent Handling

The above fragments of "fieldwork," or "deep hanging out" (Renato Rosaldo, quoted in Clifford 1997a, 188), reflect the texture and flow of my "social insertion" (Dumont 1978, 6) in a remnant serpent-handling community, and of the everydayness of the encounter with these quintessential "Others" (see Birckhead 1993, 1997, 2000; Tidball and Toumey 2000). But these were only two trips: I also went back briefly in 1974, 1979, 1982, 1987, and 1991. Each of these trips had its own tone and mood; its challenges and adventures; its events, big and small; and its current country songs on the car radio. My main "fieldwork" between 1971 and 1973 was similarly cast, except that I spent more time systematically observing in formal settings, tape recording, and writing "field notes" in my scientistic quest to "crack the code" and produce the "final" and "definitive" reading of serpent handling (Crapanzano 1992, 43).

But as I became intersubjectively drawn in to this fragmented "community of saints," I reconciled myself to the more existentially realistic goal of grasping "truth on the margins" and in fleeting encounters (Jackson 1987, 24). Long-distance trucking with Liston Pack, for example, revealed to me a saint singing Holiness songs and speaking in tongues while gearjamming, and also perilously relying on the anointing power to protect us as we pounded down a steep grade on I-24 in neutral at 90 mph.[1] Similarly, there was the Thursday afternoon of July 26, 1973, when I watched Alfred in his backyard shoot Rudolf, a western diamondback rattlesnake, as he had seen this serpent in a dream viciously strike dead a young handler—providing an exception to the rule that "no serpent handler had ever been known to kill a reptile intentionally" (Williamson 1999, 102). But, for me, my "deep hanging out" translates uneasily into writing about the religion. It highlights "the gap of engaging others where they are and representing them where they aren't" (C. Geertz 1988, 130). How do I move from the "thick" particularities of my encounters with saints, the dialectical interplay between "I" and "they" (Dumont 1978, 5), to texts which assume a single, transcendent, "controlling voice," which do not easily allow for "the inconstancy of the self and the instability of our vantage point" (Crapanzano 1992, 9). Writing is a "solipsistic operation" (Ong 1982, 101). I sit alone in front of the blank computer screen, 13,000 miles from my "field site," as I prepare to go camping with my family in nearby Mt. Buffalo National Park, sorting through stacks of scribbled notes, typed transcripts, audio and video tapes of long dead saints, photographs, and drafts that lead off in a dozen directions; and I confront a mountain of texts on postmodernism, existential philosophy, the new physics and cosmology, the ever growing popular and scholarly texts and Internet sites on serpent handling, and the kaleidoscope of images and memories in my head and in my dreams.

Yet, writing, rewriting, and writing about writing and experiencing serpent handling have engaged me for some 32 years. I have lived angst fully with such questions. What are the ethical implications of "our" desire to penetrate, invade privacy (be a voyeur of sorts), and interpret this reality to the world in the name of social science and career? As a character from an Alice Walker novel reflects: "I think it is ridiculous and ultimately insulting to study people. I think you would only need to study other human beings if you were worried you were not human yourself" (1998, 187). While I feel fully human, some "bad faith" and unease come in here, as I question the perhaps perverse desire to experience vicariously other people's deep religious meanings, meanings that are not available in a post structuralist, rationalistic university world. And as serpent handling at times veers off "beyond the limits of rationality" (Stoller and Olkes 1987, ix) and provides glimpses of a "'real' lie beyond academic analysis" (Stewart 1996, 73), many of its meanings are grasped only at an inchoate or tacit level, which words fail to capture.

Serpent handling also implies a displacement geographically and from my other self or selves in negotiating the tension between self and other, and in enduring the shifts, shocks, and states of liminality experienced in moving back and forth between worlds. Although an "ethnography at home" topic, it has always represented for me long distance travel, first from western Canada and now from Australia. As with my work on Aboriginal spiritual connection to "country" in Australia (Birckhead 2001), entering the serpent-handling world is like emerging into a parallel universe through a wormhole. Traveling half a world away from my home in Albury, an hour's flight from Sydney, then the 14-hour through flight to LA, followed by hours on the ground, and a long flight east, in the opposite season, driving on the wrong side of the road, is very dislocating. I feel the pull of home as I go through this inevitable metamorphosis of the self, never knowing what I will find in east Tennessee.

Once there, I quickly snap into the self that emerges through discourse with Holiness selves/"others" and is attuned to appropriate interactional norms and cues. A schizoid self, perhaps, but Asch (2000, 4) suggests this is a more normal reading of self-making: "We become who we are, *and are always becoming,* through interaction with others." And part of that interaction is learning to walk with death and take as commonsense the type of metaphysics described by Brother Ray to a BBC reporter:

> In the *natural world*, if I took up a cup of cyanide or strychnine and drink it, I will surely die, unless they're very fast with a stomach pump. In the *real world*, the world created by God, the world established by Jesus Christ In that world, when I am in the real spirit world of God, I could drink battery acid and do nothing but clean my teeth. (Esler 1983, 3)

Yet, death is suspended in serpent handling; as Alfred put it to me in 1973:

It's a feeling like no other feeling in the world. It is peace and joy, and faith, and confidence. It's a tremendous feeling to know for that period of time you're immune to death.

But, "when the hedge is broken, a serpent will strike" (see Hood 1998; Schwartz 1999). Indeed, death is always stalking and palpable. As Brother Tim of Jolo, West Virginia said to Ruby Wax:

When I'm holding a serpent, that's my life I'm looking at my life. It can take you. It can take you out of this world. And it don't take it very long to do it after one bites you. It will take you out of this world if God don't intervene. (Wax 2000)

As a final reflection, I have to concur with Loring Danforth, that death dissolves the distance between self and other:

I was conscious at all times that it is not just Others who die. I was aware that my friends and relatives will die, that I will die, that death comes to all, Self and Other alike. (Cited in C. Geertz 1988, 15)

In passing time with saints, I can say in the end, "it's life and life only" (Dylan 1965).

NOTE

1. See my "Midnight Tennessee Trucking" sketch (Birckhead 1997, 58–9).

Chapter 12

Voicing Spiritualities

Anchored Composites as an Approach to Understanding Religious Commitment

Marion S. Goldman

Social scientists investigating novel religions face the dilemma of presenting members' lived experiences to readers with very different standpoints from the people we describe. Good presentations of the subjective realities of spiritual commitment often include vivid personal details. The subjects of research on novel religions, however, are particularly vulnerable to personal and legal pressures, so in many cases confidentiality may be essential. Traditional academic approaches to writing life histories protect respondents' anonymity, but those approaches almost invariably diminish the authenticity of their voices. The taken-for-granted sociological conventions of presenting specific themes and isolating examples of those themes through brief quotations or descriptions protect confidentiality at the price of full understanding.

I encountered this problem while writing about my research on the short-lived community of Rajneeshpuram (Goldman 1999). I found that traditional approaches did not do justice to the vivid life histories of the high-achieving women who had followed their spiritual master, Bhagwan Shree Rajneesh, to this remote spot in central Oregon. Unless I could present a clear picture of these women's shared journeys, I could not show why they chose to leave careers, friends, lovers, and sometimes families to follow a radical spiritual path. It was crucial to convey the complexities and many dimensions of their lives, how those different facets fit together, and how each woman constructed and reconstructed her personal world. Yet, the many personal and legal conflicts associated with Raj-neeshpuram made it essential to conceal the women's identities.

So, I developed composite characters anchored in the details of devo-tees' stories. From my original transcripts, field notes, and documentary materials on the lives of 24 male and female sannyasins, I first decided to focus on 11 women. I then captured these women's lives in three compos-ite life histories. I used the 11 women's own voices, words, and life experi-ences, mixing them to construct characters that protected the originals, without adding unnecessary fiction.[1]

In this chapter, I will briefly describe my research questions, my find-ings, and the context in which they unfolded. By understanding the his-tory of Rajneeshpuram, readers can better evaluate the necessity for bal-ancing confidentiality and authenticity. Then I will examine the specific methodological guidelines that made anchored composites a valid ap-proach to qualitative research at Rajneeshpuram and a possibility for re-search strategies in other contexts. I hope that other ethnographers who investigate religion can benefit from my strategies and develop their own in order to give voice to the subjective realities so central to religious ex-perience.

Rajneeshpuram and Bhagwan Shree Rajneesh

Rajneeshpuram, located on a remote highway about an hour drive from the tiny hamlet of Antelope in central Oregon, was the most controversial utopian community of the 1980s. About 2,500 sannyasins lived at Raj-neeshpuram, and as many as 15,000 more pilgrims participated in four annual summer festivals for two to four weeks. They were briefly joined by an estimated 2,000 street people who were bussed in to live very briefly at the Ranch during an abortive attempt to sway the county election of November 1984.

The communal city was designed for visitors and residents to absorb the presence of Bhagwan Shree Rajneesh, the controversial master, who advocated blending materialism and spirituality in the service of per-sonal actualization and self-transcendence. Its buildings, which have since been torn down or reconfigured to serve as dorms and gathering places for Christian teens belonging to Young Life, once housed fashion-able boutiques, excellent restaurants, a huge meditation hall, and a uni-versity for personal growth.

Rajneeshpuram began when Bhagwan's personal secretary, Ma Anand Sheela, purchased the 64,000-acre Big Muddy Ranch for $5.9 million on July 10, 1981. From the date of purchase, Rajneesh, his sannyasins, and their communal city sparked media attention and vastly different responses from different groups. Local ranchers believed that the sannyasins' experimental farming and regular water use threatened their families' livelihoods. Residents of Antelope, the neighboring town, feared that sannyasins would destroy their small community and its public school. Worried politicians and clergy speculated that the group could take over state and local government. Law enforcement officials at federal, state, and local levels grew increasingly concerned about fraud, coercion, and weapon stockpiling (Carter 1990; Shay and Shay 1995).

Rank-and-file sannyasins and their sympathizers in other parts of Oregon experienced something quite different. They assumed that the residents of Rajneeshpuram were unfairly stereotyped and harassed by conservative central Oregonians, who mistrusted both the group's religious practices and the sannyasins' cosmopolitanism. Officials at Rajneeshpuram justified the accumulation of conventional and semi-automatic firearms in their communal city as necessary protection against dangerous neighbors, irrational lawmen, or vigilantes. Many sannyasins saw the invitations to the homeless as an opportunity to rehabilitate people who were down-and-out and demonstrate the power of their spiritual practice, while disconcerted outsiders accurately envisioned political plots (Fitzgerald 1986).

In most cases, differing perceptions were sincere, reflecting convictions grounded in the standpoints of various actors (Carter 1990, xviii–xxi). Jonestown was still fresh in the minds of both sannyasins and their opponents (J. Hall 1987). At their most apprehensive, devotees imagined lethal persecution by the government, while their antagonists feared that Rajneesh and his followers could be caught up in suicidal violence, killing opponents and their loved ones along with themselves.

These tangled, multiple realities overlaid a chronology of cumulative deceit and crime, much of which came to light after the spiritual leader had left the United States. The experiment was over by late fall of 1985. Rajneeshpuram began to close down shortly afterward. Rajneesh officially blamed his personal secretary, Ma Anand Sheela, for a catalogue of bad decisions and crimes, along with other abuses of power. He had retreated into meditative silence in 1981 and only spoke to Sheela, his personal physician, and a handful of others, until October 1984. So, Sheela effectively controlled the organization until Bhagwan began to speak publicly and internal resistance to her grew. Nevertheless, Rajneesh's complicity in many dangerous activities remains a matter of fierce speculation (Fitzgerald 1986, 373–81; Carter 1990, 230–31).

Although individual sannyasins and the attractive elements of their collective vision sustained my research, I recognized or intuited some of its darker side. At least three of the women I interviewed were under U.S. government surveillance through most of the 1980s. Another was involved in child custody litigation after Rajneeshpuram collapsed. Moreover, everyone I interviewed disclosed some details that might have been painful to their families or close friends in retrospect. Disclosure is often an issue in social science research, but Rajneeshpuram was unusual because of tensions with the surrounding society. Because of the many concerns about confidentiality, as well as legality in some cases, I pushed against sociological conventions in order to present sannyasins' stories as accurately as possible, without revealing their identities.

Why Follow the Bhagwan?

From its beginning, Rajneeshpuram attracted outsiders' attention. One of the most important reasons was the presence of high-achieving baby boomers, who had forsaken their careers to seek personal truths. They hoped to blend materialism and spirituality in a utopian community and agricultural experiment where everyone enjoyed basic physical comforts, meaningful labor, and possibilities for self-actualization through connection with their spiritual master.

Outsiders often marveled that sannyasins seemed like a lost tribe, wandering from India to Oregon in order to recapture the hopes of the late 1960s. Most of their contemporaries had already abandoned their earlier commitments to personal and social change. This unlikely continuation of the baby boomers' great aspirations to combine good personal lives with a good society provoked outsiders' wonder and anger.

Many Americans could not understand why women and men who had achieved recognition and economic security would willingly abandon those hard won rewards to recreate themselves and fill some invisible spiritual void. However, as the writer Frances Fitzgerald (1986) observed, the residents of Rajneeshpuram actually lived out long-standing American values of endless possibilities and rebirth through spiritual commitment.

Like it or not, second chances and new lives are embedded in our culture. Cherished popular icons have often redefined themselves and discovered new identities several times over, just as the sannyasins did.

Something in Bhagwan's message drew extraordinarily talented women to his movement. Many had developed careers when the upper reaches of the occupational structure were just opening to women. Their abilities flowered and their needs grew in the context of a monumental historical transition, when middle class American women had a range of choices that they neither anticipated nor fully understood. Yet, they gratefully turned away from their accomplishments.

Through participation, observation, and long conversations, I learned that these women were deeply dissatisfied with their relationships and their work until they became sannyasins. No matter how successful they were, every one of them experienced frustration and dread with each new achievement. They told me that they had attempted to define their identities in terms of each new commitment, yet they could not receive the love and recognition they desired because their desires were endless. They possessed fragile selves, needing sustained appreciation and applause in order to feel good about themselves.

This emotional fragility reflected the women's childhood experience of mothers whom they defined as unresponsive and fathers who made them feel unique and special. All of the women feared becoming like their mothers. They invested themselves in education, professional training, or interesting jobs in order to differentiate themselves from their mothers. Their achievements surprised their fathers, whom they idealized as much as they resented their mothers. The sannyasins' fathers had always reinforced their daughters' femininity, but they had never encouraged them to strive for occupational success.

When the women discovered Bhagwan, they found that they could be loved and appreciated because of their intellectual and intuitive abilities. He protected them symbolically, while encouraging them to explore themselves and strive to be the best they could be. Thus, they could resolve the tensions between work and love. This story took shape differently for each woman who talked with me. In order to tell its details, while still protecting them, I developed three composite sannyasins, Shanto, Dara, and Tanmaya. Each composite was created from a group of women who shared the same historical experiences, growing up within no more than five years of one another. The quotations were all taken directly from the respondents, and everything I described actually happened to one or another of them, though I changed some fine points in order to protect their anonymity. The details in their stories capture the essential experiences of each group of women. Each of the 11 respondents was part of only one composite, and it was the single composite most emblematic of her life. Thus, each composite had a separate life history.

The oldest, Shanto, grew up in the 1940s and 1950s and dropped out of college to marry a successful contractor and have three children. However, she thirsted for education and self-discovery, so she divorced him and embarked on her own quests.

Dara was an early baby boomer who went to graduate school in Berkeley and was active in movements against the war in Vietnam and in support of women's liberation. She married, had a child, and then divorced after she discovered a meaningful career. Like many other women of her generation, she tried to fuse the personal and the political in numerous ways. Eventually, her yearning to combine self-actualization and social justice led Dara to Bhagwan.

The third woman, Tanmaya, came of age during the Sixties. Although she always expected to have some kind of a career, her success as a fashion model in London took Tanmaya by surprise. No matter how much she earned, Tanmaya's work was always secondary to relationships with men. For many years, she only felt strong when she was involved with a man who she believed possessed the powers to help and protect her in some way. Tanmaya had used relationships with men to feel safe, but she did not find contentment until she connected with Bhagwan.

As I wrote, the three composite women assumed lives of their own. My descriptions were physically vivid, because the respondents' appearances and their overall presences were equally striking. I developed physical descriptions reflecting what was important to the women themselves, while cloaking their actual identities. Thus, for example, all three women who comprised Shanto actually had distinctive physical characteristics that brought them both joy and ambivalence, although none had long copper-colored curls like Shanto's.

The sannyasins were intelligent, articulate women, who talked about many parts of their lives. When they described their experiences, I sometimes had to change specifics: Transplant them from other Midwestern cities to Chicago, place a lover in the legal profession when he was actually a corporate executive, or transfer them from the University of British Columbia to the University of Washington. When the women provided animated descriptions of people and places, I developed equally colorful images that were very close to their own.

These composites allowed me to write for a number of different audiences: sannyasins, scholars, students, and general readers. And I could do so without complicating my interviewees' efforts to go on with their lives—which could have been imperiled by using identifiable personages. Because of the importance of sustaining traditional standards of precision and accountability, however, I included detailed methodological appendices, tables, and references at the end of *Passionate Journeys*.

Research Conversations

Every woman whom I invited to take part in the research participated. "Research conversation" or "extended discussion" describes my interactions with the respondents far more accurately than the term "interview." "Interview" implies formality, hierarchy, and structure, all of which were notably absent as I recorded sannyasins' life histories. I developed a list of questions from academic resources and from my early discussions with sannyasins, and those provided rough guidelines for our conversations. Although I introduced some topics and sometimes requested clarifications, our discussions were usually mutual and reciprocal.

Each research conversation provided a framework for both of us to understand more. Sannyasins engaged in explaining their decisions to themselves, as well as to me. In our encounters, they witnessed to the meaning of their commitment and affirmed the choices they had made. Our talks became vehicles for self-definition, and women sometimes gained sudden insights into specific relationships between past and present. All of them talked with me after crimes were disclosed publicly, and Rancho Rajneesh was in turmoil. The interview process became a useful forum to discuss their enduring devotion to Bhagwan in the face of so many negative revelations.

The sannyasins and I started our long talks with the first question from the list, guiding all of my focused conversations with the 11 women. I asked, "Tell me about the day you took sannyas." This usually prompted an elaborate description and ensuing discussion, providing preliminary answers to some other questions. From that point, I occasionally steered the conversations back to a topic that was on my list, but usually I let them flow.

I imposed structure in only three places: At the end of our first research conversation and in the middle of first and second conversations.
At the end of our second conversation, each sannyasin and I went over
demographic information about things like her year of birth and number
of sisters and brothers. In the middle of the first and second discussions, I
asked sannyasins to make up stories in response to cues from six Thematic Apperception (TAT) cards.[2]

The sannyasins revealed themselves during the interviews, through the
TATs, and when we simply hung out together. Our casual encounters
often provided as much information as our formal conversations. Fortuitous interactions, shared meals, and even my occasional *faux pas* sub-
stantially supplemented our scheduled discussions. When I spilled coffee
on her prized antique oriental rug, I learned about a sannyasin's grace
and tact, as well as the luxurious life she led before finding Bhagwan. On
another occasion, a pile of velvet I assumed to be drapery material, actually turned out to be cloth for Bhagwan's robes. In both cases, the women
glossed over my tactlessness, showing me the ways in which sannyasins
savored their spiritual choices and revered Rajneesh.

The success of the research conversations reflected the therapeutic
sensibility characteristic of the Rajneesh movement. Introspection, reflection, and self-disclosure were essential parts of sannyasins' paths to
actualization and enlightenment. Most of the women respondents had
partaken of some forms of psychotherapy before becoming sannyasins,
and almost all of the men had, as well. Sannyasins saw our discussions as
a fresh opportunity to explore their feelings, often discussing the meanings of their TAT stories in subsequent conversations (Runyan 1982).

The intrinsic value of our meetings, however, was only one reason why
people spent time with me. Some sannyasins with strong social science
backgrounds were interested in research on gender and spirituality. Two,
who stood at the edge of Sheela's inner circle, kept a watchful eye on me
and my project and tried to present positive information about Rajneeshpuram. Others saw our discussions as reasonable acts of rebellion against
the current regime. All of the women I interviewed were motivated by
mixed combinations of these three reasons, along with more personal,
idiosyncratic desires. For the most part, however, the sannyasins' motives
did not detract from their merciless truthfulness about their lives.

Throughout every part of the research, sannyasins and I learned about
one another and also about ourselves. Our focus on personal life histories
and the length of our acquaintance made it unlikely that sannyasins

would deliberately lie to me. Nevertheless, the frantic secrecy and quiet desperation that lay just below the surface of life at Rajneeshpuram undoubtedly influenced our encounters.

Still, I trust each woman's overall honesty, in the face of some general reasons to doubt it. Authorities in relatively small, closed communities like Rajneeshpuram sometimes encourage members to present the same viewpoint or even instruct them explicitly in a common rhetoric. Certainly, honesty was not the order of the day at Rancho Rajneesh. This would not have been the first time that Sheela tried to control information and orchestrate responses (Fitzgerald 1986, 354; Carter 1990, 274–75 and 284).

Deception, however, was more likely to have skewed some of the answers to anonymous questionnaires given to hundreds of sannyasins rather than the highly individual, extended personal interviews that were central to my research. I selected respondents because of their documented educational credentials or high personal incomes. They spoke for themselves and did not represent the whole commune. They told their own life stories and not the story of Rajneeshpuram, so Sheela or her subordinates could not easily orchestrate systematic distortion.

Mutual trust unfolded because I talked with each of the 11 women a number of times, over many months, and with each meeting they disclosed more. In most cases, we came to know one another beyond the interview situation, although our mutual respect did not completely compensate for the official ambivalence toward the project, which lasted until Sheela left.

Because of the many pressures on them, sannyasins would not have talked so openly with me unless their anonymity were protected from Sheela's scrutiny, other sannyasins' curiosity, and outsiders' ability to identify them. Although Sheela's displeasure is no longer an issue, and almost all criminal charges involving sannyasins have been settled, anonymity remains a problem. Sannyasins did not want to hurt their families, friends, comrades, or lovers, but they wanted to discuss those relationships openly and honestly. Anonymity also became important in the aftermath of Rajneeshpuram, as some people had to patch together new resumes, and even after two decades, some are still in the process of integrating their sojourn in central Oregon into their personal narratives.

Organizing Composites

I did not group the women into composites by some predetermined criteria, such as their ethnicity, age, social class, religion of origin, former occupation, or role at Rajneeshpuram. Instead, I read transcripts and listened to tapes in order to discover how they should be combined. My decision to organize the composites in terms of the women's ages reflected the strongest thread linking particular sets of women. In other studies, decisions might be made in terms of some other criteria.

I was surprised at how much women in each of the three groups forming the composites sounded like one another, using the same words and articulating similar concerns, even compared to women in the other two composites. They used language and images that reflected when and how they had come of age, and even a few years could create marked differences (Whittier 1995). American women's worlds changed so fundamentally between 1950 and 1980 that the sannyasins' ages during those times defined the range of their life choices. Historic experience washed away most of the social class differences within each group of the women. The most notable contrasts in social class were among the five individuals who comprise Dara. Three were working class, one was upper middle class, and one was born to the new American aristocracy, but their lives were all remarkably similar. Relative economic security and the availability of student subsidies smoothed class distinctions in their educational experiences and their youthful hopes. Both the daughters of workers and the child of a successful capitalist studied abroad during high school, graduated from outstanding universities, earned professional degrees, and anticipated limitless possibilities in useful, meaningful careers and satisfying egalitarian marriages.

The number of respondents is so small that many patterns within each generational group may be matters of chance. It is probably chance that all of the Shantos were Jewish, four of five women who became Dara were raised as Roman Catholics, and two of three Tanmayas had mild liberal Protestant affiliations when they were growing up. However, the women were bound together by something far deeper than their original religions. Age ultimately defined each of the three composite sannyasins. In fall of 1985, at the time of our last conversations at Rajneeshpuram, the oldest of these women was 49 and the youngest was 33. The three oldest women grew up in the shadow of the Great Depression, and their early biographies were connected more closely to the past century than to the next one. They matured to become wives and mothers, having been taught that marriage was a goal that was morally and materially superior to any other "feminine" career.

The five early baby boomers had a very different experience. While they were growing up, they shared the spreading national affluence and optimism that marked the 1950s. Their mothers were housewives, who wanted their daughters to do well in school before they became home-makers themselves. But the 1960s changed the young women's lives, as they questioned their old assumptions and redirected their energies to-ward changing the world.

The final three women were only slightly younger than the earlier boomers. From the time they were in elementary school, however, they ex-pected to work outside the home just as their mothers did. They were of high school age when feminism claimed the covers of all the national news magazines, and by the time they were 21, these sannyasins took the issue of women's equality for granted. They were interested in personal, not social change. Some of their old friends became yuppies. They became sannyasins.

Even with a much larger number of respondents, I believe that the three different generational categories would remain important defining classifi-cations. The women in each cohort resembled their times, even more than they resembled their parents (Bloch 1953, 157), and the historic changes in American women's roles heavily influenced these women's personal lives.

Thus, *Passionate Journeys* was not a conclusive history of Rajneeshpu-ram, although participants explored their personal responses to the com-munal city. I discovered no definitive answers about the movement's de-mographics nor about the educational attainments of most sannyasins. But I did find patterns, which the composite approach allowed me to flesh out. It made possible a detailed answer to my main research ques-tions: Why and how accomplished women turned their back on affluence and social recognition as they sought to redefine themselves.

Boundaries and Voices

Ethnography involves implicit alliances between the researcher and those she interviews. At Rajneeshpuram, that connection began because of some key biographical similarities that we discussed. Like many of the san-nyasins I met, I had grown up expecting to make marriage and children my profession. When the second wave of American feminism opened new possibilities to women, I was at the front of the line, struggling through those recently unlocked doors. But over a decade of work I had learned that occupational mobility didn't provide everything I needed. I had two children in my mid-thirties, and I had begun to rethink the priorities in my life. In the early 1980s, thousands of women my age were also reflecting on their decisions. The women who talked with me had already reordered their priorities, often leaving behind hard won educational credentials, lucrative careers, lovers, husbands, and children, in order to create meaningful, integrated lives. Their extreme choices could allow me and other women to examine our own.

The sannyasins, as they themselves often noted, were possibly the most interesting single group ever to settle in Oregon. One of my major identifications with them was as an urban outsider, caught in a relatively bland state that seemed to be peopled by individuals of Northern European descent, who told me things like, "I've never met anyone Jewish before. Do you mind if I stare at your nose?" If I was unusual, the sannyasins were positively inexplicable in this homogeneous social landscape.

Despite these similarities, I differed from them in fundamental ways. Not surprisingly, the greatest distances involved the fact that I did not develop a charismatic connection with Bhagwan Shree Rajneesh. I certainly "went native" in terms of empathy with sannyasins and recognition of our mutuality. But I did not share, or even understand, their fundamental allegiance. I think that this actually helped my research, as the women themselves had to supply the thick descriptions that illuminated the process of living as a devotee (C. Geertz 1973b). Their charismatic connections also made their own voices essential to their unfolding stories.

Some sannyasins who only met me casually assumed that I was also a devotee, because I was a frequent visitor, and I picked up the community's argot fairly quickly.[3] Without thinking about it, I began to use words like "juicy" for full of life or "conditioning" to signify past socialization. My language was not a careful research strategy, but it was instead a natural adaptation to conversations in a bounded social group (Richardson et al. 1978).

Keeping Secrets, Speaking Truth

In the context of Rajneeshpuram, ordinary, formal guidelines for the protection of human subjects had to be expanded. I informed each participant about the broad outlines of the project, the protection of respondents' anonymity, and any risks that I believed sannyasins might face through participation. In most research contexts, participants sign a form indicating that they have been informed about those issues. Because of their unspoken knowledge of internal surveillance and the continuing investigations and lawsuits by state and federal agencies, some sannyasins suggested that I take unusual precautions to protect them. I guaranteed complete anonymity, consistently substituted pseudonyms on tapes and transcripts, and gave every respondent a statement documenting their rights. Both of us signed and dated two copies of an agreement, and I kept a copy signed with only their non—sannyas name. This process increased my sensitivity to the need for sustained confidentiality, long after Rajneeshpuram had collapsed.

Federal human subjects' guidelines require both informed consent and also special sensitivity to topics involving sex, drugs, or crime. Once again, established guidelines did not fit research at Rajneeshpuram. Because of Bhagwan's support of open communication about intimate matters, the sannyasins, to a woman and to a man, took pride in the ways in which they had come to terms with their own sexuality. I offered to turn the tape recorder off during florid descriptions that sometimes made me blush, but they laughed and made comments like "No, you must hear this!"

Sannyasins also offered candid discussions about their consumption of street drugs before finding Bhagwan, possibly exaggerating their use in order to affirm the positive effects of spirituality. Some admitted that they still used recreational drugs on occasion, and those conversations went unrecorded. Until Sheela was deposed, sannyasins were cautious about their slips of criticism against her or her entourage, and they shied away from any topic touching on the internal or external politics of Rajneeshpuram. After Sheela and her inner circle fled, some sannyasins talked at length about how they had felt while she was ascendant, often blaming themselves for their tacit compliance with her arrogance and impulsive decisions. A few women briefly described their complicity in minor crimes, and I immediately forgot the details of those conversations.

Although I had sent early respondents transcripts of our interviews, most did not reach them. I discontinued mailing copies to Rajneeshpuram in June 1985 and then resumed in September of that year. This interchange was an important part of mutuality in research. The sannyasins who returned transcripts to me usually corrected grammar and spelling and amplified their comments. Only one sannyasin deleted our substantive discussions, taking out references to a convenient marriage to a foreign national and to personal financial arrangements for supplementary income. She was unusually cautious, and other respondents described similar marital and financial arrangements without reservation.

One of the women who returned her transcripts after she had left Rajneeshpuram voiced a positive response shared by other respondents. She wrote, "Thank you for sending the huge transcript. It has helped me to read about my life in this time of transition."

The Case for Composites

My explicit promise to guard respondents' identities was in tension with my implicit pledge to present the women's life histories as clearly and accurately as possible. I had to conceal identities without diminishing the full impact of the devotees' life histories, so I developed anchored composites.

My creation of composites is a disputed form of presenting data. Recent criticisms of composites in news reporting have been particularly bitter. Janet Cooke returned her 1981 Pulitzer Prize for feature writing, after confessing that she had entirely contrived a six-year-old heroin addict. In 1998, Phillip Glass, a rising star in journalism, confessed that he had made up numerous individuals and incidents in stories published in magazines ranging from *The New Republic* to *Rolling Stone* (Bissinger 1998).

Although sociologists Richard Sennett and Jonathan Cobb (1972) created composites grounded in actual interviews and observations, they received criticisms that were as harsh as those leveled at the journalists who passed off imaginary characters as real composites.

Sociologists usually pull together quotations from a number of individuals to illustrate a particular point. Thus, in order to depict the fact that the sannyasins had difficulties with their mothers, I might make a statement about those tensions and present two or three illustrative quotations. This type of organization sustains respondents' anonymity, but it does not illustrate the ways in which personal visions are inevitably enmeshed in changing life stories.

I believe that this standard method of presentation is neither more nor less accurate than responsible composites. Quotations drawn out of the context of people's life histories are constructions that distort their voices. I used composites in order to present all 11 of the women's voices in terms of life histories similar to their own. I changed some aspects of women's histories so that they could not be identified, but no major event such as marriage, divorce, or childbirth was recorded unless it was shared by the majority of sannyasins in a group. Because of journalists' fabrications and the many questions raised about composites in academic work, I presented my strategy in some detail in methodological appendices, to allow readers to evaluate both the general approach and also my specific strategies.

Composites built on actual life histories and accurate quotations permit people to speak in their own ways. When sannyasins talked with me, they were organizing and reorganizing their experiences in the same fashion that sociologists examine and classify respondents' accounts. Almost everyone considers and categorizes, trying to learn from the past, consider the present, and anticipate the future. We configure and reconfigure our lives, as the construction of social meaning becomes a daily project.

In qualitative sociology, the search for theoretical meaning is embedded in the research process itself, but it becomes most important when transcripts and ethnographic materials are finally analyzed, organized, and presented. Qualitative sociology is an endless spiral of research and reflection, in which analysis and writing are as important, possibly more important, than data collection (Becker 1986; C. Geertz 1988).

Narrative almost inevitably reflects writers' own language and perceptions. Composites offer solutions to some of these narrative distortions by providing readers with access to actors' voices, while anchoring each voice in a collective biography. The composite approach was the best way to introduce the sannyasins as multidimensional actors engaged in the process of shaping their own lives. I am committed to allowing readers to hear, appreciate, and understand their compelling personal histories.

NOTES

1. This form is grounded in postmodern approaches that move beyond the confining structures of traditional ethnographic narratives (Denzin and Lincoln 1994, 575–86). I was inspired by Karen McCarthy Brown's *Mama Lola* (1991),

though I circumscribed my inventions, grounding each major life history theme in explicit biographical information.

2. The TAT is a collection of ambiguous pictures that cue people to invent relatively long stories, which can reveal central emotional issues, such as their desires for affiliation, intimacy, power, achievement, or transcendence (Murray 1943). The *sannyasins* enjoyed devising elaborate tales, and they all scored well within normative ranges on every variable, while also demonstrating their considerable intelligence and imagination (Sundberg et al. 1992).

3. Indeed, I was more than just a visitor, but in most cases I was less than a friend (Becker 1967; Neitz 1987; Reinharz 1992).

Chapter 13

Against Univocality
Re-reading Ethnographies of Conservative Protestant Women

Julie Ingersoll

Women, Fundamentalism, and Ethnography

The growing interest in women and religion and the rise in popularity of ethnography as a research method are inextricably tied to each other. Since the experiences of women are often neglected in documentary and textual sources, ethnography is a key tool for those who would examine religious cultures with an eye toward gender inclusivity. This is especially true of sociological and historical studies of women in conservative religious traditions, as those women are even less likely to be given voice in the formal structures of religion.

The earliest scholarship on conservative religion and gender emphasized the patriarchal character of those communities. As feminist scholars grappled with questions about why women seem, at times, to be at home in such traditions they resorted to a variety of explanations that rarely took seriously what the women said about their own lives. The women in conservative religion were seen as misguided dupes or as disingenuous manipulators who benefited personally from the oppression of their sisters. Post-modern critical reflection has led scholars in many fields to recognize that scholarship, by its very nature, tends to assemble vast amounts of data into singular narratives and thereby silence counter-hegemonic voices. In the study of religion, for example, David Hall (1997) calls for scholarship that avoids imposing univocality on social systems as though they were monolithic. David Chidester and Edward Linenthal (1995) have challenged scholars to focus on conflict and contestedness as an essential component of culture. Furthermore, postmodernism has challenged us to take seriously the "insider/outsider problem" and be more cognizant of the ways in which our work is shaped by our own values and perceptions (McCutcheon 1999).

Ethnography, as a method, is held up by many as a potential answer to these long-standing criticisms; "ethnographers can give voice to the otherwise voiceless," or so the story goes. And so it should come as no surprise that the many fine recent studies of women and religion have, at the very least, significant ethnographic components. Christel Manning (1999), Brenda Brasher (1998), and R. Marie Griffith (1997) examine these issues in conservative Protestant contexts. In similar studies, Debra Kaufman (1991) and Lynn Davidman (1991) explore the stories of women who convert to Orthodox Judaism.

These recent ethnographies represent a move away from a simple feminist critique of patriarchal religion toward an effort to make sense of the women in these traditions on their own terms. Each of these authors expresses her own feminist convictions and then seeks to give voice to those with whom she would disagree. This recent scholarship on women in American conservative religion has begun to show how women recast the conservative doctrine of women's submission in ways that are ultimately empowering. Often with a focus on converts, these studies have asked: "How is it that women would chose to embrace a religious tradition that is predicated on their own loss of power and seeming oppression?" These feminist scholars have begun with the assumption that the experiences conservative women claim for themselves are authentic and that (despite how we might feel were we part of such traditions) the women who choose these life courses do so because they find something of value in them. For example, Davidman and Kaufman found that the women they studied value a sense of community among people who see their work as wives and mothers as important. Griffith, Kaufman, and Brasher argue that what looks like powerlessness from the outside has its own processes of empowerment.

However, when I have used these works in the classroom—especially the works on Protestants—many of my students, having grown up in these traditions, object that such arguments just don't ring true. They know from experience that many conservative Protestant women do not find "power in submission." They know that these women often feel limited, discounted, and redirected when they express the sense of calling for which men are encouraged and rewarded. Many know all too well how these women struggle with frustration and depression as a result of their gendered worlds.

My own research suggests that these students are correct. While what authors like Griffith and Brasher have found is certainly true for some (even many) women in these conservative communities, the story is much more complicated than their studies indicate. Many women do not find the empowerment that these authors promise. While contributing to our developing understanding of conservative Protestant women, in important respects, each of these authors, in the end, imposes a univocality on the women she studies. Such univocality not only marginalizes alternative views, but it also masks important aspects of religious phenomena.[1] It has had the paradoxical effect of silencing the feminist women within these traditions.

It is my argument that ethnographers (specifically those studying women in conservative religious traditions) need to take this challenge to avoid univocality to heart; that unless we move to incorporate the conflict and complexity that characterizes gender norms, expectations, and ideology in conservative Protestantism, we miss an opportunity to observe the process by which these religions produce and reproduce themselves. Factions with the most power inevitably try to create the illusion that theirs is the only possible interpretation of reality. By failing to tease out the hidden counterhegemonic voices, we become complicit in their effort to maintain the status quo.

To recognize the real import of gender as a core aspect of culture in American Protestant Fundamentalism, ethnographic research must move from an effort to find women's empowerment amid structural limitations, to exploring the experiences of women in the subculture who participate in the process of change. We need also to study conservative women who challenge gender norms within their religious traditions, the fallout they experience as part of the ensuing conflict, and the significance of the conflict over gender for the development and character of culture.

Case Studies: Two Ethnographies of Conservative Christian Women

In *God's Daughters: Evangelical Women and the Power of Submission*, R. Marie Griffith (1997) argues that if we look at the practical outworkings of the doctrine of submission in the lives of pentecostal women, instead of just the doctrine as it is articulated by religious leaders, we can see ways in which those women reshape submission to create a space of empowerment. Griffith's approach goes a long way in helping us to take seriously the convictions and values of these women without dismissing their viewpoint as some form of "false consciousness." For this reason, it is an important contribution to this growing list of titles on women in conservative religion.

Griffith began her fieldwork with an interest in the prayer lives of women, but her study developed in such a way as to explore a multitude of issues. These include gender and power relationships, the role of religion in a therapeutic culture and the impact of the therapeutic culture on religion, the history and ethos of Women's Aglow Fellowship, and the themes of healing, transformation, secrecy, and intimacy as they play themselves out in the women's experiences. She paints a textured picture of the lives of the women in Women's Aglow, and most of the time that picture fits with what we might expect from women in an international pentecostal prayer organization. But Griffith gives a surprising twist to her narrative as she pieces together her argument that, to these women, submission is really freedom; that, in actuality, it is empowerment.

She grants that the doctrines of submission have softened over time as religious leaders have emphasized the loving character of "responsible male headship." But Griffith doesn't hide the fact that significant differences exist between the forms of "empowerment" available to Aglow women and feminist notions of equality. As Aglow women confess their dissatisfaction with their lives, they still do so in ways that conform to accepted narrative conventions that assume that "domestic unhappiness stems largely from stubborn willfulness, so that healing can occur only when a wife pliantly consents to obey her husband and lets him reign as leader of the home" (172).

So how is it that submission is inverted—transformed into empowerment? When exploring the related issue of weight control, Griffith explains: "Surrender and discipline appear to harmonize as the will of God is internalized in the will of the individual" (147). And she does not miss the point that, in this subculture, the power in submission applies to all Christians, not just to women, as she calls our attention to the "paradox of surrender and control so deeply ingrained in evangelicalism" (150). The inversion of power relations has long been an important theme in Christianity. The meek inherit the earth, the church leaders are really servants, and most centrally, the power of death is overcome by resurrected life.

But there are hints throughout that, although hidden from view by the Aglow rhetoric, there are other forces at play as well. Griffith points to the significant "lampooning of male behavior" and the jokes about "men's 'nature' that have a rather sharp edge" (155). In her insightful discussion of the impact of the "therapeutic culture" on the women she studies, Griffith explores evasion and denial of anger (her example is a case in which a women had forgiven a man who had raped her). Griffith recognized that the stories the women tell "end on a more cheerful note than their subject might warrant" (95). Indeed, she writes, "all narratives end with joyful professions of victory and transformation" (120). Those to whom she gives voice (and those to whom the organization gives voice), tell their stories in the institutionally approved narrative format. Whatever the problem, the love of Jesus has overcome it. But a reader is left wondering whether the biting humor might not be an outlet for otherwise "inappropriate" expressions of anger.

Despite the seeming autonomy of Aglow, a women's ministry, it is overseen by a board of advisors that is all male. Griffith documents the variety of explanations for this fact, as well as the variety of views on the role the board actually plays (152–156). But with some women leaders believing that the board's role in merely symbolic, while others believing that the men oversee Aglow's theology as a "protection and covering," it seems inevitable that there would have been conflicts over control. Griffith's narrative left me wondering how this really works and whether all the women are equally happy with it.

Griffith deals, adeptly, with two groups of women: those in conservative Protestantism who embrace patriarchy and submission, and feminists outside those traditions who insist on understanding the conservative women on their own (feminist) terms. But she imposes univocality on pentecostal women when she gives no voice to the women within the tradition who have chafed under patriarchy—and have been sometimes nearly destroyed by it. Evangelical Feminists and others who have studied them (e.g.: Scanzoni and Hardesty 1992; Groothius 1994; Hearn 1979; Malcolm 1982) have documented high rates of depression and anxiety disorders. Conflict is rampant, brought about by the inability of many conservative Protestant women (including evangelicals, pentecostals, charismatics, and fundamentalists), to reconcile what they are taught about the Bible with what they believe to be true about their own identities and callings.

Brenda Brasher's *Godly Women: Fundamentalism and Female Power* (1998) is another such example. Brasher gives depth and nuance to the literature on the lives of conservative Christian women. She struggles to step out of her own world and into theirs, presenting their stories much as they might tell them. She finds that, though the women she studies are excluded from congregational authority, they are by no means without power. Brasher effectively demonstrates the significant differences between authority and power, shows the workings of female power in the congregations she studies, and then explains that this is due, in large measure, to the highly developed network created by the women's ministry enclaves. In her words, "the . . . primary thesis of this book is that to Christian Fundamentalist women, the restrictive religious identity they embrace improves their ability to direct the course of their lives and empowers them in their relationships with others" (4). And, "again, women's interviews divulge how submission increases rather than decreases a woman's power in the marital relationship" (6).

But, here too, there are hints that the story is more complicated. For example, by Brasher's own account, the separate women's sphere in which these conservative Christian women find empowerment includes only a fraction of church women—one-third of the women in one congregation and one-fifth of the women in the other (13). Brasher hints at "communal social pressures" faced by these women but doesn't elaborate on what those might be. She refers to "rebellious impulses" but doesn't spell them out (69).

She explains that she believes the women spoke openly (7) but never explains why she believes this to be true. Given the emphasis conservative Christians place on making a positive witness of their faith, there are significant forces that obfuscate tension, conflict, disagreement. Brasher even notes that her respondents told her repeatedly that they valued the opportunity to have their "testimonies" "on the record" (41). If the stories of these women were told from a different perspective, emphasizing the variety of voices to be found within this world, Brasher would have asked how much this motivation to have "testimonies" on the record led the women to sanitize their views on gender issues so as to not draw attention away from their emphasis on the necessity of a "personal relationship with Jesus." At one point in her research, when a female Women's Pastor deferred to a decision made by the male Pastor, everyone said that the woman's decision was an autonomous one. But Brasher suggests that this seemed implausible and that an accurate reading of the politics of the situation "eluded" her (71). In another incident, when women in one congregation drew on their enclave power to influence a pastoral decision, Brasher even notes that she doesn't believe she would have learned the details of the story had she not actually been there (88).

So when women claim that the restrictions put on them "do not bother [them] because [they] don't find [them] limiting," or that being banned from pastoral ministry or church governing positions didn't keep them from "meaningful religious participation" (63), a discerning reader is left wondering if the respondents were being completely straightforward. In other words, the women have reasons to tell their stories in ways that deemphasize gender conflict and there are likely issues not visible to an "outsider" researcher.

Brasher reports specific instances that beg for more elaboration. When one church went back and forth on the question of women leading the house churches (72), there was no real discussion of how the ousted women really felt. When the pastor at the other church limited working hours for staff women with children, the decision was clearly unpopular (134). Did all of the women just fall into line on these points or were there conflicts to which an outsider could never be privy?

In an example where the women did not "fall into line," Brasher explores the fallout from a situation in which a pastor became inappropriately involved with a women he was counseling. The pastors' wives led an effort to eliminate the practice of male pastors counseling female parishioners, and this was represented as an example of the successful exercise of female power. The pastors' wives first began to teach the other women in the church that women shouldn't seek counsel from men because the men did not understand their problems anyway. "Don't cast your jewels before them," one of the women taught in Bible study. Brasher didn't comment or elaborate on the implicit hostility in the statement. The Women's Pastor was referring to the biblical passage "don't cast your pearls before swine." Was she, in effect, calling the male Pastors pigs? Furthermore, while the pastors' wives prevailed in this conflict, it is a bit more ambiguous as to whether the women generally prevailed. Women who do not necessarily feel "better understood" by other women thus lost their choice as to whom to seek for counseling; they could no longer seek the counsel of those with the most training and experience. As a result of this decision, women had even less access to those in the congregation who held most of the authority.

Brasher mentions a few women who expressed some dissatisfaction with the gender norms and expectations, complaining about sermons "harping" on submission and expressing support for alternative styles of family and equality within marriage. I am not arguing that the fact that she did not follow up on these stories is a shortcoming of her book. On the contrary, I am advocating a subsequent move. Having taken seriously what the majority of these women say about their lives, we now need to take seriously the counterhegemonic voices.

Against Univocality

In reality, there is tremendous evidence, within these traditions, of heated conflict over these issues. When the Southern Baptist Convention passed its recent resolution on women's submission and then its subsequent resolution opposing women's ordination, they did not do so because Southern Baptists agree on these issues. On the contrary, they passed such resolutions because these issues are so contentious; even inside the tradition they divide people according to ideological camps in ways that even the battle over biblical inerrancy could not. There is a long-standing feminist movement within conservative religious subcultures—a movement that criticizes patriarchy and calls for women's equality at all levels including family, church, and society. These feminists range in conservatism from what might be called "fundamentalist" to those who would more appropriately be called "evangelical." They are represented by a number of groups, some of which exist to promote what is called "Biblical Feminism" and others exist to help women caught in the crossfire deal with the fallout. These feminists often embrace doctrines of "inerrancy" about the authority of the Bible. They use traditional conservative hermeneutical approaches to argue that, "properly understood," the Bible demands equality and justice between men and women, that it does not preclude women from certain forms of ministry, and that husbands and wives should practice "mutual submission" in marriage. It is somewhat difficult to measure the level of support for these views, especially insofar as people are influenced by them without realizing that they are. It is clear that these views are significant at all evangelical and some fundamentalist educational institutions; in fact, they are the dominant view at many such institutions (Hunter 1987). Most conservative Christian publishers have published books on these issues and a response to this version of feminism (Piper and Grudem 1991) was named "Book of the Year" by *Christianity Today* in 1993.

While scholars have noted this biblical feminist movement (Stacey and Gerard 1990; Bendroth 1993), they have not explored it in depth. As a result, the contestedness of gender norms, expectations, and ideology that arises as a result of these divergent commitments within these subcultures has been completely neglected. There are at least four reasons for this gap in scholarship on conservative women.

The first has been alluded to: there is a natural tendency on the part of scholars to find a single narrative thread with which to tie together their data. Scholars tend to observe what they think is "the big picture" and try to write coherently about it. While producing a well-crafted narrative, this approach does not necessarily produce the best scholarship possible. Second, the institutions and the people in power (who are likely to be disproportionately represented among those interviewed and influential over all who are interviewed) have a vested interest in keeping the conflicts under wraps. Those who become leaders in these organizations are, by necessity, those who are supportive of it and relatively content within it. Third, much of the work in this field has been done by feminist scholars who are, by definition, outsiders to these traditions. When conflict and disagreement is well hidden, scholars' attempts to respect the integrity and authenticity of those they study may lead them to be insufficiently critical.

Finally, situations such as hiring decisions, tenure decisions, firing decisions, and so forth are typically very difficult to document. I have struggled with this fact throughout my research. Can I believe any individual woman's account of gender discrimination in the circumstances that surrounded her? If not, does this mean that these issues are beyond the reach of scholarship or is there another way to explore them without being able to prove gender discrimination in any given case? In my own work, I have chosen to focus on themes and recurrent problems and issues. My rationale has been that while any individual case might not be provable, when taken together, the stories get at something important, if only by virtue of widespread recurrence and similarity.

My research documents widespread anguish and turmoil among evangelical and fundamentalist women. I have studied women pastors in conservative churches, women faculty and administrators at conservative Christian colleges, and women students at those Christian colleges. These are not feminists outside these traditions, but women who remain within their religious traditions and try to work around the doctrine of submission as it has been presented to them. Some of these women identify themselves as feminist and some do not, but they emphatically do not find the demand that women must submit to men to be empowering.

Conservative Protestant religious institutions—even those which officially endorse women's equality—that permit "doctrinal disagreement" on what is seen as a "nonessential" issue create circumstances in which women are precariously placed in leadership positions. Those who reject the authority of women over men on biblical grounds are often permitted, in the interest of not rocking the boat, to undermine the women's ability to function effectively. Such stories abound among professional women who maintain their ties to this subculture; they are especially poignant among women in pastoral ministry and among women in academic posts at evangelical colleges and seminaries. Because these conflicts take place at the intersection of these women's work, family, and spiritual lives, the toll taken by them is often tremendous.

During the course of my fieldwork, I encountered many women who sought me out because they desired to have their stories "on the record." They told me of the roadblocks they encountered in pursuit of their callings in pastoral ministry (even in conservative religious organizations that ostensibly support women as pastors.) There was the female youth pastor who, at church camp, was to speak before the young people. When she went to the podium, some male youth pastors from sister congregations, who did not believe females should ever be in authority over males, stood in the back of the room and turned their backs to her. There were women who went to their church leaders for support when they believed they had been called to the ministry and were then told that they should just marry a minister. There was the young woman who had won a preaching contest at seminary and was then invited to speak at a local church. Her sermon didn't go well and she fumbled. After beating herself up over this, she came to the realization that her male colleagues had been given opportunities to preach from the day they had "received a call." Preaching before a congregation was a new experience for her. Her conclusion was that while she had been invited to preach because she had won the contest, her male colleagues often won contests because they had had so much experience preaching.

Sometimes women seem to get bombarded from both directions. There was one woman who is a professor and recently married. She left her tenured job to move to the town where her husband taught. She had been hired by the administration to teach at the same Christian college at which he taught. When the board later voted on her appointment, it was denied because the board (unlike the administration) believed that women should not be teaching college. She was told that she could only teach if her husband supervised her classes and that she "had really only been hired because he worked there anyway." A woman administrator, on the other hand, was threatened with losing her job because she and her husband were employed at different colleges. In her first year on the job, she and her husband lived apart (as many academic couples must) with the intention that after a year, he (and their son) would relocate. At the end of the year, they decided that it was better for the family to stay put. The college's board of trustees met to discuss the matter because the long distance relationship made her "not a good role model for the female students." Then there are the cases where marriage and family are considered markers of good Christian character, which is, in turn, an essential component of hiring and tenure decisions. Family responsibilities, which fall disproportionately on women, end up being an informal aspect of job evaluation, but since it is only an informal aspect—unlike scholarship, for example—institutional accommodations for such responsibilities are not necessarily made.

It is not these individual instances though, that make the case that not all conservative Christian women view submission as empowerment—and it is difficult to make such a case in a short essay. In fact, it is the pervasiveness of the stories, and the similarities between them, which leads me to the conclusion that recent ethnographies tell only part of the story.[2]

Conclusion

Perhaps it is true that all our scholarship is, to some extent, autobiographical. As a former "insider" to evangelical Protestantism, I had firsthand experience with the frustration and discouragement at the limitations placed on me as a woman. I am sure those experiences led to my interest in the topic as a field of study. In the end, it may have been those limitations on women's roles that led me out of the conservative Christian subculture altogether. So when I present ethnographies arguing that submission is really empowering in class, and my students balk, it is difficult for me to defend the studies against the students' criticisms.

It is clear from the existing ethnographic works, that the doctrine of submission *may* function to empower some (even many) conservative

Christian women. But in their effort to take seriously what conservative Christian women say about submission and the limitations on their public roles, existing ethnographies are not sufficiently critical and, therefore, they miss an important part of the picture. These authors end up arguing that women are really content in their limited roles and that women in these traditions do not believe they are disempowered, oppressed, or significantly limited. While the women given voices in each of the studies express relative contentment with their positions in conservative religion, there are hints that the overall picture is murkier, more complicated, and more conflicted than the studies let on.

If the questions are: Does conservative religion meet the spiritual needs of some women? And can these women build purposeful, meaningful lives in these contexts, which demand their submission to men? The only answer that does not arrogantly override what such women say about their own lives must be a resounding "yes." But if the questions focus on the doctrine of submission and ask: Is this a clear and complete picture of the ways in which women in these communities experience the doctrine of submission? And is the doctrine of submission really a force for the empowerment of all women? Or if the questions focus on women's public roles and ask: Are these women really content with the limitations placed on them? Do they feel a sense of calling in their own lives that is thwarted by the traditions of which they are a part? Then the answer is much less clear.

Both Griffith and Brasher point to the "bargaining" that conservative Protestant women do in coming to accept the demands of their religion's gender ideology. However, scholars have yet to explore the stories of the women who fare less well in the bargaining: to explore the costs the women pay and to explore the implications of those costs. When we focus only on women who find more meaning than discomfort in traditional religion, we not only do an injustice to the women we silence. We also lose sight of the way in which gender ideology is central to this subculture and in which gender conflict is symbolic conflict for control of the subculture itself.

NOTES

1. See Colleen McDannell (1995) for a discussion of some other ways in which elite biases for theology and "high religion" have silenced "women, children

and other illiterates" and, in the process, created an image of religion, which is distorted.

2. When the first version of this essay was presented to the Annual Meeting of the Society for the Scientific Study of Religion in 1999, several women came up after the session to tell me that they had had similar experiences and that they were glad someone is writing about this.

Chapter 14

A Conscious Connection to All That Is

The Color Purple *as Subversive and Critical Ethnography*

Cheryl Townsend Gilkes

> Believing with Max Weber, that man is an animal suspended in webs of significance he himself has spun, I take culture to be those webs, and the analysis of it to be therefore not an experimental science in search of law but an interpretive one in search of meaning.
>
> —Clifford Geertz (1973a, 5)

> Experience is messy. . . . When human behavior is the data, a tolerance for ambiguity, multiplicity, contradiction, and instability is essential. . . . We must constantly remind ourselves that life is "unstable, complex, and disorderly . . . everywhere."
>
> —Margery Wolf (1992, 129)

In the tenth anniversary edition of *The Color Purple*, Alice Walker expresses her own dismay that a book that began "Dear God" was not immediately grasped "as a book about the desire to encounter, to hear from, the Ultimate Ancestor" (p xi).[1] For Walker, her book was a "theological work examining the journey from the religious back to the spiritual." This work of fiction can also be read as a subversive and critical ethnography. Although the book is not an ethnography in the technical sense and is not always what many anthropologists would consider "anthropologically correct," it does accomplish what anthropologist Margery Wolf stresses is central to ethnography: the inscription of a culture into respectful existence in the modern world and the assertion that any group of human beings is "suspended in" what Clifford Geertz calls "webs of significance."

The Color Purple is about these webs of significance and their complexity within a people and among peoples who are often dismissed from the human family. Embedded in a society whose material and symbolic dimensions are suffused with racism, African Americans are repeatedly dismissed as a people without a history and without defensible norms, values, customs, and traditions. *The Color Purple* shows us the lives of women who represented the foundations of the Black middle class in the South. In a society that offers nothing but disrespect and flat images in its manifestations of racism, an ethnography of Black people that grasps complexities, presents a nuanced humanity, and offers a critique of oppression is subversive of that society. Alice Walker as ethnographer provides, in the tradition of Zora Neale Hurston, what Henry Louis Gates (1988, xxv, 112) calls a "speakerly text," a text that allows us to hear the voices of those who persistently constitute and construct culture and who carve out discursive spaces somewhat free from the intrusions of the oppressors.[2] Ethnography provides descriptive detail organized in an interpretive framework, and *The Color Purple* offers an interpretive framework that takes seriously the intersection of spirituality and humanism in the African American response to oppression (see Wolf 1992).

A critical approach to culture involves identifying the stresses, strains, contradictions, and antagonisms that constrain and motivate the participants, particularly in a situation of inequity and oppression. Such a critical perspective seeks to identify the forces within and without a culture that may, particularly in situations of colonial oppression, deform or assault certain aspects of social organization, such as kinship, economics, religion, and politics, and that may prevent the meeting of basic social and individual needs. Regardless of the political or self-reflexive standpoint of the anthropologist, sometimes the simple act of writing the culture and its members into existence can be an act subversive of the inhumane consequences of marginalization and domination.

The Color Purple carefully details the webs of significance and connectedness that shaped and constrained the lives of Black landowning families in the Deep South during its most violent and repressive period of history. Walker provides unusually thick descriptions of the private milieu and structural ambiguities that gave rise to those whom Evelyn Brooks Higginbotham (1993) identifies as "the female talented tenth" in the late nineteenth and early-twentieth centuries and whom Stephanie Shaw (1996) points to as the Black professional women workers of the Jim Crow era. Walker also describes the conditions from which such African American women had to cut themselves "loose" in order to save their lives and eventually the lives of others. She highlights the importance to these women of the discovery of agency, resources, and social position through a variety of experiences in the life of one Black woman, poor by her own definition, who insists, "I'm pore, I'm Black, I may be ugly and can't cook, a voice say to everything listening. But I'm here" (205). Walker does not ignore the oppression of the White world, with its lynchings and violence toward Black people, but she puts it in perspective, expressing her faith and hope in the ability of Black people to constitute and construct lives that persist in subverting oppression through the healing and uplift of one another.

The Doctor Aunt, the Lynched Daddy, and Persistent Misreadings

The complexities of social class leap from the very first page of Alice Walker's novel. Celie begins her correspondence with God, attempting to explain her transition from "a good girl" to someone in search of "a sign letting me know what is happening to me" (1). Celie's mother, after refusing to engage in sexual relations with her husband because of her fragile physical condition and her fear of pregnancy, goes "to visit her sister doctor over Macon." This little detail signals webs of social relations in early-twentieth-century Georgia that are grounded in the emerging complexities of African American intragroup class relations and a larger political context of exploitation and vulnerability. There is a connection, through this aunt who is a doctor, between Celie and the Black professional class that emerged during the rise of Jim Crow. The daughters of landowning farmers contributed disproportionately to the educational leadership during this period, and the community often, according to Stephanie Shaw's (1996) analysis, sponsored these women's mobility from the farm to the college in order that they might "uplift the race." Disadvantaged communities that were unable to defend all of their daughters often made choices for a few women that were simultaneously empowering and constraining.

With the reference to Macon, we become part of the movement between the countryside and the town, and eventually the city, that women were making at the time in far larger numbers than men. Men, especially men without land, were more firmly tied to the land than were women.[3] Some of the men who emerged as educational leaders during this period describe personal struggles that arose in their homes because their fathers did not feel the family could afford to lose their labor if they went away to school (e.g., Mays 1971). For landless families, the positions available in the town or city for women and girls sometimes provided the only cash that the family ever had. For families with resources, such as land, the desire to educate daughters so that they would not be trapped in rural labor or domestic service also coincided with the historical needs of the Black community.

The controversies over the novel obscure, mask, and mystify this larger socio-historical context. The novel was most often labeled "the story of . . . a poor, barely literate Southern Black woman who struggles to escape the brutality and degradation of her treatment by men." Although it is a complex novel, male critics often reduced it to one major theme, "the estrangement and violence that mark the relationships between Miss Walker's Black men and women" (Gates and Appiah 1993, 16, 17). The controversies over the depiction of the relations between Black men and women and a related subtheme, the state of the Black family, began almost the day the novel was published. The tensions continue to this very day, with many people still complaining that Alice Walker, the author, is too hard on Black men.

Poorness and Blackness are so fused as interacting terms in American social consciousness that the class complexities of Walker's novel are largely overlooked by hostile reviewers and sympathetic readers alike. We call Celie "poor," and Celie calls herself "poor." However, there is land and there is food, and Alice Walker's "poor" pay far more, morally and psychically, for their material advantage than can ever be imagined. If there was ever an answer to the question as to whether Black elites or members of "the Black middle class" were oppressed, Walker seems to answer with a resounding "Yes."

The time period of the novel, from the late nineteenth century through the first half of the twentieth, is full of contradictions and enigmas. The violence leveled against the former slaves and their families was unprecedented. Every effort toward their political participation was met with a myriad of creative strategies to exclude them. The predatory sexual activities of Whites were so great that one writer argues that the raping of colored women was "as common as the fish in the sea" (Dash 1992). Yet at the same time, Black Americans worked with White philanthropists and missionaries to build colleges, universities, and schools for Black youth. Women in the various Black denominations, the same women who were raising money for schools and preachers' salaries, challenged the male supremacy of their church bodies, either by carving out new spaces in the form of missionary societies and auxiliary conventions or by creating new denominations or new roles in the emerging Sanctified Church.[4] By 1896, when the Supreme Court enshrined "separate but equal" as the right of states to establish segregation, Black women had developed a network of more than two hundred clubs working on the problems of survival, participation, and social change that confronted the Black community (Shaw 1995). That network of clubs became a socioreligious movement called the National Association of Colored Women's Clubs whose motto was "Lifting as We Climb" (Riggs 1994; Davis 1933). How could women, caught in the oppressive web of experiences and structures that characterized the horrendous constraints on African Americans in the rural South, construct a movement that educated a nation within a nation, institutionalized women's public leadership, challenged racism, fostered internationalism, and reached across the ocean to reclaim their African kinship? The novel *The Color Purple* provides an ethnography of the personal dimensions of women's experience that is a partial answer; it is both a description of suffering and its organization of experience and an account of spiritual rebellion and transcendence.

One can read many accounts of the ways in which Black people were cheated, terrorized, and otherwise coerced into giving up land that a small proportion of freedmen and -women owned at the end of slavery and during Reconstruction. The Black masses were, for the most part, a landless peasant class, and every effort was made to keep that class landless and subject to all sorts of political and economic controls. Roger L. Ransom and Richard Sutch (1977) have argued that the sharecropping system that developed in the rural South was the outcome of a dynamic class struggle between former slaves seeking economic autonomy and political personhood, and former slave owners working to reinstate slavery. Those Black families that acquired land and retained it did so in a milieu that saw the economic independence of Black men and their families as a provocation to murder. This is the motivation that Ida B. Wells-Barnett (1997) identified as the basis for lynching in the South, a motive masked by the myth of the Black rapist.

One wonders why Celie's mother left home to visit her sister, leaving Celie and the other children alone with her husband. At the beginning of the novel, we readers do not know that Celie's "father" is really her stepfather. And we do not know that the title to the land and the house is in her mother's hands and not her "father's." This stepfather never gets control of the property; he manages, through an ironic accommodation to White power, but he never owns.

The plaintiveness and moral poverty of Celie's situation often overshadow the little details that signal the ambiguity and complexity of social class. First of all, when Celie marries, she brings her own linens and her own cow. Ownership of a cow was a critical component of economic independence and implied a level of self-sufficiency that made a big difference. James Comer (1988), writing about the experience of his mother's family and the little details of economic life that allowed her to survive in the rural South, pointed to his mother's ownership of a cow as a critical element in the family's economic survival that loomed as large as land ownership. Fannie Lou Hamer's father's escape from sharecropping to renting was short-lived because hostile Whites poisoned the family mule. The critical importance of ownership of farm animals to economic position in the rural South cannot be overstated.

After Celie's marriage to Mister, we meet his sisters, Kate and Carrie. They like Celie and are quite critical of Mister's treatment of her and his late wife. From the exchange between Celie and the sisters, we learn about the complexity of Celie's household and the considerable skill that she has brought to this marriage. We also learn how hard Black property-owning women must work "to keep a decent house and a clean family" (19). Failures of effort and discipline lead to households full of children with "colds, they have flue, they have direar, they have newmonya, they have worms, they have the chill and fever. They hungry. They hair ain't comb. They too nasty to touch" (19). Celie is diligent, disciplined, and very hardworking, and the sisters convince Mister to buy Celie some clothes. Celie, of course, wants to buy the "color Shug Avery would wear" (20). Although she wants a red dress, Celie eventually chooses blue. She writes (to God):

I can't remember being the first one in my own dress. Now to have one
made just for me. I try to tell Kate what it mean.
I git hot in the face and stutter.
She say, It's all right, Celie. You deserve more than this. (21)

The custom-made dress and the interaction between Celie and Mister's
sisters are the kind of details that point to class position and, at the same
time, depict the varieties of female presence in that class and the tensions
associated with being a woman of that class. When Kate and Carrie become a threat to Mister's untrammeled oppression of Celie, they are sent
home. Celie is admonished to struggle: "You got to fight them, Celie . . .
You got to fight them for yourself" (21). Part of Celie's eventual emancipation process involves her discovery of the resources that she and her
sister Nettie possess. In spite of the assaults to her personhood that sexual
molestation and marriage bring, the ennobling elements of Celie's
world—education, spirituality, and humanism—persist as positive life
forces.

We also discover that the vulnerabilities and personal damages Celie
and Nettie experience are also the consequences of lynching. The isolated
and highly ambiguous position of Celie's family comes about because her
Daddy was lynched. Everyone in a Black community knew that no one
deserved lynching. However, the terror of lynchings was effective precisely because communities were placed in such a state of fear that the
normal funerary rites were impossible. Lynchings immediately smashed
the supports that follow normal deaths—the comforting hands, the sharing of food, the celebration of life, and the promises of help toward healing in the future. Lynchings and, by extension in Alice Walker's world,
other forms of deadly violence are so wrenching that they destroy the opportunity for the basic human interactions that sustain the community.
We learn that Celie's lynched Daddy was buried in an unmarked grave,
and the fear and the terror were so great that Celie's mother never said a
mumbling word about their biological father to her children. Not only
did a lynching terrorize an entire community—usually as an assault on
an independent and advantaged Black man, as Ida B. Wells-Barnett
(1997) persuasively demonstrated. But also the lynching also ripped away
the protections and controls that made a normal and liberating family
life possible. We learn later that perhaps Celie's mother married this man
for protection. And protection she has, as we see him go hunting with a

group of White men from the community, after which we find pregnant Celie vomiting and dressing game.

Overall, one realizes that the problems faced by both Celie's family and Mister's family are tied to the terror attached to Celie's father's death and the scandal attached to Mister's first wife's death. Both families are isolated from the larger community, one of the most effective and dangerous consequences of terror and violence. Celie's family is particularly isolated. With a sick mother, Celie points out, "Don't nobody come to see us" (2). Actually, the local schoolteacher, Addie Beasley, does come and try to persuade Celie's stepfather to send Celie back to school. She relents in her pleadings when she realizes that Celie is pregnant.

The novel is written in such a way that one has to "look back and wonder" about many of the details that are there all along. The small detail that Celie's mother's sister is a doctor over in Macon signals the beginning encounter with a wide range of late-nineteenth-century and early-twentieth-century Black women who populated the towns and cities of the South. These same women also were the "farmers' daughters" who sought higher education and became the army of Black schoolteachers who were responsible for the great surge of literacy in the Black community after the Civil War (Du Bois 1924). When Mister comes to ask for Nettie, Celie's stepfather, monster that he is, refuses, saying, "I want her to git some more schooling. Make a schoolteacher out of her" (7).

Significant class ambiguities abound within this family. The story takes place among families who have material resources and access to literacy. Furthermore, in the first few pages we discover that in spite of the moral degradation and ambiguity attached to Celie's stepfather, even he upholds and affirms the value of education and the importance of women educators. And it is clear that somewhere deep down in all of this sickening misery, there is an understanding that education is a liberative pathway, especially for women.

A Novel of Black Women's History

Walker's novels have always been about women and their social worlds. She brings through the pages of The Color Purple a parade of Black women, especially educated Black women, who represent significant points along the time line of Black history in the United States and the world. The role of schoolteachers as prophetic and instrumental leaders inspires long discussions. Bernice Johnson Reagon (1982), in an essay pointing to the importance of diverse women in her community in shaping her life, writes extensively about Mamie Daniel, the schoolteacher who came to her community and brought improved health and broader cultural exposure along with literacy. Daniel organized the entire community to participate in the children's education. They built a theater and a playhouse and organized trips for the children. Reagon thought as a little child that her teacher was old, but she later learned that Daniel was only in her twenties. Daniel was not unlike other members of that army of young women who taught throughout the South. Many of these women trained for the mission fields at places like Spelman College and spent their summers teaching school in rural communities (Higginbotham 1993). Walker connects Celie's life with these kinds of women. We not only meet Miss Beasley, who comes to plead for Celie's attendance at school, but we also then meet Corrine, the first woman Celie has ever seen use actual cash in an economic transaction.

Cash money is a small but critical detail in this story. When telling Nettie where to go to escape Mister, Celie tells her to find Corrine precisely because she had handled cash money. The ambiguities of cash are at the nexus of much racial oppression in the late nineteenth and early twentieth centuries. For the most part, a lack of cash kept African Americans in the position of a debtor class. Poll taxes could not be paid without cash, and in those areas of the South where Black people could vote if they paid their poll taxes, families went without eating to have that money. Bail could not be paid without cash. The lives of African American women, the poor and the not so poor, were tied to their participation in the labor force in ways that provided access to cash for their families— for parents and siblings as well as husbands and children. For most rural Black people, economic life was mired in farm tenancy, sharecropping, and contract labor situations. Sometimes, as in the case of Sofia, Celie's daughter-in-law, the criminal "justice" system allocated the workers for domestic and farm work. In a letter to Nettie, Celie tries to explain whom she saw working as "the mayor's maid." Celie writes:

> The mayor and his wife and a lot of other white people get labor free from the jailhouse by pretending a colored person jumped on them or cussed them out so they had to have them locked up. After they're locked up these same white people come up to the jail and get them out and make them work for them for nothing. It's just like slavery, except they sign a paper with the sheriff. They call it contract labor. (193)

In the early decades of the twentieth century, Black people had no cash for poll taxes, bail, and material goods unless some, usually female, member of the family found work that provided cash. Women could be released from farm labor, especially young, unmarried women, more easily than skilled men and older skilled women. Although bootlegging, prostitution, and other "shady" pursuits were conduits for cash, aside from domestic work the only real honest and honorable option for women was teaching school. Everybody in Black communities, even Mister, understood those harsh realities. Therefore, if the route of escape through education was open, there was a cultural consensus that women should take it.

In the course of telling Corrine's story, Walker connects us with Spelman and its history of missionary and teacher training.[5] We know we are in the world of the talented tenth when we meet "Dr. DuBoyce" on the Spelman campus. Nettie, in her letter to Celie, places these women in the context of African American history and world history, writing:

> [Spelman] was a very interesting place . . . Started in a church basement, it soon moved up to Army barracks. Eventually these two ladies were able to get large sums of money from some of the richest men in America, and so the place grew. Buildings, trees. Girls were taught everything: Reading, Writing, Arithmetic, sewing, cleaning, cooking. But more than anything else, they were taught to serve God and the colored community. Their official motto was Our Whole School for Christ. But I always thought their unofficial motto should have been Our Community Covers the World, because no sooner had a young woman got through Spelman Seminary than she began to put her hand to whatever work she could do for her people anywhere in the world. It was truly astonishing. These very polite and proper young women, some of them never having set foot outside their own small country towns, except to come to the Seminary, thought nothing of packing up for India, Africa, the Orient. Or for Philadelphia or New York. (231-232)

In her discussion of Spelman and its community work, Walker also deconstructs the false consciousness surrounding color that characterized this community and others like it and, in the process, connects the history of these talented women with the history of the oppression of Native Americans of the southeastern United States. Walker identifies the source of the false consciousness of color in the prurient interests and sexual violence of White power. That false consciousness not only deformed the self-understanding of Black people about their substantial Native American heritage, but also operated powerfully in the world of Shug Avery and the blues queens of the twentieth century (Harrison 1988). While Sofia is incarcerated, Squeak's color and her family history of sexual oppression become a site on which the eventual liberation of Sofia is mapped. The dialectic of kinship, even an unspeakable kinship, becomes a resource for ending Sofia's incarceration. Liberation by any means necessary sometimes means the subversion of indignities for a higher purpose. In the process of liberating Sofia, however, Squeak/Mary Agnes is raped by her White uncle, the warden. Although not part of the more visible and honorable segments of the lighter-skinned Black elite, Shug Avery and the other blues queens represent a critical group of women whose freedom was meaningful to the larger Black community. Their opportunities to shake themselves loose from oppressive reality were disproportionately tied to their skin color. According to Daphne Duval Harrison, "Complexion and hair that approximated White standards of beauty continued for decades to be plus factors for women who sought stage careers as singers, chorus girls, or actresses" (1988, 32).

In spite of the colorism and cultural politics that shaped their marginal positions in the Black community, Shug is a blues singer, and blues singers, particularly the blues queens of the 1920s, are a vital segment of African American women's history. Education was one motivation for women to leave the farms and towns and migrate to cities. Opportunities in the entertainment industry were another. Women of both genteel and peasant upbringing sought careers as blues singers and entertainers. Most women were the same age as Celie, twelve, fourteen, and sixteen, when they ran away to become stars. Walker's novel gives us some idea of what they may have been running from, not only with regard to the oppression and degradation visited upon them by Whites but also with regard to the problems of coming of age sexually in an oppressed Black community and the limited opportunities for the most exploitative work.[6]

Evelyn Brooks Higginbotham points out that the church women of the talented tenth engaged in a "discursive effort of self-representation" that opposed the humiliation of the "social structures and symbolic representations of White supremacy," identifying this self-representation as the "politics of respectability." Furthermore,

> the politics of respectability emphasized reform of individual behavior and attitudes both as a goal in itself and as a strategy for reform of the entire structural system of race relations. . . . Such a politics did not reduce to an accommodationist stance toward racism, or a compensatory ideology in

the face of powerlessness. . . . The Baptist women emphasized manners and morals while simultaneously asserting traditional forms of protest, such as petitions, boycotts, and verbal appeals to justice. (Higginbotham 1993, 186–87)

While church women generally and Baptist women particularly were "privileging respectability and particularly the capacity and worthiness of poor, working class Black women for respect" at the same time that they were emphasizing "a critical message . . . namely that self-esteem and self-determination were independent of contexts of race and income" (Higginbotham 1993, 191), the blues women were engaged in a different set of oppositional practices that often drew the wrath of the church.

The blues women, queens and empresses to their audiences, were engaged in a politics of elegance. Although they did not reject outright the politics of respectability, their lifestyles and the contents of their singing did not garner the approval of the church community. The discussion of Shug Avery by Mister's respectable sisters reflects this disdain:

Shug Avery, Shug Avery, Carrie say. I'm sick of her. Somebody say she going around trying to sing. Umph, what she got to sing about. Say she wearing dresses all up her leg and headpieces with little balls and Lassies hanging down, look like window dressing. (20)

Later, when Shug Avery is sick, no one wants to offer her a place to stay. Her estrangement from her parents becomes apparent, and the women at church claim that she is afflicted with "some kind of nasty woman disease." Her alienation from the church is even more pronounced: "Even the preacher got his mouth on Shug Avery. . . . He talk about a strumpet in short skirts, smoking cigarettes, drinking gin. Singing for money and taking other women mens. Talk about slut, hussy, heifer and streetcleaner" (41).

Celie, on the other hand, reflects the response of those who filled the audiences of tent shows, juke joints, and theaters when she writes, "I think what color Shug Avery would wear. She like a queen to me so I say to Kate, Somethin purple, maybe little red in it too" (20). Later, when "Shug Avery is coming to town," the anticipation of her presence briefly provokes a new civility in the relationship between Celie and Mister. Mister gets all dressed up, and Celie tells him how nice he looks. Mister actually appreciates her opinion. Celie then spends the day walking around with an announcement of Shug's performance in her pocket. Celie's description reflects the emotional impact these women had on their communities:

Shug Avery standing upside a piano, elbow crook, hand on her hip. She wearing a hat like Indian Chiefs. Her mouth open showing all her teef and don't nothing seem to be troubling her mind. Come one, come all, it say. The Queen Honeybee is back in town.

Lord, I wants to go so bad. Not to dance. Not to drink. Not to play card. Not even to hear Shug Avery sing. I just be thankful to lay eyes on her. (25)

These women who were "like a queen" to their audiences wore beautiful jeweled gowns and dresses when they sang. According to Harrison (1988, 14), "they raised the status of Black women entertainers to a new height and were adored at home and abroad for a brief moment in history." In a way that the church women could not, the blues women engaged in the messiness of life, the disrespected underside of African American women's experience. Furthermore,

> The blues women . . . brought to their lyrics and performances new meaning as they interpreted and reformulated the Black experience from their unique perspective in American society as Black females. They saw a world that did not protect the sanctity of Black womanhood, as espoused in the bourgeois ideology; only White middle- or upper-class women were protected by it. They saw and experienced injustice as jobs they held were snatched away when White women refused to work with them or White men returned from war to reclaim them. They pointed out the pain of sexual and physical abuse and abandonment. They sought escape from the oppressive controls of the Black church but they did not seek to sever their ties from home, family, and loved ones. They reorganized reality through surrealistic fantasies and cynical parodies. (Harrison 1988, 64)

In a way, the discursive practices of blues women were as prophetic as those of the church women. Blues women, Harrison points out, "were able to capture in song the sensibilities of Black women—North and South—who struggled daily for physical, psychological, and spiritual balance" (1988, 221). They gave voice to the troubles that people experienced in an oppressive social structure at the same time that they provided an alternative vision of Black women—a rich elegant one—in a world that insisted on their poverty and humiliation. Often, the language of the biblical prophets was harsh and shocking as it addressed the consequences of apostasy and oppression. At the same time that these women embodied opposition to the cultural humiliation, they spoke forthrightly of the troubles endemic to their lives: "Alienation, sex and sexuality, tortured love, loneliness, hard times, marginality, were addressed with an openness that had not previously existed" (Harrison 1988, 221).

"But I Don't Never Git Used to It"

There are multiple manifestations of oppression in the lives of Black people. Walker reveals these oppressions and their intersections in the everyday lives of rural Black people, in the operations of larger systems of violence and exploitation, and in the political economy of an imperialist world system.[7] We see the ambiguity of Black dependency in a context of White supremacy. We see the violence used to enforce that system and its reverberations throughout the community as it latches onto false moral visions and pretensions to respectability. We see the basic, everyday humiliations that come in the form of White harassment of all Black people regardless of their class or precisely because of their class. We see the difference between White paternalism in Christian missions and Black communalism in their differing approaches to Christian missions. We see the way in which the expanding international colonial order often heightened contradictions on mission fields, producing a cloud of witnesses who could speak against the brutality and cultural genocide of colonialism. Walker constructs a world where the poor Black person who is *here* is connected to "all that is."

In the process of naming oppressions, Walker also links the near-destruction of Sofia with her husband's violence against her and with Celie's collaboration with that violence, a collaboration not disconnected from her own victimization. It is a "dry bones in the valley" phenomenon wherein the interconnections of oppression cannot be ignored. As the family comes together to rescue and reclaim Sofia, the family must manipulate the history of sexual exploitation that has shaped Squeak/Mary Agnes's story (193–194). In her own act of liberation, Celie reminds Harpo that "if you hadn't tried to rule over Sofia, the White folks never would have caught her" (195). Thus, through the lives of women, fully credible lives when seen in the context of African American women's history, we see the way in which oppression breeds and feeds oppression. The roots of what Deborah King (1988) calls Black women's "multiple jeopardy" are carefully described, contextualized, historicized, and then subjected to very creative criticism. Walker does not accept the received wisdom of disconnections between Black people of different classes; the simplistic dichotomy between the house slave and the field slaves, or more accurately their descendants, is unacceptable. Walker reiterates the voices of Mary Church Terrell and Ida B. Wells-Barnett when she points to the real targets of lynching and then explores its consequences in the lives of the women left behind. Lynching and rape are no longer issues of male suffering contrasted with female suffering; they are interconnected and interlinked, and they shape the personal worlds of several generations. Both lynching and rape function together as an assault on "the survival and wholeness of entire people, male *and* female." Walker also protests against the tendency to dismiss the suffering of privileged Black people, especially those whose color distinguishes them from the masses. To be loved for one's color is also an aspect of dehumanization that is dialectically linked with the self-hatred among Black people manifested in antipathy toward dark people. In a manner similar to that of the biblical prophets, Walker points out that brothers' mistreatment of their sisters and women's collaboration with violence against other women have consequences that can literally, as through Celie's and Nettie's letters, stretch across oceans. The book's ethnographic vision provides a cautionary tale about judgments that dismiss and therefore disconnect members of the community as either privileged or disreputable. What Higginbotham calls "the politics of respectability," when carried too far, can be hazardous to communal health.

Every aspect of suffering in Walker's multifaceted model of oppressions is also a site and an opportunity for resistance and subversion. The pretty light-skinned blues woman can articulate the suffering of the masses of women. The unspeakable kinships between Black and White people can sometimes be manipulated to sustain life—always a revolutionary act in a death-dealing system. The woman labeled hussy and heifer from the pulpit is the one with the spiritual vision for raising the dead. Even the most dissolute sinner man is able to share a vision of empowerment through educated women. No matter the limited comfort zones that are carved out of segments of personal experience, people, Walker points out, are never really comfortable with suffering. The fact that people "don't never git used to it" is a catalyst for activism or, at least, for the support of someone else's.

Finally, Walker demonstrates that it is important to provide those who seem to be "the least of these" a vision of something, if only just a sign, beyond the boundaries of one's own personal pain and suffering. The book begins because Celie, ever the obedient daughter, doesn't tell anyone about her troubles but God. But her world grows. She acts to save her sister and in the process begins to save herself. She hears the prophetic voice of the blues woman. Her sisters-in-law urge her to fight. The reflexive process grows. She repents and reconciles through the production of a quilt. Celie's humanity grows. And, eventually, there is rebellion, resistance, and a new order. What Walker tells us in the opening pages of her book is that our journey and our connectedness by way of Celie's story to an oppressive world order that can be described, named, and challenged all happen because one sexually abused, pregnant fourteen-year-old "don't never git used to it" (1). In the process, Walker also lifts up the significance of African American women's history for the liberation of the entire community. The entire community must be constantly challenged not to become complacent with oppression and not to develop strategies of internal and internalized oppression that further reinforce the power of larger, more alien structures in all our lives.

Ultimately, the resistance to oppression, the saving and sustaining of lives, and the persistent humanizing of community are problems of the Spirit and of our spiritual freedom. Nettie, assessing the impact of her experience in Africa on her life, writes to Celie:

> God is different to us now, after all these years in Africa. More spirit than ever before, and more internal. Most people think he has to look like something or someone—a roofleaf or Christ—but we don't. And not being tied to what God looks like, frees us. (256)

The critical dimensions of Walker's ethnography challenge us to recover the details of our everyday existence in all their messiness in order to understand fully our humanity. The subversive dimensions of her ethnography seek to free us to reshape and to liberate our communities and our existence. We are products of our history, but our spiritual journeys also make us shapers of history—historical subjects—who have the power to challenge and reshape the world beyond our immediate milieu.

NOTES

A longer version of this chapter appeared in *Embracing the Spirit: Womanist Perspectives on Hope, Salvation, and Transfiguration*, edited by Emilie M. Townes (Maryknoll, NY: Orbis Books, 1997). Reprinted by permission.

1. All quotations from the novel are from the 1992 tenth anniversary hard-

cover edition of the book, and page numbers are henceforth provided in the text. Misperceptions about the book are exacerbated because of some of the terrible miscastings in the movie based on the book. In order to demonize Celie's stepfather more dramatically, for example, he is played by an actor whose age, color, and demeanor are not the same as those presented in the book.

2. I believe that the ethnographic continuity between Alice Walker and Zora Neale Hurston is no mere accident. Zora Neale Hurston has been criticized for her "ethnographic intrusions" into the text by Eric Sundquist (1992). However, the description of African Americans as cultural and cultured beings is the mission of both novelists as they inscribe the humanity of Black people into the Western consciousness. For White people or any people affected by White Western racial hegemony, ethnography must be part of a writer's mission.

3. Walker points out, through the relationship between Mister and his father, that being the son of a large landowner was not the same as being a large landowner. Mister's father is a very domineering and oppressive presence who imposes on Mister the kinds of relations that Mister imposes on Celie.

4. See Higginbotham (1993); Dodson (1989); Dodson and Gilkes (1986); and Gilkes (1985).

5. The work of historian Sylvia M. Jacobs (1982) is vitally important for understanding the roles, relationships, and responses of African American women who worked as missionaries in Africa. People like Mary McLeod Bethune and Mamie Garvin Fields also trained to work overseas. Bethune was told by the Presbyterian Church that there were no openings for Negroes in Africa.

6. In my classes I also use Christine Dall's film *Wild Women Don't Have the Blues* (1989), which provides enough information on blues singers' class backgrounds to make the point about the mix of women who sought careers on the stage. Those who were more advantaged were better able to manage their own lives and to hold on to their money.

7. Dorothy E. Smith (1987; 1990), a feminist sociologist, suggests that the problematics of everyday life are the starting point for a critical perspective on the world and its power structures.

Part IV

Beyond Personal Knowledge

New-Old Directions in the Social Scientific Study of Religion

Ethnography, Phenomenology, and the Human Body

Meredith B. McGuire

"Was it as incredibly good for you as it was for me?" Why is this trite expression about sexual experience readily recognized in our culture as humorously naive, while the parallel question about the religious meanings, values, or feelings of others is the stock-in-trade of social researchers of religion? Of course, the intent is different: Social researchers have a heuristic goal. In order to understand others' deeply felt religious expressions, we need to find out "how it was" for those others. We also have some strong norms about the quality of our evidence and how we know what we claim to know. "Good" evidence should not distort the other's expression of meaning; it should not misrepresent our respondents' experiences, beliefs, and feelings. It should not represent as "fact" descriptions that are merely the product of the researcher's prejudices and bias.

Ironically, researchers who operate "experience-distant" are often more likely than those who work "experience-near" to presume that they are accurately describing the "real" religion of the other. For instance, using secondary analysis of a large quantitative data set, one can sit in an office in Michigan and describe, in the aggregate, remote respondents' beliefs and behaviors as reported on a nationwide survey conducted by a research center in New York. Researchers do not need to meet, observe, or interact with survey respondents in order to produce a highly reliable and reproducible set of quantitative descriptive comparisons. Are women more likely than men to believe _____? Do Baptists report more experiences of _____ than do Roman Catholics? Are church-at-tenders more likely to report valuing _____ than nonchurch-attenders? And so on.

Are these "experience-distant" representations "good" evidence about real people's experiences, practices, and feelings? Do they adequately capture what is religiously important to the respondents themselves about their individual experiences, beliefs, and practices? Can they show the interpersonal interaction and the synergy that may occur when these individual survey respondents gather with others in a community of faith and practice?

The scientific study of religion is replete with examples of how quantitative research methods can result in misunderstanding and misrepresentation, obscured by (or deliberately glossed over with) sampling, data-gathering techniques, coding categories, indices, and seemingly "objective" numbers. Why do I get angry, in answering a survey, when I feel forced to select from a set of precoded categories, none of which corresponds to my own response? I am not merely irritated that the questionnaire was prepared incompetently. I am angry at the subtle *violence* implicit in the research method. A number of years ago a hapless young man interviewed me for a Gallup poll. Each of its substantive questions—on politics, religion, and other issues—was phrased such that I challenged either the wording of the question or the options for answers. It made me angry to realize that the final report would most likely represent my opinion as "other" or "don't know" or "none of the above." And the final report would equally misrepresent the expressions of other respondents who allowed their complex, nuanced answers to be stuffed into one of the questionnaire's categories.

"Objective" research methods should be evaluated by the same hard questions that we pose for fieldwork methods: Does this very method suppress the respondent's "voice"? Does the methodology privilege the distant research designer's autonomy and control of the situation, while denying the respondent's autonomy and control (short of complete refusal to cooperate)? Does this method of gathering, coding, combining in indices, and reporting of these findings create the sense that these quantitative data are somehow more "real" or "true" than the respondents' subjective meanings and understandings that they purportedly represent? The sociology of religion must be especially self-critical to guard against the misrepresentation and methodological reification of people's religious beliefs, practices, and experiences.

Experience-distant research methodologies risk serious misunderstanding and misrepresentation. Experience-near methodologies, however, inevitably involve the subjective self of the researcher. The highly personal role of the ethnographic researcher impels us to grapple with issues of bias and representation, relationships and "objectivity," and it problematizes the very grounds of our knowledge and understanding. The essays in this volume demonstrate why the social scientific study of religion is advanced only when we confront these issues critically.

Ethnography is not unique, however, in this requirement. I would argue that *all* methodologies in the social scientific study of religion should be held up to the same critical light. We need to develop, not only in ourselves as individual researchers, but also in the entire discipline as a community of scholars, a commitment to critical self-awareness and integrity in our quest to understand people's religious meanings, practices, and experiences.

How Do I Understand Another's Lifeworld?

The trajectory of learning experiences that brought me to my present stance has been very different from that of most American social scientists. Perhaps that is why this essay may appear to be less radical than some others in this volume. Rather than overcoming, much less overthrowing, the limitations of the "received wisdom" that I learned in graduate school, I find myself returning to it. I do not do so uncritically; yet I return with new appreciation, in order to build upon what my teachers taught me.

"You studied Research Methods with *whom*?!!!!" My colleague, a Columbia Ph.D., thought it hilarious to imagine a Research Methods course taught by Thomas Luckmann, a brilliant theorist (she admitted) but hardly well known for his empirical research. But what I learned about method at The New School for Social Research was, for me, formational. I still thank Tom Luckmann and Debbie Offenbacher for this personal, as well as theoretical and methodological, foundation; other New School faculty whose teaching still informs my approach include Peter Berger, Carl Mayer, and Aron Gurvitch—all phenomenologists or in conversation with phenomenology. They taught me:

1. an abiding commitment to the goal of *verstehen* (though, hopefully, with more refined methods than those of Grandfather Max);
2. an attention to the epistemological grounds of all method;
3. a critical awareness that the "social construction of reality" implied rethinking (the then-standard positivist) methods of social research;
4. a special emphasis on human language, bodies, and subjectivity, as both objects of our search for understanding and vehicles for accomplishing understanding.

My experience of trying to put these methodological underpinnings into practice has increased my respect for that foundation. I find myself returning to some of these bases to suggest future directions for ethnography and other fieldwork methods in the study of religion.

As I launched my research career, I had no methodological "toolkit," no recipes for producing or organizing the complex and seemingly subjective evidence that *verstehen* required. I was clear about why quantitative methodologies would not produce the kind of deeper understanding I sought of people's religious experience and expression, but I wanted my research evidence to be at least as grounded, as "true," as quantitative data. I had, early on, discovered my sheer enjoyment of the interpersonal interactions of the research encounters themselves. I found field research simply fascinating—whether observing a worship service or social activists' demonstration, interviewing a woman at her kitchen table about her healing experiences, listening to believers witnessing or praying, or learning about how people made sense of their lives and their worlds. How, then, could I use these interpersonal interactions to accomplish a genuine understanding of others' subjective meanings? How could that interaction produce solid evidence, as meticulously rigorous and precise as the best quantitative data, but with the contextual richness and depth of a fine ethnography or social history? Thirty years later, I am still working on the "how to" part of the research process. And I am yet asking the same critical questions of my methods: How well does this methodological approach help me understand the religious meanings, practices, and experiences of others? How adequate is the specific way I am practicing this method for the apprehension of knowledge? How is what I experience—in observing, conversing, sensing, and interacting—usable as authoritative evidence, as the grounds for understanding peoples' religious or spiritual lives?

Refining Field Research Methods

Though my co-editors have portrayed anthropology as the leader in methodological self-examination,[1] until relatively recently, few anthropologists have felt the obligation to tell their readers how they obtained their evidence. Nor have they noted the limits of the author's reporting that the reader should keep in mind. It was only in the last quarter of the twentieth century that anthropologists began to unpack the concept of "ethnography" (literally, the writing of culture) and critically examine its assumptions.

As a field, anthropology has found itself (sometimes uncomfortably) in two completely different camps—science and humanities—each implying very different norms about how to deal with "truth" and "fiction."[2] Meanwhile, sociologists who used nonquantitative methodologies had to be particularly attentive to methodological issues. Sociology's dominant stance was "science," and—especially in the United States—positivism and empiricism were the norm well into the 1960s. Thus, unlike anthropologists, sociologists using fieldwork methods were on the defensive, consciously choosing them over quantitative research approaches standard in the discipline.

Many wrote thoughtful "methodological notes" in which they described problematic issues that arose during fieldwork. In retrospect, those notes seem somewhat naïve. Many implied that—if only the researcher could have controlled the interaction, could have kept a confounding factor from intruding, could have eliminated a problematic human variable—then, the resulting evidence would be more "pure," i.e., more objectively accurate. Such methodological notes were, however, an important part of the process by which researchers grappled with how they knew what they claimed to know. The experience of articulating methodological limitations, sources of bias, and one's social location as researcher is, today, still a useful exercise, even if it is not the ethnographer's chosen form of reporting. My earliest "methodological note" described, among other issues, one of the most difficult methodological problems of all my experiences as a field researcher of religion. My first post-doctoral research was a study of groups of Catholics practicing pentecostal style prayer and prophecy (later, the movement called itself the Catholic Charismatic Renewal; see McGuire 1982). During the first three years of this research, I had attempted an "ethnography of speaking" (Hymes 1962). This approach (in principle, usable with communication in any cultural setting) seemed particularly apt for a religious group that had special meanings for valued speech events, such as witnessing, prophecy, and speaking in tongues.

After extensive observation and some participant observation in several prayer groups, I began interviewing members and leaders. I asked specific open-ended questions of all interviewees, followed by further questions to clarify the meanings they expressed. I tried using respondents' language "back" to them to ascertain "Do I understand . . . correctly?" After a while, I could express, somewhat proficiently, what I had learned from interviewees. I could use their language in a way that reflected that I understood their meanings. Wasn't that what I wanted?

The methodological issue came, however, from the members' equation of "understanding" with "conviction": If I understood their experiences so well, why didn't I become one of them? I began to receive pep talks to "let go and let the Lord." With one prayer group, I became the object of intensified pressure to receive "baptism in the Spirit." I had become a problem for them. Because I spoke as though I really understood, they assumed that such understanding compelled me to believe, but that I was resisting the conviction that understanding implied. My unwanted role as unconvinced-nonbeliever-who-understands-too-well had evolved into a serious methodological problem for me, so I had to end my research with that group and focus on other groups in my study "sample."

That experience shook me. I had naively assumed that, by maintaining an open—not disguised—role as researcher, I was fulfilling my ethical responsibilities. The experience reminded me that, while our "presentation of self" is part of the field researchers' method and deserves to be reported, we cannot control the identities and roles that others impute to us. I had believed that my detailed attention to their ways of expressing their deeply felt meanings would produce connection, not distance. Yet, my methodology inadvertently resulted in locating me in a threatening role. My very presence could harm their religious world, by making them aware that their conversion and commitment to it was not an inevitable, god-given product of simply understanding that worldview.

That prayer group may have been an extreme instance, but I suggest that many religious groups—especially those whose image of faith is particularist and conversionist—pose similar methodological issues.

Mind/Body/Self in Ethnographic Interpretation

It is virtually impossible to do ethnographic research while holding one's own self utterly aloof. Thoughtful ethnographers have always struggled with this necessary dilemma, asking themselves such questions as: How can I really understand these people and live with them these many months, while their everyday life is shaped by values I do not share (or even abhor)? How can I retain my sense of my own identity while living out the identity they have assigned me in their family and tribe? Can I "be myself" and let down my guard with some of my new friends in this culture without reducing the accuracy of my fieldwork data or without jeopardizing my chances for further fieldwork with these people?

Although the ethnographer's subjective self has always been problematic in anthropological fieldwork, it has been simultaneously an indispensable part of ethnographic methods for comprehending and interpreting cultures. Anthropologists have long agonized over the personally painful conflicts between their subjective self-identities and their fieldwork community's assignment of their identities (see Whitehead and Conaway 1986). One ethnographer, Jean Briggs (1970) could work among Eskimos only in the imputed role of adopted, carefully protected daughter of an elder. She chafed at being treated as a non-adult. Although this assigned identity was temporary, it was painful—not only because the role limited her access to important information about the people's way of life, but also because it challenged her own self-understanding and, perhaps, her self-esteem. Other ethnographers (especially males) have struggled with their imputed roles as vulnerable, weak, ignorant, or lowly, even though they recognized that these roles helped reduce social distance between them and the people.

It may be easier for women than men to allow themselves to be identified as weak, since that ascription is consistent with most societies' cultural bias. Women in academia, however, often succeed precisely by being "like" men—strong, decisive, goal-oriented, self-directed. In retrospect, however, I believe that the community's perception of the ethnographer's weakness does not matter so much as the ethnographer's own *experience* of vulnerability and the resulting interpersonal interactions produced by that experience.

My own experience of being "weak" occurred during ethnographic research in the late 1970s in rural Ireland, where I was interviewing farmwomen and their 15 to 21-year-old daughters about their aspirations in a time of rapid change, both for the economy and for gender roles. [This study was not about religion, but it turned out to be about women's beliefs, practices, and experiences far more than I initially realized.] At that time, It was culturally anomalous for a married woman with three children even to be employed, much less to be a professional in rural County Kerry, interviewing in remote townlands with a four-week-old baby on her hip. My then-husband came only long enough to help us move to the community and returned to the States to look for work. It was, in effect, a trial separation, but I could not reveal any marital distress to my Irish neighbors. My son (8) and daughter (6) quickly made friends at school, and I made many helpful contacts in the study area, but my community-assigned identity as researcher/foreigner/superwoman was frustratingly distant.

I felt subjectively linked with the farmwomen through parts of my self-identity—as mother, Midwestern "farm girl," of Irish (and Welsh and Scots) descent, homemaker who knitted and sewed my children's clothes, and lover of Irish music and dance. Other parts of my self-identity, such as my valued career as university professor and author and my relative financial independence and autonomy, made better sense in my own culture than in theirs. I needed to understand the life-worlds of my neighbors, but how?

The fortuitous development that shifted my relationships in the field cannot be recommended as a "strategy" to fledgling ethnographers. Barely two weeks after going into the field, I fell seriously ill; both I and my eldest child had acute hepatitis. I was virtually helpless, and the neighborhood mobilized to help me—bringing the doctor, shopping and cooking, washing the baby's "nappies," and minding the children after school. By the time my mother arrived to help out, I was nearly well and in the debt of nearly all my country neighbors and several townsfolk, too. My genuine vulnerability, temporary dependency, and sense of obligation to reciprocate immediately linked me with my neighbors—especially the women—with bonds I could never have created with words alone. As I recuperated, neighbor women came to "call." They chatted about babies and child-rearing, gave me pointers on the Aran sweater I was knitting, and enjoyed a "fine crack," while swapping recipes—all of which helped me frame my questions for the interviews that I hoped to begin the next month. The obligations I felt to reciprocate enabled me to offer (and them to accept) such mutual help as transportation to market or hospital, hand-me-down baby clothes, and help caring for a sick infant and an ailing elderly neighbor. My women neighbors and I discovered our commonalities, which then became my foundation for a far better understanding of their social worlds.

My vulnerability was a necessary, but not sufficient, factor in my new role in the community, however. Had I been a single woman, had I been a man, or had I been a childless married woman, I would not have been incorporated into the neighborhood as I was. In retrospect, I believe that it was not only the *fact* of my being a mother, but also their *experience* of my mothering that allowed for a closer mutual identification. One neighbor and her daughters had been present when, early in my illness, I argued adamantly with the doctor (making a house call) that I would continue nursing my baby throughout my illness. By the time I was convalescing and receiving frequent neighborly "calls," the women's grapevine had informed virtually all my women neighbors of this episode, and even total strangers remarked approvingly about my insistence on breastfeeding.

When I began interviewing, with my infant (and, often, my mother) in tow, women welcomed us, and they gave a quality of response to interviews that was beyond my highest hopes. Part of this enthusiastic response was because I was genuinely interested in what they thought and felt. It felt strange, at first, to have so many of my respondents thank me so profusely for the interview and beg me to visit with them again if I could find time. One woman, almost in tears, said "No one—not my parents, not my husband, not my neighbors—no one has ever asked me what I think about any of these things. Just talking to you about my thoughts and feelings makes me realize how important they are, even though no one else does." But these often-profound interviews and my new ascription as modern-educated-mother-who-also-breastfeeds-her-baby were not unproblematic in my field research.

One of the norms of field research, emphasized even in my undergraduate education, was to avoid changing the "host" culture.[3] Yet, my very presence and work had an impact. For instance, I had to drive a car to do interviews in remote townlands. Women asked me how I had learned to drive, how hard was it to learn, how difficult was it to manage my "huge" VW bus, and so on. They had seen that I was not so different from themselves, so every aspect of my behavior raised possibilities for them. Subsequently, not a few women in the community began to press their husbands to let them learn to drive and have use of the family car. At the time, I was uncomfortable with that influence: Was I inadvertently doing these women a disfavor? Was I promoting marriage or role conflicts? Or were these conflicts already underway? Were these very issues about women's roles and identities perhaps clues of what I needed to understand?

Interestingly, my unintended modeling of the role of nursing mother had particular appeal for many respondents—and led to some important understandings of women's issues in that setting. Shortly before the interviewing phase of my research, I was visiting in the kitchen of a nearby neighbor. As she made tea—the ubiquitous stimulant for women's conversations—I was nursing my baby on the settle (a long, cushioned bench) beside the cozy peat-burning "cooker." I asked about her hopes for her daughters. She talked briefly about her elder daughters' education and about her wish that they could be accepted in post-secondary training programs not too far from home. She spoke of fears about cities and emigration, and she was torn between wanting her daughters to settle near home, yet wanting them to have a better way of life than her own.

Then, watching me intently, she added: "I'd want them to know that they could be happy doing just what you're doing now and not be of no account." After several halting starts, she asked would I mind letting her girls (four teenagers) watch me nurse and talking to them about what the experience is like. I hesitated—not out of modesty, as she surmised, but because I was uncomfortable being cast in the role of advocate for a practice I had (incorrectly) assumed was already valued in their society. It had not occurred to me that I may have been the only mother in the entire valley who was breastfeeding! Her plea, however, was not merely about the value of breastfeeding for the well-being of the infant. It was about a dramatic change in societal values—promoted by the medical profession and the mass media—that had, in less than a generation, resulted in disvaluing the role of breastfeeding mother. More relevant for my research, I learned that many of the middle-aged mothers I interviewed felt that their daughters loved them but disparaged their mothers' central roles in life. They feared that the same socioeconomic changes that brought opportunities for their daughters reduced the value of their own contributions to their families and diminished their very identities.

What now stands out in my memory of that moment in my neighbor's kitchen was the sheer physicality of our mutual understanding. We understood each other, not only cognitively or emotionally, but also with our bodies. Indeed, I would have to say that I remember this moment now with my body/mind, not just mentally. This body/mind connection is strong. I have myself just recently remembered this moment as I watched my son's wife nurse her newborn. The memory came, not merely in my mind, but also as a bodily experience. I literally re-experienced the sensation of the baby nursing, the warmth of the turf fire in the cooker, the taste of the strong Irish tea, the morning light streaming through the kitchen window, the sound of the woman's voice, and the sense of pain she shared.

That two mothers—from different generations, cultures, and social statuses—shared an experiential sense of nursing suggests some important methodological possibilities. Ours was not exactly the same experience. We could not, for instance, experience the other's memories. But the shared physical experience was a critical bridge that enabled me to understand my neighbor more deeply, drawing on my own body/mind experience. It strikes me that this may be an unexplored avenue by which ethnography goes beyond the purely personal knowledge of the ethnographer.

Kleinman and Kleinman (1991) argue for doing "ethnography of experience" as an antidote to the dehumanizing tendencies of scientific ways of knowing. Significantly, their research focuses on the physical suffering experienced by Chinese victims of political oppression. Thus, they aim to understand both the culturally different Chinese emotional/physical constellation of pain and the subjective meanings of respondents' concrete biographical experiences. They argue that scientific ways of knowing euphemize victim's pain—for example, by calling it "post-traumatic stress syndrome" and implying that the suffering is "all in their head," i.e., fundamentally unreal. Their ethnography of experience, by contrast, treats bodily/physical aspects and mental/emotional aspects as completely melded:

> We live in the flow of daily experience: we are intersubjective forms of memory and action. Our experiences are so completely integrated—narratized moments, transforming narratives—that the self is constituted out of visceral processes as much as expressed through them. (1991, 293)

The Kleinmans argue that what I call the "mind/body/self" (McGuire 1996), as a unity, can be intersubjectively understood and that it can intersubjectively know others. My later studies of illness and healing (McGuire 1988) convinced me of the possibility and validity of this way of knowing. I cannot claim that all (or even most) of the evidence I presented in those studies resulted from the "ethnography of experience" (whether mine or my research assistants'). I do believe, however, that many of our best insights came from such experiences. Participating in a yoga-meditation group, I discovered experientially what my respondents had described about their *practice* of yoga postures (*asana*). Superficially, yoga poses appear to be merely physical—like "exercising." In the context of yoga practice, however, the poses involve the entire mind/body/self in an experiential transformation, that is, according to my informants, the essence of the experience of healing. It was only when I experienced just such a mind/body/self transformation (admittedly, a minor one compared to those in my respondents' narratives), that I could comprehend their stories of illness and suffering, healing and transformation. I did not need literally to "have" my respondents' illnesses or to be healed by each and every form of healing I studied, but I did need to connect with their narratives of experience. I needed to know their illness and healing as subjectively meaningful and real. To comprehend others' illnesses, suffering, transformation, and healing, I had to be open to the experiential grounds of understanding.

Is (Women's) Intuition a Body/Mind Way of Knowing?

Some scholars have begun to explore "intuition" as an immediate "sensing" or direct way of knowing (Davis-Floyd and Arvidson 1997). They suggest that it can provide knowledge unmediated by conscious logical analysis or by awareness of the steps by which one arrived at that "sense." Our positivist intellectual heritage has made us suspicious of intuition, but even such "hard" sciences as physics rely upon it (Monsay 1997; see also Dunne 1997). Intuition may be particularly useful in experience-near field research methodologies.

In the middle of my fieldwork for the pentecostal Catholics study (McGuire 1982), I obtained a small grant[4] allowing me to hire a research assistant (a rare experience for those of us who teach undergraduate students). Trying to articulate for her my approach to doing field research was a valuable experience for me, because it forced me to spell out when and how I worked by intuition. At the time, I did not have a clear sense of *why* intuition should be a valid part of social research, but since my research assistant had an uncommonly strong intuitive grasp of social interactions, I focused on teaching her to report with precision what she was observing.

For example, after several observations in one group, Linda commented that she wondered if part of the basis of the charismatic leadership of the male group leader might be his sex appeal and his sexually tinged ways of paying attention to female followers. I was taken aback— and felt appallingly matronly (then, mother of two and about 30 years old!)—that I had not even noticed the man's sex appeal. But as soon as she mentioned it, I agreed that she was accurately describing him. At that moment, Linda could not say what was the basis for her hunch; it was just a "feeling" or a "sense" she got when she was in the group in his presence. What observable behaviors and interactions might be underlying her "sense"? If her "feeling" was mistaken, what observable behaviors and interactions might we discover to lead to a better understanding? We both observed the next few prayer meetings, specifically attuned to displays of sexuality and attention-giving-and-receiving. Linda's intuition proved well founded, substantiated by our subsequent recording of such interaction patterns as eye contact, mutual postural alignment, touching and personal distance, flirtatious gestures, vocal intonations and speech patterns (e.g., addressing, complimenting, joking, and so on).

Here, intuition alone did not let us understand a social setting, but it was a valuable tool for insight. Intuition can provide a shortcut for focusing the research effort toward evidence necessary for fuller understanding.

I raise the issue of "women's" intuition, not merely because women are socialized to be more intuitive than men, but because it reminds us that the reigning ideology in science is gendered male. Western societies generally, and Western science in particular, have valorized rationality, objectivity, and linear thinking. Furthermore, emotionality, subjectivity, and intuitive thinking have been disvalued and identified with women. Keller (1985) reminds us that masculinity is attributed to science as an intellectual domain, because science is ideologically linked with power, control, and the rigidified autonomy and emotional distance of the "objective" observer. Note the gendered metaphors: Facts are "hard," feelings, "soft"; a man using a nonrational argument is "thinking like a woman." Keller (1985, 87) asserts

> adherence to an objectivist epistemology, in which truth is measured by its distance from the subjective, has to be reexamined when it emerges that, by this definition, truth itself has become genderized.

The approach to ethnography advocated by most of the authors of this volume eschews this ideology. I agree that the social scientific study of religion is not well served by ideological links with power, control, and false objectivity.

What we call "women's intuition" may be, in part, an instance of what Narayan (1989) calls the "epistemic advantage" of women and other marginalized people. She observes that women and ethnic minorities not only learn their own culture, but also often learn the culture of the dominant group—as a survival skill. The colonial master does not need to acquire the language, religion, or folkways of the colonized people, but the subjugated people need to learn at least enough of the colonial rulers' culture to protect themselves and to survive.

Anthropologist Ruth Behar (1996) notes how her own ethnographic insights have been greatly expanded by her own marginal position: as a woman in the male-dominated Academy, as a Latina in an Anglo world, as a Jew in a Christian-dominated society, as the child of immigrants in a xenophobic America. Being marginal and disempowered does not itself produce ethnographic understanding, for not all women have developed intuition, and some men have greater intuitive sense than the average woman. Generally, however, women in Western societies are more likely than men to have and use more developed intuitive "senses" of social situations, emotional and bodily experiences, and some gendered practices (such as midwifery).[5] Such knowledge and skill may be experienced as "intuition" or "gut-level hunches" or "sense," only because the person is not aware of *how* they know it. Ideally, by raising intuition to the level of consciousness, we can train ethnographers—female and male—to have and to use greater intuitive grasp of their research settings.

Women's uses of intuition may also be gender-linked, due to the culturally patterned ways that women attend to their bodies and use their bodies to attend to their world. Our bodies are intimately involved in how we apprehend our world, and women's bodily ways of knowing their worlds are different from men's. My Irish neighbor's identification with me as nursing mother may be an instance of how women experience bodily connections with others. These ways of knowing are not biologically determined, arbitrary, or culturally universal differences. Rather, they are learned subtly, as part of gender socialization, and (like all socialization) there is enormous individual variation in what is internalized. Pierre Bourdieu (1977) suggests that our very senses (our physical senses, not just our "common sense," "sense of justice," and "sense of taste") are socialized and culturally patterned. If this is the case, then women may indeed attend to their world differently.

Thomas Csordas (1993) argues that the body may even be directly involved in certain "somatic modes of attention." Elsewhere (McGuire

1996) I have discussed how such theories of bodies and emotions may help us understand religious experience and expression. For present purposes, however, I suggest the possibility that bodily ways of knowing may produce intuitions, a form of knowledge that could be sound bases for ethnographic exploration and analysis. Perhaps our discipline's research endeavors would be greatly enhanced if men and women alike were socialized to attend carefully to bodies and emotions, to develop better and more precise "women's" intuition.

Epistemological Homecoming: Grounding Method in Phenomenology

My research at least for the last twenty years has focused on religion and the human body—in healing, in religious experiences, in sexuality, in ritual practices, in eating, dancing, and journeying. No research topic could be laden with more subjective meanings! How can I—as a researcher with my own mind/body/self experiences and my own embodied meanings and identities—best understand others' experiences, meanings, and identities? And how can I do so without losing myself in those meanings (for our commitment to integrity as researchers must not override our personal integrity)?

I find myself returning to a phenomenology that shows us not only that body/mind/self intersubjectivity is possible, but also that it occurs regularly in socially structured ways. Where the phenomenology of my graduate school training was in Husserl and Schutz, I now find Merleau-Ponty, combined with Bourdieu, more immediately useful—though Schutz's emphasis on the phenomenological grounds of intersubjective understanding remains a useful basis for amplifying how *verstehen* is possible (see Spickard 1991b). If our bodily senses and our emotions are socially shaped (Bourdieu 1977; Jaggar 1989), then a close study of how they work may produce useful tools for intersubjective understanding.

Unfortunately, too much sloppy research in sociology and, especially religious studies, has been justified as "phenomenological," so we need to develop a methodology with far more precision and rigor about exactly *how* we know what we claim to have apprehended. I must admit that I have not fully succeeded in doing so. I offer two recent studies to suggest the potential of phenomenology as a basis for sound fieldwork.

About two decades ago, Thomas Csordas began his study of Catholic Charismatic healing, using rather standard anthropological fieldwork methods. He has since developed a sophisticated synthesis of phenomenology and semiotics undergirding his methodological approach. His attention to the "immediacy of embodied existence," apprehendable in the context of cultural (thus, shared) meanings, make his data and interpretations compelling (Csordas 1994). I find them compelling, not merely because his reports are corroborated by my observations when I studied similar groups years earlier. More important, Csordas tells the reader, with considerable specificity, *how he knows* Charismatic Catholics' distinctive cultural meanings of ritual body practices, postures, and performances, of constitutive language and other signs, of such Charismatic ways of knowing as the "gift of discernment" (Csordas 1997). Although I do not agree with some of his interpretations, I consider his explicit and careful use of phenomenological apprehension to be exemplary.

Similarly, James Aho's (1990) ethnography of right-wing extremists, together with his thoughtful methodological reflections on that and other encounters with hate groups (Aho 1994; 1997), suggest the promise of phenomenology for achieving *both* a genuine understanding of a culture's meanings and, yet, enough distance to be able to name those meanings "evil."

This last point is important. How can we remain true to our values, our relationships, our very selves, while we accomplish phenomenological understanding in the field? Our commitment to integrity as researchers must not override our commitment to human integrity. It is my earnest hope that both such commitments, reflected through continual—indeed, lifelong—reflexive attention to challenging and refining *how* we know what we professionally claim to know, will transform our ways of exploring the social sciences of religion, no matter which methodologies we select.

NOTES

Thanks are due to Sheryl Tynes, Richard Reed, and Jim Spickard for their thoughtful comments on an earlier draft of this chapter.

1. Field research methods would not include all "qualitative" research methods, because such methods as analysis of personal diaries and letters often do not involve the researcher's interaction with the authors and, thus, resemble history research methods (see Tweed, this volume).

2. In this respect, epistemological and methodological issues in ethnography resemble those in historiography.

3. I say "was," because this norm was impossibly naive and has since been rethought and reframed. It is still a useful reminder that social researchers—especially those doing ethnographic field research—have serious moral responsibilities and professional ethical obligations toward the people they study.

4. Special thanks to the Society for the Scientific Study of Religion for what was, I believe, one of the first small grants for research funded by that Society.

5. An excellent essay on intuition as authoritative knowledge in midwifery is Davis-Floyd and Davis (1997); see also Cooey (1989) for an epistemological treatise on embodiment as a basis of authority.

Chapter 16

Greening Ethnography and the Study of Religion

Laurel Kearns

"We are about human concerns; there are plenty of environmental groups out there to work on ecology issues." In the mid-1980s, as a researcher on religious political lobbying, I accepted the premise of this statement on the lobbying priorities of the Friends Committee on National Legislation (FCNL). One year later, however, the organization had a part-time volunteer lobbyist whose focus was on environmental issues. This shift in FCNL priorities marked the beginning of my research into Christian ecological activism; for, although my religious beliefs spoke to the compatibility of religion and environmental activism, until then I had assumed that environmentalism was a secular concern (Smith 1987). Many of those I have interviewed over the years spoke of their own confrontation with the same assumption, and the difficult acceptance of their stance by both environmentalists and others of their faith tradition. This chapter, then, is a tale of how research changes the researcher. As such, it is a tale of conversion, for the people and organizational literature that I have encountered in my research have convinced me that a growing environmental crisis presents a challenge to the way we think and do research in the social sciences.[1]

Research and Rethinking

Throughout my research, the world of religious environmentalism has challenged many of the sociological assumptions that I was taught. For one, religious environmentalism does not respect the classical conservative/liberal divide in American Protestantism. As one evangelical activist explained in an interview, "I completely disagree with [those who say that Christianity should be about things other than environmental concern]. It's our job description" (Kearns 1996). Here was a conservative evangelical telling me that "to be saved means saving the creation," thereby contradicting the surveys that would predict otherwise.[2] Some evangelicals lobbied against New Christian Right-supported anti-environmental legislation and work with the National Council of Churches (Kearns 1997). Other "truisms" also fell. I encountered wealthy suburban churches crossing lines of denomination, class, race, ethnicity and geography to work alongside poorer urban churches to combat environmental degradation. I encountered African-American congregations, often thought of as being unconcerned about "White" environmental issues, that were deeply involved in fighting for cleaner, safer environments (Kearns 1999a). In all of these cases, groups moved beyond the assumed boundaries of their worldview and ethos because of a new recognition of what they had in common with those labeled as "Other."

In addition to confounding the assumed borders within the world of Christianity, my recent research has broadened my understanding of what religious environmentalism entails. Religious environmentalism is not just "star-gazing" and "tree-hugging," as one activist named it in an interview. Rather, as she pointed out, there is also that critical eco-justice vein of religious environmentalism, which cares about poverty and about those persons living near hazardous or toxic waste sites—the majority of whom are people of color (UCC 1987). The activism of grassroots groups and churches in these areas, and that of the National Council of Churches Eco-Justice Working Group (EJWG), is largely responsible for the birth of the eco-justice or environmental justice movement (Kearns 1999a), a movement that has changed the demographics and focus of many environmental organizations.[3]

Eco-Justice: Rural and Urban

The investigation of religious responses to environmental injustices has begun to reshape my understanding of the discipline of sociology in general and the practice of ethnography in particular. Through the EJWG, I had the opportunity to visit with Jesus' People Against Pollution (JPAP), a group of African-American women living in Columbia, Mississippi, home of one of the first Superfund cleanup sites. JPAP was formed by a group of women in a local church who noticed that skin lesions and unexplained rashes were becoming common and that there was an unusual number of people dying of cancer in their community. The town had allowed a predominantly African-American senior citizen home to be built on land that turned out, upon later investigation, to be part of the industrial site that had not been marked on the maps given to the EPA. Although the EPA had pronounced the Columbia Superfund cleanup site finished, barrels of the hazardous wastes removed from the site were later found floating in or buried near local water sources. Many in the White neighborhoods near the condemned land had been relocated, but an elementary school and the African-American community that it served were still located right next to the fence surrounding the site.

When the women formed Jesus' People Against Pollution to seek redress from the EPA, they chose the name quite deliberately. In talking to them, what was clearly evident was that the intrusion of the biophysical world around them into the bodies of their loved ones and themselves had transformed their religious faith. Despite what their Baptist preacher said about salvation and keeping their eyes "on heaven above," it was impossible for the women to maintain a solely otherworldly religious focus when the givenness of the natural world around them—their water, soil, and air—so impinged upon their lives. For them, pollution was a faith concern because they now saw that environmental issues were justice concerns; Jesus came to save the powerless, in this instance, from strange diseases and oddly formed garden produce, from corporate pollution and irresponsibility, and from government neglect. Addressing this realization, however, meant worldly, political involvement and thus battles within their churches about such a focus.

In the course of listening to the women's stories, I realized that it was not just the content and practice of their faith that was being challenged, but rather their very sense of the safety of the world around them. Their conceptions of the soil as a source of nourishment and water as a source of purification or sustenance were being radically challenged. With this changed realization went their sense of security about being able to make it through hard times by at least being able to provide for their family through gardening and fishing.

In Newark, New Jersey, there is no illusion that the natural world is benign, pure, or sustaining. Newark will long be prisoner to its history as one of the first industrialized cities in the nation. Newark's industrialization, and its slow decline, happened primarily before the era of "heightened" environmental awareness and regulations. The magnitude of the environmental degradation caused by this legacy is easily demonstrated in the Diamond Alkali site in Newark's Ironbound section, now a predominantly Portuguese and Brazilian neighborhood, where the company manufactured DDT and Agent Orange. In the process, DDT and dioxin—a toxic by-product of Agent Orange—were dumped into the river or allowed to seep into the ground. The level of contamination at the site is thought to be the largest concentration of dioxin in the world. Currently, about 357,000 people live within a three-mile radius of the site, 40,000 within one mile. Sixteen years after condemning the site, the EPA began overseeing the building of a sealed six acre, fifteen foot high "toxic tomb" to house the materials until safe ways of destroying dioxin can be found (Masnerus 1998).

The Diamond Alkali plant is not the only hazardous or toxic site in the city of Newark, nor is it the only one in its Ironbound neighborhood of 55,000 people. The Ironbound alone contains 110 sites. Yet, in addition to dealing with such a toxic legacy, the neighborhood has been host to other environmental justice struggles. In 1990, they lost a prolonged battle against the building of the state's largest garbage incinerator, but successfully fought the placement of a tire incinerator, a medical wastes disposal facility, a sludge landfill, and a dock and additional incinerator to handle 4,000 tons per day of New York City garbage. One of the neighborhood's two parks and its only public swimming pool were closed due to contamination.

Rather than forming a separate religiously based activist group, some area churches joined with Ironbound Community Corps and often played a key role in these battles. Churches provided public meeting space and a ready pool of potential activists. Their bulletins offered a valuable means to communicate with the community, and their pastors spoke on the issues with a moral voice that was harder for elected officials to ignore.[4] In other words, several churches within the Ironbound acted as movement midwives (Smith 1996). In the campaign to push for EPA-mandated remediation of the park, banners with religious symbols of hope and children's murals were hung on the boarded-up fence around it. In an effort to bring together religious congregations on environmental issues, an interfaith eco-sabbath was held each year both to commemorate creation and to witness to its local degradation.

My research in Newark is part of Drew University's "Newark Project," in which present and future anthropologists and sociologists are engaged in a detailed mapping of the religious landscape of the city. Among the many insights revealed by this collective research is that healing is a central concern among religious groups in the city. Whether it is the *botanicas* throughout the city that provide herbal materials for santería, voudou, and candomble practitioners, or the lead testing and cancer screenings (because of abnormally high local rates) hosted by Protestant churches and neighborhood organizations, health and healing concerns are a vital part of the religious landscape. I soon realized that my own mapping of Newark's hazardous waste sites shed insight into understanding the larger religious landscape of the city. It became clear to me that one cannot fully understand the prevalence of health concerns, or the religious landscape of Newark in general, if factors such as the condition of the soil, dirt and dust, the quality of air and water, the lack of green space, or contact with non-human nature are ignored.

The larger implications of this research were obvious: it is not enough to understand the social and cultural dynamics of religious groups in Newark; the short term and long range implications of such a toxic environment are also factors. In conversation with other Newark Project researchers at the time, however, it became apparent that they had no grasp of the toxicity of the city. In Newark, the environment is detrimental to human health and has pervasive effects on human reproduction; it provokes crises of meaning, even without conscious awareness of it, for which religious answers are often sought. As a result of this research, I would at least suggest that scholars studying religions, with a focus on issues of health and healing, need to include analysis of local and regional factors of environmental pollution and deterioration that might be relevant to the particular illnesses showing up in a congregation, or that are implicated in the rate of birth defects, types of illnesses, or deaths.

What my research on JPAP and Newark has further helped me to see is that there is a general need to "green" ethnography, that is, to make an awareness of the seen and unseen physical environment a factor in all of our research. As German sociologist Ulrich Beck (1992, 41) contends, "'ecological blindness' is a congenital defect of sociologists." This means that a re-examination of our disciplines as a whole is needed; for far too long, as social scientists, we have generally disregarded the "natural" world as a given, concentrating instead only on "human" concerns.

Nature/Culture

At the core of our disciplines is the dichotomous distinction between human/nature, or culture/nature, further reinforced by the mind/matter division at the heart of Enlightenment thought. Historically, the realms of human, culture, society, and mind have been seen as the subjects of the social sciences, whereas nature or matter belonged to the biological sciences. As dichotomies, these terms are seen as mutually exclusive: humans are viewed as separate from nature; mind can transcend nature. This has led not only to an institutional separation, but also an intellectual separation that still remains at the core of much of the scholarly work being done (Little 1999). For many, to bring "nature" back into the social sciences would muddy the waters between the social and biological sciences.

This adamant division is a result of the shared historical roots of sociology and anthropology. Hannigan (1995) points out that in the nineteenth century, natural factors in understanding the development of societies and individuals were quite prominent. Both geographical determinism and varieties of Social Darwinism drew upon "nature" or biology for explanations of human society and culture. The implications of Social Darwinism and the large flaws in geographical/environmental determinism, however, soon led to a strong aversion to theory based on nature or biology.[5] Subsequent arguments about biological determinism, such as eugenics or race-based intelligence, provided plenty of evidence of the dangers of arguing from nature. This tension is still quite evident in the debate between constructionism and sociobiology or between "nature" versus "nurture" in feminism. The assumptions and aims of the Enlightenment strongly shaped the emerging fields of sociology and anthropology. The founding theorists were products of the Enlightenment, with its belief in human mastery over and freedom from natural constraints. There is little significant recognition of the environment or nature in the founding theories of Durkheim, Marx, and Weber. As one recent reviewer of the field of environmental sociology comments, "classical sociological theorists essentially disregard the physical environment, place human society 'outside' of nature, and even take nature out of human beings" (Canan 1996, 33).[6] Reflecting the Enlightenment focus on mind over matter, sociology and anthropology developed notions of human actors that were distanced and disembodied from their physical selves so that in fact they seemed to have no bodies, gender, sexuality, hormones, cycles, disabilities, etc. (Adams 1994; McGuire 1990). In an effort to correct this false and flat universalistic erasure, recent innovative scholarship strives to include the excluded. Nature is absent not only in our theory but also in our methodology. The fields of ethnography and qualitative methodology (Denzin 1997; Clifford and Marcus 1986) reflect the larger social science bracketing of nature. A survey of texts discussing ethnographic or qualitative methodology reveals little if any mention of taking environmental conditions into account, or considering nature as a factor.[7] As indicated by this volume, the current climate change within ethnographic work to recognize gender, subjectivity, reflexivity, embodiment, etc. (Behar 1996; Olesen 1994) has the potential to open the door for the recognition of nature as being an excluded "Other," as we wrestle with how humans are shaped by both "natural" and "cultural" factors.

Like many feminist ethnographers, those involved in bringing the environment into our disciplines are involved in advocacy work and continue to challenge the paradigm of the distant, objective researcher (Fonow and Cook 1991).[8] In distinction to a focus on environmentalism, the effort to introduce an ecological worldview into the social sciences is often referred to as ecologism. This has many facets: Little (1999) calls for an effort at "epistemological symmetry" in our work that seeks to balance the poles of the social-culture/nature dichotomy, and Gellner (1995, 252) states that the "social construction of reality needs to be complemented by the natural construction of society."[9] There is call for the recognition of "natural agency" in our study of human culture and societies and the increasing recognition of the human construction of "nature," including the fact that human processes now interfere with the very complex, interrelated workings of the planet itself.

The Sociology of Religion

Yet, even as the influence of environmental sociology and anthropology broadens, it has little affected the sociology of religion. Sociological or ethnographic research on topics related to environmentalism and religion are still scarce.[10] In addition to being shaped by the dominant paradigms suggested above, the sociology of religion, more so than the anthropology of religion, has been further influenced by the shadow of Christianity that haunts our thinking about "religion." As well as reinforcing the mind/body, spirit/matter divide, this Christian shadow may have influenced the exclusion of nature from our thought. With some exceptions, the strong anthropocentric focus of Christianity (more so than Judaism) privileges humans over nature (Santmire 1985). Some scholars argue that Jewish and Christian understandings of God have focused on human history as the stage for divine acts in distinction to nature, which was the stage for the acts of "pagan," "heathen" deities. This understanding certainly influenced Weber, Durkheim, and Marx in their analyses of religion. They also shared an evolutionary understanding of religion in which religions that related more to nature were seen as "primitive" or elementary—this view was shared by anthropologists such as Tyler and Fraser—and more advanced religion bore a semblance to Christianity (e.g. Bellah 1970).

As Carolyn Merchant (1990) persuasively argues, Christian theological concepts and worldview helped shape a dominant scientific worldview that emerged in the late eighteenth century. The drive to understand nature and, in so doing, the "mind of God," was transformed into a focus on dissecting and controlling "nature," so that nature played an ever-decreasing role in human affairs (Swimme and Berry 1994). This reigning scientific paradigm strongly influenced the discipline of sociology: nature was seen as a backdrop to human affairs. The struggle between science and religion also shaped the discipline: religion was assumed to be about faith and "unseen" matters; science was about the physical, "real" world. Feminists, womanists, Native Americans, and post-colonial theorists further point to examples in Christian thinking where nature was connected to race and gender so that people of color and females were less than "human." A similar assumption of white, male humans as the normative model of "mankind" has also haunted both the social and natural sciences.

Additionally, as a discipline shaped by the study of Christianity, U.S. sociology of religion has focused on institutional and organizational aspects of religion, or, as Karen McCarthy Brown (1998) suggests, "religion in buildings." This often leads to the assumption that the practice of religion takes place inside buildings and is little connected to the physical world in which it occurs. This assumption is not surprising, for historically, the design of Christian churches has tended to reinforce the dismissal of the natural world as part of religious practice. Gothic architecture, designed to suggest heaven to believers, completely redirected all of the senses from the outside world. Ascetic Protestant design, seen in the simple and austere lines of a New England church, ordered and shut out the unruliness of nature (while trying to do the same with human nature). Similarly, most contemporary church architecture is designed to block out the outside world, and even if one could see outside the windows, especially those of large scale, mega-churches, all that would be seen is acres of parking lot pavement with a few ubiquitous shrubs. In church architecture, it is still radical to design a church so that congregants can see the outside world clearly and easily. Much of the sociology of religion also reflects the Christian (and post-exilic Jewish and Muslim) assumption that religious practice and worship are not place-related and are therefore portable. As proselytizing religions, Christianity and Islam both carry within them the notion that their faith can be practiced anywhere. For post-exilic Judaism, there was no choice but to maintain the faith wherever possible. This "portability" stands in stark contrast, for instance, to many Native American religious practices and systems in which to perform a rite outside of the "natural" context is to render it meaningless or to change fundamentally the nature of the rite or practice. In other words, most Native American traditions are connected to landscape and place, although the massive relocation of Native Americans severed the continuity of these ties for many, many groups, thus changing, or extinguishing, their religious practices (Weaver 1996). Assuming that religious practice is not place-related allows sociologists of religion to ignore the physical environment in which it is practiced.

Nature-oriented religions are usually treated as non-institutionalized religion, thus carrying the denotation of lesser importance. A glance at the history of religion in North America, for example, reveals how often non-mainstream religious movements focus on how humans relate to the natural world, incorporating that which the dominant Christian culture saw as heretical (Albanese 1990; Berger 1998; Bloch 1998).

Bigger Questions

Not only did my research lead me to rethink the practice of ethnography and the human/nature divide within the social sciences; it has also generated a range of questions for my future research. What is the impact of recognizing that the "natural world" around oneself is no longer a backdrop, able for the most part to be controlled, and that the change is human induced? Some scholars suggest that the only "acts of God" left are earthquakes and volcanic eruptions. All other "natural" disasters are now partially caused by human actions. (Hurricanes and massive storms are thought to be connected to desertification and greenhouse-related ocean warming; mudslides are made worse by deforestation from population pressures; destructive flooding is linked to river control, irrigation channeling, and surface paving). The vision of wilderness afforded to more affluent countries varies from a source of inspiration and escape from human society to the ultimate testing ground of our high-tech equipment and SUVs. We are surprised when real people get hurt in nature, or when insects once again are more than vague nuisances. The crisis of meaning caused by recognizing that humans are not in control of their own fate is central to religions, but how does it change now that these forces are ones that we have in part created?

The eco-justice advocates that I encountered in my research no longer shared such an illusion of the "natural world" as a backdrop to human wants. Poisoning was now making their immediate biophysical environment the enemy once again; the world around these communities was not to be trusted and taken for granted. As a result of my research, it is clear that this has effects on identity and on understandings of salvation, security, safety, destiny, the afterlife, or hope in the future. Kai Erikson (1995) points out that the effects of this new class of human-caused disasters not only affect the current generation but future ones as well. This recognition has implications for one's sense of parenthood and generativity. Often toxins are stored in human body fat and passed on through breastfeeding; what does it mean for women to realize that their own bodies can poison their children and that breastfeeding is not necessarily natural and safe? These are all questions that I ponder not only about the "subjects" of my research, but also that I now ask myself as researcher.

Furthermore, what does it mean for those in both rural and urban settings when nature is mainly weeds, rats, and roaches? As the United States becomes an increasingly urbanized society, what will this mean for our cultural understandings of nature—Central Park as "nature"? For religious vision and experience?[11] For the motivation and sympathy for ecological activism? Individuals working in youth or camp/retreat center ministry tell me that "nature" is an alien, and annoying, experience for many on retreats, because going into the "wilderness" means having to be unplugged and disconnected. They report that participants frequently don't like the silence or are extremely afraid of bugs and creatures. What does it mean when virtual reality is more real than the "reality" of nature?

Experiences of "nature" are often an important part of religious inspiration, and the majority of advocates that I interviewed reported that the loss of a piece of land, a landscape, a way of life, motivated their faith-based activism. They wonder how increasing suburbanization and urbanization will affect future activists. Will religious visions of the goodness of creation even make sense to future generations?

Finally, environmental problems, whether global or local, respect no boundaries. The nature of environmental problems muddies the illusory demarcation between researcher and researched. Before I even go to my "research" site in Newark, some of the same problems of the region's deteriorating environment are inscribed in my lungs and body, as well as in those of Newark's residents. We all live in the New York City metro area, which has the fourth worst air quality in the nation plus above average cancer rates. We live in the New Jersey county that has half of the state's asthma cases; my four-year-old son is one of them. We all live within the radius of the Newark incinerator's particulate discharge and now have respiratory problems. It is not just *their* environment that is hazardous. And when I get "there," I am aware that I take home some of the Ironbound neighborhood's toxicity; the unjust contaminants in the air, water, and dust respect no person. There is no neat divide between nature and society/culture, between researcher and subject, and I cannot remain a distant, objective researcher, unaffected by my research.

This awareness has made me once again an activist. I do not mean to say that there is no difference in impact, for certainly age, gender, race, ethnicity, and class play a role in who suffers the effects of environmental degradation the most. I can "escape" and drive an illusory twenty miles away to the cleaner, greener, and higher ground of Drew's forested campus, where I write articles about what I have learned of my sense of self, my research, my "calling," and my academic field.

Conclusion

I have shared how my research on religious environmentalism in general, and on environmental injustice in particular, led me to the conclusion that an understanding of local environmental issues and environmental quality is important for any ethnographer, not just ones working on environment-related topics as I am. This will require a different level of awareness from the researcher than we have learned in the past. And since many of these environmental factors are relatively unseen, the construction of their "presence" (or "absence") are factors that must be taken into consideration.

I have argued strongly for a rethinking of the nature/society dichotomy that runs through the social sciences, and in particular, for a recognition of how the exclusion of the natural world has shaped our discipline. Such a rethinking of how nature is "Other" is a continuation of the innovative work included in this volume. The recognition that nature cannot be excluded also has many implications for how we see ourselves as researchers.

At the same time, I have tried to introduce some of the important voices in sociology and anthropology that call us to wrestle with the implications and effects of human interference in the intricate eco-system of the earth. We need to do so, if we are to understand human cultures and societies. As the nature of the environmental problems facing us so clearly indicates, to ignore these problems and the related complicated effects on human institutions and societies will increasingly be to keep our head in the sand.

I am suggesting, therefore, that human/nature interaction should be recognized as both the subject and context of our work. In this process of challenging the nature/culture split of our fields, as ethnographers in particular and as sociologists/anthropologists in general, we will also need to examine what are the understandings of nature and culture that are implicit in our research. Our ears, eyes, and brains have not been trained to be aware of ecological issues, and ecological thinking is still foreign to most of our scholarly minds. It is past time for "greening" ethnography.

NOTES

This chapter could not have been written without the assistance and insights of Matthew Immergut and Beth Beall.

1. While I will continue to use the terms "environment," "ecology" and "nature," I recognize that all three are not without problems: "environment" and "nature" are problematic because they are used to denote the world around humans, as if humans were separate. "Environment" and "ecology" are often used in the social sciences with no reference to the natural world.

2. See Eckberg and Blocker (1989) or Guth et al. (1995) for references to other surveys.

3. Religious involvement is left out of the majority of accounts of the environmental justice movement (Kearns 1999b).

4. Newark Project researcher Matthew Immergut (2000) has done follow-up research on these churches to help understand their current inactivity.

5. The discipline of human ecology, developed by Robert Park and the "Chicago School," sought to use insights from the natural sciences but still remained focused on the human. Hannigan (1995) sees this approach as a precursor to environmental sociology; however, Catton (1992) argues that nature was mostly absent in their analyses. Anthropologists Roy Rappaport (1979) and Andrew Vayda (1975) further developed this approach.

6. Some scholars argue otherwise. Klaus Eder (1996, 128), for example, argues that "nature mattered in Montesquieu, Marx, Spencer, Durkheim/Mauss, and Simmel. . . . After [these] classics, nature vanished from sight in sociology." Environmental sociologist Raymond Murphy (1997, 3) describes the field as "sociology as if nature did not matter," but exempts Weber.

7. In addition to those already cited, see Burawoy et al. (1991); Denzin and Lincoln (1994).

8. See the Winter 2000 volume of the journal *Sociology of Religion* for extensive reflection on feminist approaches.

9. See Redclift and Benton (1994) for perspectives from several fields. In addition to those previously cited, see: Milton (1993) in anthropology; MacNaughten and Urry (1995) and the many efforts of Fredrick Buttel (1987) and Riley Dunlap (1992) in sociology.

10. It is not, for example, mentioned in Sherkat and Ellison's (1999) recent review of the field. There are, however, exceptions, among them: Berger (1998); Beyer (1994); Bloch (1998); Gould (1997); Kearns (1996; 1997); Shibley and Wiggins (1997).

11. Robert Orsi (1999, 42–43) comments that the long association of religion with nature by theorists such as Eliade skewed the perception of religion in the city, so that it has been viewed as alienated religion.

Chapter 17

As the Other Sees Us

On Reciprocity and Mutual Reflection in the Study of Native American Religions

Armin W. Geertz

The insights and problems addressed in this chapter arose in connection with an in-depth study of Hopi Indian millennial prophecy.[1] After discovering a whole series of questionable evidence, statements, and interpretations of and about Hopi prophecies, I noticed that one of the major reasons for the fluid nature of these supposed revelations was politics. Inter-Hopi politicking was understandable and did not prove to be a serious obstacle to my study. And the presence of Euro-American interest groups that believe in, or at least claim to believe in, Hopi prophecies about the end of the world complicated the matter somewhat, but could be more or less explained as just another example of Western cultural madness.

But when scholars likewise become involved in the local politics of prophecy, then we are faced with more serious problems. Richard Clemmer—one of the radical proponents of action anthropology during the 1970s—was an anthropologist who analyzed the Hopi movement that promoted Hopi prophecy, the Traditionalist Movement. His book, *Continuities of Hopi Culture Change* (1978), strikingly insists on defending the notion of the absolute precognitive value of Hopi prophecy. His otherwise cogent insights on the cultural nature of myth and tradition and its undulating, dialectic nature did not mesh with his efforts to replace Hopi theology with a "planetary field-of-mind theory" which postulates that everything in the cosmos, from material to morals, are integral parts of a vast network of energy fields. On delving further into his career, I found out that Clemmer was an activist for the Traditionalist Movement and that his work was highly ideological, containing stereotypes about the Hopis as well as about Americans.

In focusing on Clemmer's errors, I was forced to take a critical look at the way in which the Traditionalist Movement was using its own prophecies to manipulate others. It struck me then that my own critical, skeptical activity was itself political, as it is based unconsciously on a cultural countercritique. I was forced into the battlefield of stereotypes whether I liked it or not. And even if I did not perceive my arguments as being political in nature, they would nonetheless be understood as such both by Clemmer and by the Hopis. To complicate matters further, my study of the situation out on the Reservation during the last 100 years has shown that not only has the Traditionalist Movement changed its prophecies, but so has everybody else! This situation raised questions in my mind about the nature of prophecy in the Hopi context and in religion in general and about whether we, as historians of religions, are also guilty of idealizing religion (see A. Geertz 1994a).

My conclusion was that much of my wonderment about these apparent contradictions stems from inflexible conceptions about indigenous peoples and their religions that our culture and our discipline hold. We forget that religion, tradition, prophecy, and so on are ways of thinking, speaking, and acting by humans situated in intricate webs of significance, to borrow Clifford Geertz's (1973b, 5) phrase. Religion in this sense is discourse conceived as social praxis. Prophecy is tradition that is spoken by someone to someone else for specific purposes whether for moral, ideological, or political reasons (A. Geertz 1989; 1991a; 1992/94).

I believe that the generation of essentialistic stereotypes and the implicit or explicit political dimensions of this activity—whether produced by politician, journalist, or scholar—should move us to re-evaluate what the study of religion is all about. The fact that the history of religions was created in the ferment of the orientalisms of the last century should warn us that there are aspects of our science that are not altogether as ideal as we would like them to be. Orientalism is understood here both as the tendency to dichotomize humanity into we—they contrasts and to essentialize the resultant "Other." Orientalism is a way of thought that justifies political action, but it is also a method of defining self or own culture. Finally, it is also a way of writing. The problem I am addressing, then, is the cultural construction of the exotic and whether we can ultimately escape from it.[2]

We can begin our reflective efforts by questioning the somewhat simplistic and idealistic conception of an objectively empirical search for scientific truth with no concern for problems of meaning or relevance in relation to the needs of the people we study or of our own people.

Scholars who are involved in controversial issues perceive the problem more urgently than others do. One is not only confronted with the existential and other needs of the people under study, but also with the existential needs of our own civilization. Our own culture obviously uses the study of foreign peoples as one of its methods of self-reflection. Since our fellow culture-bearers will do this whether we like it or not, then it must be our duty to provide the most trustworthy data possible. However, "others" can manipulate data as well as truths. Therefore, I have come firmly to believe that we should not entrust the task of interpretation and opinion-making to novelists and journalists (A. Geertz 1990c).

As Michael Agar (1980, 256) notes about anthropology, regardless of the problems of the hermeneutic circle, some interpretations are better than others. Although meaning is always contingent and situational (Tyler 1978, 364), what constitutes the ethnographic pursuit is a "shared implicit commitment to make sense of group meanings" (Agar 1980, 269). In other words, it is an attempt to make sense of the meaning produced by others. Therefore, scholars who are trained in dealing with the products of culture—texts, discourses, performances, actions, and objects—should be in the position to report on the meanings of other cultures in a reasonably objective and accurate manner. More so, anyway, than the tabloids and literary canvasses.

The claim that some interpretations are better than others is based on the assumption that such interpretations are the result of systematic field methods, linguistic expertise, comparative analysis, and theoretical sophistication. I hold that if any writers are in a position to provide accurate information and explanations of exotic cultures for our own audiences, then surely it must be professional cultural analysts! If this is not the case, then what are we doing in the academy?

Poetics is not science. It is another discipline with different methods and goals. It is by definition concerned with the esthetic interpretation of the world and in many instances constitutes a commentary on the world. Our job is not to produce social commentary or to write inspiring books—although such might be the by-product of our work, and legitimately so. Our primary job is to study and describe aspects of human societies that support, improve, or supplant general theories about human society and religion. If we can popularize our cultural analysis, that is good. Nevertheless, it should contribute to an understanding of the world that neither romanticizes nor misrepresents other cultures. Romanticizations and misrepresentations have been known directly to cause cultural misunderstanding and even in some cases cultural conflict and tragedy. Native Americans, for instance, who do not live up to contemporary romantic American stereotypes know of the indignities that follow (see Rose 1984).

Having said this, we must not forget that in our choice of subjects, we are not only choosing material for historical study and relating it to an important theory or paradigm, we are also communicating our results and activities to different audiences. This means that we must pursue our hermeneutics in a self-conscious manner, not only within the framework of academic discourse but also at all other levels of communication. In other words, we must learn to communicate meaning to our own culture through the expert analysis of the meanings of other cultures. We must educate our own tribes about ourselves through the existential lenses of foreign peoples, and we must do it in a talented manner.

The Problem of the Other

The study of religion is, as John Van Maanen (1988, ix) noted about ethnography, "the peculiar practice of representing the social reality of others through the analysis of one's own experience in the world of these others." Admitting this, the scholar of religion must also admit a series of relationships, all of which have equal bearing on the job of describing other religions and cultures. Following Van Maanen, these relationships are composed of four factors: the observed, the observer, the ethnographic text or tale, and the audience. These four factors are all highly complex processes that require clarity and acknowledgment in the pursuit of a self-conscious discipline. Furthermore, matters such as university career opportunities, institutional funding practices, editorial policies of journals and publishing companies, the idiosyncrasies of peer reviewers, academic fashions, and issues in the general public all play important roles in the type of observations made and the style chosen for the ethnographic text.

I would add a fifth factor: the role of reciprocity and mutual reflection in the study of indigenous religions. For while we have been engaged in battles with non-academic interpreters of the "Other," we have paid little attention to the serious problems with the concept of the Other and the role our study of it plays. While anthropologists and even historians of religions have been debating what role the natives' understanding is to play in cultural accounts, the natives have, in the meantime, been voicing their unwillingness to remain, in Edward Said's (1985, 17) words, the "silent Other" of Europeans and Americans.

Orientalists and scholars of American Indians and African peoples have most frequently met the criticism that what we are doing is in reality a science of imperialism. The attitude that the people under study lack the capacity for self-representation and therefore must be represented by others who know more about them than they do about themselves is in the words of Said

> ... neither science, nor knowledge, nor understanding: it is a statement of power and a claim for relatively absolute authority. It is constituted out of racism, and it is made comparatively acceptable to an audience prepared in advance to listen to its muscular truths. (Said 1985, 19; but see Mudimbe 1988, 16ff.)

I meet with such statements all the time, and I am forced to admit that colonialism and imperialism nourish the very attitudes and language that our discipline employs.

This realization is in full agreement with the latest works of self-reflection by social anthropologists. As James Clifford wrote in his collection of essays on writing culture, the newer anthropology sees

> culture as composed of seriously contested codes and representations, they assume that the poetic and the political are inseparable, that science is in, not above, historical and linguistic processes ... and that the writing of cultural descriptions is properly experimental and ethical. Their focus on text making and rhetoric serves to highlight the constructed, artificial nature of cultural accounts. It undermines modes of authority, and it draws attention to the historical predicament of ethnography, the fact that it is always caught up in the invention, not the representation of cultures. (Clifford 1986, 2)

These are points well taken, and they clearly question the idea of an objective, dispassionate, and nonpolitical science. On the other hand, we must also beware of excessive breast-beating. I disagree with the tenet, for instance, that personal commitment or agreement gives special access to the truth of a religion. I also disagree with the tenet that experience somehow makes description more accurate in an absolute sense. Instead, I hold with scholar of religion T. Patrick Burke (1984, 631) that "adherents of a religion do not necessarily understand their religion, and a person who disagrees with a religion does not necessarily misunderstand it." Whether one is interested in an account of a religion's historical development, or of its practices or beliefs, or of the truth of those beliefs, or of the faith in which they are found: in all these cases, Burke argued, being a believer is no unassailable qualification. In almost every case, the observer will encounter disagreement and in many cases conflict. When doing fieldwork we meet this situation all the time. Being born a Hopi does not guarantee the quality of the information given. In fact, competent scholars sometimes are asked by the Hopis for their opinion, advice, or help in political and cultural matters. In each case, whether native or fieldworker, it is a question of cultural competence and the methods one employs. It is also a question of analysis. We will tend to ask questions that the natives have not thought about, unless they themselves are cultural analysts. Or we ask questions hidden by their cultural blind spots.

Outsiders can, indeed, be greatly mistaken about a foreign people. Most often, they fall victim to what Robert LeVine (1970, 389) called "loyalistic misperception" and "errors of hasty judgment." Nevertheless, the advantages of being an outsider are legion when and if they are tempered by training in the use of comparative, independent control measures. No one is infallible, it is true, but it is equally true that outsiders are not disqualified per se to study other peoples. Neither are unbelievers.

A second problem, however, is more difficult to address: the issue of authority that is often raised by indigenous scholars (A. Geertz 1991b). In most of the societies studied by anthropologists and scholars of religions, knowledge, being a prerequisite of authority and power, is often hard-won physically, economically, and socially. Authority and cultural competence are not something an indigenous artist has, just because many Americans happen to buy and read their books or enjoy their paintings. If they have a special standing in their own communities, it has little if anything to do with the talents acclaimed by Euro-Americans. Charles Loloma and Fred Kabotie, both world famous Hopi artists, were respected by other Hopis because of their clan and sodality standing and not necessarily because of their artistic talents (which, by the way, often got them into more trouble than not). As the Vietnamese feminist Trinh T. Minh-ha complained:

Commitment as an ideal is particularly dear to Third World writers. It helps to alleviate the Guilt: that of being privileged (Inequality), of "going over the hill" to join the clan of literates (Assimilation), and of indulging in a "useless" activity while most community members "stoop over the tomato fields, bending under the hot sun" (a perpetuation of the same privilege). (Trinh 1989, 10)

The Problem of Representation

If our discipline is truly international, then our dialogue must be so, too. I do not claim, with Said, that it is necessary to break up, dissolve, and reconceive "the unitary field ruled hitherto by Orientalism, historicism, and what could be called essentialist universalism" (1985, 23). Rather, I think that much less ambitious goals, pursued with old-fashioned courtesy and openness, will suffice.

Years ago, I believed that if our science could liberate itself from its andro/eurocentrism, then perhaps we would find ourselves in a truly unique situation in the history of the West, where we would be able to transcend the limits of our epistemology through a truly global dialogue. The application of this idea is practiced by only a few.

Feminists and others engaged in gender studies have attempted to break out of the confines of our epistemology, and they have helped to raise cultural and religious studies to a more competent level. But their struggles with the scientific assumptions of our times are still going on. The same thing can be said about most African and American Indian writers and scholars who have not, as yet, departed from Western paradigms. My point is that where we might expect to find significant advances in departures from Western assumptions, we find, instead, people engaged in the same struggles as the more reflective andro/eurocentrics among us.

As James Clifford wrote in his sympathetically critical review of Edward Said's book *Orientalism* (1978), Said seems to support the ideals of comparative humanists:

But the privilege of standing above cultural particularism, of aspiring to the universalist power that speaks for humanity, for the universal experiences of love, work, death, and so on, is a privilege invented by a totalizing Western liberalism. This benevolent comprehension of the visions

produced by mere "local anecdotal circumstances" is an authority that es-
capes Said's criticism. (Clifford 1988, 263)

Furthermore, Clifford argued that Said failed to question "anthropological orthodoxies based on a mythology of fieldwork encounter and a
hermeneutically minded cultural theory" (267). Clifford wished to go
further by avoiding all essentializing modes of thought and to perceive
cultures not as "organically unified or traditionally continuous but rather
as negotiated, present processes" (273). Clifford asked how we can avoid
the dichotomizations produced by Orientalism without falling into its
opposite, "Occidentalism." He argued that it cannot be done by resorting
to alternate totalities such as "humanist cosmopolitanism" (as Said argued) or "conceptions of personal integrity" (as I have argued: A. Geertz
1991b).

Stephen A. Tyler (1978; 1987) has addressed this problem in his attempts to provide a postmodern orientation to anthropology. Tyler calls
for the complete abandonment of representation (1987, 207) in order to
reach what I would characterize as "a cognitive utopia," consisting of an
"author-text-reader" construction in a kind of "emergent mind which has
no individual locus" (209). But I do not believe in this utopia! Anyway,
my ambitions are more humble. I simply want to point out that writing
bears with it certain consequences, which have little to do with reader or
writer, yet which affect the perception of the topic that is ostensibly being
textualized.

For instance, in looking through versions of the Hopi paramount
myth, called the Emergence Myth, one is left on the surface with an impression of continuity, historical rightness, and existential truth. Such is
the impression that the judicial use of rhetorical devices is meant to im-
part. However, a closer comparative look at the texts reveals fragmenta-
tion, historical contingency, chance encounters with chance audiences,
and the direct manipulation of purportedly revealed truths.

In dealing with these texts, many of the answers to the questions we
might raise are not to be found in the texts themselves but in the emergent and cooperative nature of textualization, where rhetorical devices
define historical realities. Our job must be to pursue an interpretive description of both the text and the realities of which the text is a product.

A recent critic of the so-called dialogical and discursive strategies,
philosopher Paul Roth (1989) argued that critiques of ethnographic
rhetoric confuse literary, epistemological, and political issues. Roth

claimed that "stylized self-reflection no more guarantees authenticity than does a pose of detachment" (560). The discursive paradigm helps secure representativeness in a political sense but does not necessarily secure methodological fruitfulness or desirability. Furthermore, Roth argued, a sophisticated literary analysis of voice does not solve the ordinary questions of method, in other words, of validity, warrant, and proof. Clifford (1989, 561–63) retorted that arguments about validity, warrant, and proof are historically and politically conditioned, and Stephen Tyler (1989, 566) asked how we can find any representation that is not already an epistemology of representation—an "epistopolitics."

A way out of the Orientalism trap may very well be the one offered by Clifford (1989, 562)—namely, that the dialogical approach decenters the self and focuses "neither on the (intimate) self nor on the (distanced) other but on the historically and politically constituted field of relationships *between* (and constituting) self and other."

A Solution?

I have found no foolproof answer to this dilemma, which I believe lies at the very core of every comparative, cross-cultural pursuit. Nevertheless, I think that we should pursue the same kind of reflection as our anthropological colleagues are doing, and I suggest, at the very least, that an academic dialogue with our Other is absolutely essential if for no other reason than to clarify exactly what we are doing. Furthermore, if we wish to differentiate our activities from those of tourists, we need to emphasize a heightened sense of the political.[3] Or, as P. Steven Sangren (1988, 405) termed it, we need to employ a "totalizing" theoretical stance that "locates the logic and reproduction of power and authority in society as a whole—including academic institutions—rather than in texts alone."

The ethnohermeneutic approach that I have tried to promote (A. Geertz 1990a; 1990b; 1992/94; 1997; 1999) pays attention to theories and models proposed by both scholars and native thinkers, while at the same time applying control measures against loyalistic misperceptions and errors of hasty judgment on both sides of the issues. Ethnohermeneutics combines indigenous hermeneutics with our own. It aspires to an Archimedean platform located somewhere in between—or at least somewhere else. In other words, it attempts to locate both scholar and consultant in each of their own web of texts, traditions, meanings, and social

234 ARMIN W. GEERTZ

and intellectual circumstances, analyzing each other's blind spots in mutual criticism, and somehow trying to transcend local epistemologies in the pursuit of adequate theories about human social intercourse. The platform I am referring to has been named by the Sudanese scholar Abdelwahab El-Affendi (1991) as "agnostic pluralism." He notes that somehow our pragmatic, agnostic search for ever more information on the exotic has led us to the possibility of approaching a degree of accuracy and therefore the further possibility of the multicultural application of such an endeavor. He claims that criticizing Western representatives for their parochialism and partisanship implies that they have the capacity to be otherwise. He accepts the fact that Western tradition has the capacity to attain this kind of platform, but he personally rejects that platform for his own religious one.

According to Anindita Balslev (1991), intercultural understanding consists of two types of intellectual activity. The first is one of deconstruction and the second is constructive. In the question of the power politics of knowledge, it must be our goal to promote self-criticism and free ourselves from the indoctrinations of our training. We must also deconstruct the stereotypical dichotomies of contrasting "Eastern" and "Western" thought traditions, underplay the superficial attraction to the exotic (since imaginary differences have often been the breeding grounds of tragic hostilities), and point out which descriptions of Self and the Other are no more useful for present-day experience. On the constructive side, we must consider the difference between "insider" and "outsider" interpretations, while insisting that this distinction is not equivalent to "authentic" and "inauthentic" interpretations. We must find devices to make us familiar with each others' traditions and promote authentic understanding based on information—understood here as "an honest and genuine effort to acquaint ourselves with the central and the sub-plots of the story of those whom we seek to comprehend" (Balslev 1991, 60). Then we must introduce such information at the most basic levels of our educational institutions and continue the intellectual struggle to "redefine, redescribe human relationships in this narrative of progress and power-sharing" (69–70). In our search for alternative agendas, non-Western utopias cannot be ignored.[4]

Still, we must recognize that our pursuit is essentially ambiguous and antagonistic to religion. Even in the most Arcadian, Eliadean approach, the student of religion promotes conclusions and points of view with which specific religious people would disagree, sometimes violently so.

The comparative approach itself cannot accept information based on religious authority alone. Thus, it constitutes a threat to claims of absolute, universal authority to which most religions make claim.

Is this wrong? I think not. My attempt to move the locus of the conversation does not mean that the locus and whole reason for study should now be entirely in the hands of those we study. In giving up our independence, we would lose too much. Cooperation between scholar and priest is necessary and useful, but their interests in the cooperation—as with their separate worlds—are often radically different.

Conclusion

Yet, the people under study do not always perceive our work negatively. Many religious people actually accept the need for a non-confessional, impartial study of religion. Religions that have experienced persecution due to hostile propaganda, like many of the new religions and spiritual movements, find the humanistic study of religion a welcomed and needed relief. Many people in more traditional "mainstream" religions also understand the need for a study of religion. Furthermore, in a more global perspective, the study of religion is appreciated in other pluralistic societies, such as in Africa, India, and Asia. I make no claims of having solved the issues raised in my essay. I do claim, however, that a more human-oriented study of religion, when conducted wherever possible in cooperation with the humans under study, will go a long way to help solve not only some of our methodological dilemmas but also our ethical ones. Even in the midst of our lost innocence, we must carry on the job of recapturing the study of religion. Like our anthropological colleagues faced with the same challenge, we must truly globalize our discipline and rework our concepts and methods in response to the pressing demands of an intercultural world.

NOTES

A previous version of this essay appeared as two articles in a special issue of *Religion: An International Journal* on the theme "As the Other Sees Us: A Conversation on the Postmodern Study of Religion" (January 1994, vol. 24, no. 1). See A. Geertz (1994b; 1994c). Used by permission.

1. A. Geertz (1992/94). For my work on the Hopi, see also A. Geertz (1987a; 1987b; 1989; 1990a; 1990c; 1991a; 1996).

2. I have also dealt with these issues in A. Geertz (1991b).

3. Errington and Gewertz (1989). See also criticisms by van den Berghe (1980) and Crick (1985).

4. We may also need to reassess, among other things, our concept of rationality. See Jensen and Martin (1997), Lloyd (1990), Overing (1985), and Tambiah (1990).

Chapter 18

On the Epistemology of Post-Colonial Ethnography

James V. Spickard

Ethnography has long been enmeshed in colonial power-relations.[1] Though there have been traveler's accounts of far-off lands at least since Herodotus, ethnographic anthropology traces its rise to the end of the nineteenth century, when, after decades of colonial expansion, imperial bureaucrats needed to understand the peoples they now ruled. The problem was one of control: Western armies had conquered the world but had not been able to pacify its populace. The British Foreign Office hoped to get natives to stop fighting and pay taxes, while the American Bureau of Indian Affairs hoped to turn tribes into family farmers. French and Russian officials had similar agendas. Rulers needed data, so they hired ethnographers to record their subjects' folkways, mores, and customs, as well as their political structures, material accomplishments, and worldviews. They hoped—correctly—that such "power/knowledge" (Foucault 1980) would help Europe dominate the world.

Understanding native politics and motives made such domination easier. E. E. Evans-Pritchard (1940; 1956)—on everyone's short list of great ethnographers—studied the Nuer in part to find out how authority works in a society with no apparent political structure. Though not himself interested in ruling, he applied what he learned to organizing native raids on the Italians during World War II (C. Geertz 1988). Such practical ethnography helped Britain govern the south Sudan while it kept the other Great Powers at bay.

Not all early ethnographers served their governments. Frank Cushing (1990) is remembered as an "ethnographer gone native," in part because he refused to report his Zuni secrets to his sponsor, the Bureau of Indian Affairs. Introductory anthropology textbooks still treat him as a traitor to science, while recognizing his ethnographic expertise. Did he abandon science or was he merely more conscious than most ethnographers of the imperial uses to which his reports might be put? One can make sense of his reputation only in the context of a push for colonial control.

Sociological ethnography, despite a different origin, has a similar political birthright. Refined at the University of Chicago in the 1920s, it grew out of a concern for social problems. Unlike colonial anthropology, its main issue was not rule but assimilation: How could the "socially disadvantaged" be integrated into middle-class American society? William F. Whyte's *Street-Corner Society* (1943) was an excellent example of such ethnography, set in motion by a wish to help poor immigrants and guided by the sense that the first step in helping them was to know them. Later descriptions of poor Blacks, homeless families, and other social outsiders opened such lives to middle-class readers and built support for ameliorative social programs (Liebow 1967; Kotlowitz 1991). These sociologically informed ethnographies encouraged the notion that given the right environment and support, the "disadvantaged" would become "just like us."

Fewer sociologists have portrayed the rich and well positioned, except insofar as they appear in cities and towns studied as wholes (e.g. Dollard 1937; Warner et al. 1963). Those who do—William Domhoff's (1974) depiction of San Francisco's Bohemian Club comes to mind—seem driven by a wish to expose upper-class power or make us see the unusualness of upper-class lives. Like the desire to aid the unfortunate, this, too, grows from the American middle-class belief that everyone should be alike. But more sociological ethnographies make the lives of the poor seem familiar more than they make the lives of the rich seem strange.

In a sense, such anthropological and sociological ethnographies are just two different ways of presenting "the Other." Anthropological "Others" have traditionally lived in far-off places and been seen either as restless natives or as exotic relics that need preserving. So we control them or protect them, keeping them at arm's length because they are not "Us." Sociological "Others," on the contrary, are potential friends and neighbors. We get to know them in order to change them—to make them copies of ourselves. Thus, there is a connection between sociological ethnography and social work—both born at the University of Chicago: a little wealth and education, a better accent, a few more middle-class values, perhaps a little soap behind the ears; what sociological ethnography of poor folk does not recommend, at least unconsciously, such cures for social ills?

Such ethnography gave us, until recently, a choice between social uplift and intellectual zoology—not conscious, mind you, but lying just beneath the surface. Both are colonial relics: once the machinery and now the detritus of empire.

This is not to say that sociological ethnographers intend to patronize their informants, any more than anthropological ethnographers intend to betray them. It is merely to note that ethnography arose in both disciplines within a specific political context. That context harnessed ethnography to colonial ends, often against the wishes of those ethnographers who saw the politics most clearly. Yet traditional ethnographic methods—particularly the canons of professional objectivity and the notion that their scientific training gives ethnographers more insight than other folk—themselves have political implications. As Edward Said (1978) has shown, the idea that Westerners have a responsibility to record and catalog vanishing native customs is inherently imperialistic, for it implies that only the West has "history" and "progress" while everyone else is stuck in "tradition." Westerners justified their rule with the fiction that only they could understand the historical forces to which everyone was subject. "Objective," "scientific" ethnography encouraged this fiction, thus aiding the colonial enterprise. Matters have now changed, at least among anthropologists. The past fifteen years have seen the growth of a new, reflexive, anthropological ethnography, which has rejected its colonialist, museum-oriented roots. Where there was once a single model of ethnographic encounter—visit some exotic peoples, live with them for two years, record their lives, write up the results for the people at home—now there are many. Rather than presenting its results as a series of "facts," the new ethnography speaks of "texts," "discourses," and "narratives." Rather than taking the role of omniscient narrator, it touts "reflexivity," "pluralism," "dialogue." It broods over the impossibility of its knowledge and the inadequacy of its key ideas. Though sociological ethnographies still retain the air of the settlement house, anthropologists now write experimental works in which they appear as prominently—sometimes more prominently—than do the natives.

Take, for example, Kenneth Good's (1996) account of his fieldwork with the Yanomama, in the Venezuelan rainforest. He went to live with them as a graduate student, but stayed for twelve years, not the fifteen months that he had expected. During this time he married a local woman, enmeshing himself in local kin relations and in frequent emotional storms. His honest reporting helps us see the inner side of Yanomama life more clearly than do outsiders' tales. It also shows us the underside of American academic life—its power politics, its egos, and the hard road facing those who do not bend to its rules. It opens questions only hinted at by standard ethnographies: What is fieldwork actually like? How does one negotiate identity across cultures? What kinds of emotional burdens does cross-cultural work make one bear? Such questions, answered with truth, provide a better picture of ethnographic knowledge than does the façade of being an omniscient observer. Good does not give us a standard ethnography, showing the Yanomama as if from afar. He shows us what he really knows, rather than pretending to see it all, uninvolved.

Kevin Dwyer's *Moroccan Dialogues* (1982) recounts the author's conversations with Faqir Muhammad, with whom he lived for eighteen months during his first fieldwork. The project grew from Dwyer's realization that while ethnography takes such conversations as its primary data, they appear in none of its reportorial genres. The personal interaction that creates ethnographic knowledge is somehow supposed to vanish from research reports, sustaining the fiction that the observer knows all. Yet, he argues, one cannot know "the Other" without exposing the Self; Dwyer thus finds it more honest to present himself in dialogue with his informant than to present the latter alone. These are merely two examples, which could be multiplied. Michael Herzfeld (1998) weaves biography and ethnography in his portrayal of the Greek writer Andreas Nenedakis. Pei-Lin Yu (1997) masquerades her ethnography as a travel journal of her two years among the Venezuelan Pumé. Lila Abu-Lughod (1988) and Smadar Lavie (1990) explore poetry in two Arab societies, while appearing in their own texts and reflecting on their own investigatory roles.

Just what is going on here? Various authors have explored this change; many have grasped a part of it.[2] At times literary, at times philosophical, ethnography's recent reflexive turn has a less-noted political side. At its core, it involves a shift of allegiance. Like many intellectual offspring of the 1960s counterculture and anti-war movements, the new ethnographers do not automatically salute the Euro-American intellectual and political establishment. Moreover, they see the complicity of that establishment in the trampling of marginalized lives. From the bombing of Vietnamese and Laotian peasants to development policies that enrich the powerful, they have seen late twentieth-century capitalism's crushing effect on the world's "little people" (Wolf 1982). Not only do many ethnographers now reject this system, but they also reject collaboration with it. To say, with Clifford Geertz (1998, 72), that they now "see poking into the lives of people who are not in a position to poke into yours as something of a colonial relic" is to understate the case. Ethnographers can no longer avoid their predecessors' unintentional imperial complicity; the point, for many, is to find a new, more progressive, role.[3]

Ethnography's crisis of conscience has spawned a crisis of both method and substance. Those rejecting their discipline's closet imperialism have had to find an ethical way to ply their trade. Fortunately, their reflections have profound implications for social science as a whole.

Self, Time, Culture

This volume's preceding chapters wrestle with many issues; chief among them is ethnographic identity. In the colonial era, ethnographers were much like the journalists and tourists of today, though with deeper intellectual pretensions. They were "Civilization's" eyes and ears. They came, they saw, they reported, arm in arm with the conquerors, whose deeds they may have deplored but whose underlying missions they bolstered. They, too, fed our demand for the exotic, whether as noble savages or as heathen darkness (Douglas 1970). Apostles of the extraordinary, chroniclers of the remarkable, they told us about people in far-off places—and did so with purported scientific accuracy. They saw themselves as "scientists of social life," whose reports alone were the only credible records of other peoples' ways.

Yet—and this is the import of post-colonial anthropology—many ethnographers no longer wish to claim such an identity, for it is bound up with social repression. Ethnographers who do not wish to support imperialism find that they must rethink their role and their relationship with "their" natives. No longer is their task a matter of "us" studying "them"—and then passing on the results of such study to those in command. No longer can ethnographers pretend to be invisible recorders of an objective social world. Instead, they must discover who they are in the ethnographic encounter. The hardest part of the new vision is figuring out where to place themselves in the social picture. Who am I, in this field setting? Who are these "natives"? What is our relationship, and what differentiates my relationship with them from the various journalists, voyeurs, moralists, and others who surround us? How does my role lead to knowledge—or does it even do so? How does it change me? How might I be harming them? Is there any way to be authentic here? These questions are not trivial and confronting them allows ethnographers both to paint a more accurate picture and to oppose repression.

In any event, only fluid boundaries separate ethnographers from other players. As Jim Birckhead (1997), for example, notes, a reporter gave him his first entry into the field and he has often been pumped to return the favor. His "natives" (now his friends) sometimes expect that he will report on them journalistically—the only kind of reportage they understand. But he has qualms about telling tales that might bring them ridicule or harm. Outsiders, on the other hand, often think that ethnographers *are* natives: research on the socially marginal notoriously leads folks to suspect one's loyalty to the normal world (Wagner 1997, 94–6). This is especially true if the "natives" are not easily distinguishable from everyone else and is the case with a White anthropologist investigating White Appalachian churches. Such apparent disloyalty can have consequences: snake handling is illegal in West Virginia, and Birckhead could have been jailed for "encouraging" his informants' unlawful acts.

Formerly, ethnographers avoided such worries by representing the authorities. Having decided that this role made them glorified spies, many have given up that privilege. They may not have gone as far as to *become* natives, as did Frank Cushing, but their loyalties have changed. They no longer automatically reject Cushing's path while affirming Evans-Pritchard's. They find that their identity is not as easy as the textbooks claim.

Identity is not the only issue, however. Ethnographers must also deal with the problem of time. Old-style ethnographies were written in "the ethnographic present"—a tense which portrayed their subjects living changeless lives. This highlighted peoples' cultural rules at the expense of ignoring their histories. As a result, anthropologists missed much. Take two examples, one recent, one classic. Pierre Clastres (1998) portrayed the Guayaki Indians as timeless forest-dwellers, ignoring the fact that they were refugees who had been displaced by the Paraguayan government two years before his visit (C. Geertz 1998). Margaret Mead (1953) recorded the cultural changes between her two visits to Manus Island without seeing how the islanders' experiences in World War II stimulated their latent political discontent and focused it into religious channels

(Worsley 1968). In both cases, the presumption that non-Europeans lack history got in the way of a full understanding (Wolf 1982).

As Renato Rosaldo (1989) notes, this focus on timeless culture will no longer do. Ethnographers now recognize that their encounters are bounded in time—and that the patterns they discover in a given situation may easily change. Few current ethnographers expect to find enduring traditions waiting to be recorded. Instead, they find people wresting with an adventitious present, who call on various traditions to aid their wrestling. Such traditions are reshaped in the act of being used. Rather than static, enduring entities—the "superorganic" toward which Alfred Kroeber (1952) theorized—cultures are constantly being revised and re-created. Ethnographers have gradually learned to be true to their data, rather than reifying it into something supposedly eternal.

To do this, post-colonial ethnographers focus on their encounters. Rather than pretending to be a superior "observer" watching a subordinate "observed," their work is now clearly a meeting that expands both sides. To use a distinction that Birckhead (1997, 24) borrows from Wilma Dykeman, ethnography is not a matter of looking at others but of allowing us to live with them. For what happens when we truly encounter another way of life? As novelists and travelers have long claimed (and as even the classic ethnographers admitted in their private moments), an encounter with others always changes us. We compare our way of seeing with theirs, as they compare theirs with ours; the normal human result of such conversations is that both sides grow.

As we watch others impose meanings on their experiences, we come to see how we do the same. As we see them work to justify their worldviews, we realize that we, too, work to justify ours. Our encounters show us that neither they nor we are privileged, for our own ideas are as poorly or as strongly grounded as theirs. For all our pretensions to science, nothing much separates us from our informants. They take up serpents to test their faith; we test ours by adhering to supposedly "objective" methods. Both of us seek salvation, as we understand it. This point of view places ethnography squarely among the humanities—as a path of knowledge that seeks to understand people rather than to explain them (Dilthey 1883).

Such humanism is inherent in the stream of ethnographic writing spurred by Clifford Geertz's pathbreaking *Interpretation of Cultures* (1973a). To this way of thinking, ethnography is not as much a path to knowledge but a way to transform our own civilization through cross-cultural encounter. Recent critics have in one sense merely separated this

Habermasian "human interest" (Habermas 1968) from the scientism of their predecessors. They have shown how science and imperialism have gone hand in hand, stifling those lives that ethnographers struggled to record. Clifford Geertz (1998), himself, worries about what is lost with this separation, for anthropology is, to him, a dual enterprise: both science and humanity intimately, if contradictorily, bound. His intellectual descendants see the contradictions more than the intimacy, and so are willing to let detached description go.

Epistemology and Its Regulative Ideals

There is an epistemological point to all this, as there often is when science and the humanities square off. Ethnography has long seen itself as scientific, yet one of science's chief raisons d'être is that it is more objective than the humanities—that it provides surer knowledge. Can ethnography sustain this claim any longer, especially after so many ethnographers have put objectivity in question? Is not one of the hallmarks of post-colonial ethnography its choice for "deep hanging-out" and "lucid uncertainty" (Clifford 1997b) over any pretense of knowing the people that it supposedly studies? This is one of ethnography's finest contributions: the recognition that ethnographic knowledge, too, is socially generated; that our ideas are no more firmly grounded than are those of the natives we encounter (Douglas 1975, xi–xviii). If this is true, if ethnographic knowledge is inevitably partial, how is it possible to build a science on such sand?

To understand how, we need to revisit the notion of "ethnographic truth." Is there such a thing? Has post-colonial ethnography so relativized "truth" that anything goes?

Truth

Let us first dispose of the notion that any science gives us "true" knowledge of its subject matter. Since Peirce (1877), most philosophers have been clear that truth is available only eschatologically. That is, truth is unobtainable by mere mortals, who can at best work toward it. A scientific community accumulates wisdom by collecting the experiences of its members, then using these experiences to revise their theories. Though no straight-line matter, this continual course-correction should—in the end—move the community toward a "true" account of the-way-things-are.[4] But it can never claim to have arrived at a "final truth," for such a claim would require omniscience—precisely what we, as humans, lack. Unlike communities that anchor truth in the past or in some a priori revelation, the scientific community corrects its mistakes by systematically revising its beliefs in the light of experience—a process that, in the mortal world, never ends.

Yet, just as the calculus can speak of a curve approaching a limit, so in science one can speak of the limit of a line of inquiry. For Peirce,

> truth is that concordance of abstract statement with the ideal limit towards which endless investigation would tend to bring scientific belief. (Quoted in Feibelman 1969, 212)

We can never reach that limit—at least we can never know that we have done so—but its existence as a goal guides our efforts to achieve it. The very act of trying to do so, of directing our work as if truth were within reach, moves the scientific community forward.

"Truth" stands here as a regulative ideal, a concept that, though itself epistemologically insecure, makes science possible. Kant (1781) argued that the idea of "God" so regulates morality: one cannot demonstrate God's existence, but some faith in a supreme power is needed in order to have a moral life. In Kant's vision, all practical thought requires regulation, much as a motor needs a governor to do useful work. Though one cannot deduce the aptness of such a regulator a priori, one can judge that aptness by the results obtained. When scientists speak of "truth," they state their faith that—given limitless time, through rigorous analysis, doubt, intelligence, and careful listening to experience—humans will be able to understand the world. Without some such belief, inquiry would proceed aimlessly and without rudder. With it, the scientific community has steerage. Not that it can ever prove its theories right—Peirce (1955) and Popper (1932) agree on the epistemological impossibility of that!—but it can at least prove some theories wrong. That itself constitutes scientific progress, and "truth" is the mental ideal that makes such progress possible.

It is not hard to fit post-colonial anthropological ethnography into this picture. Its practitioners do not merely think that colonial ethnography is outmoded; they think that it is wrong. Societies are not timeless, so ignoring their history distorts them fundamentally (Rosaldo 1989). Culture does not consist of a set of impersonal rules directing human action;

instead, it consists of resources for action, subject to human choice and will (Douglas 1979). Colonial power relations are not external to so-called primitive societies; they construct those societies and so must be central to ethnography rather than peripheral to it (Wolf 1982). These and other issues separate post-colonial ethnographers from their predecessors and lead them to claim to portray more truly the people about whom they write. "Truth" here continues to regulate inquiry.

Were it to cease doing so—were "beauty," "the market," or "careerism" (to mention just three other options) to replace "truth" as the ideal guiding the ethnographic community—then ethnography would cease being a science. Ethnographers would choose gorgeous over accurate prose, salable over uncomfortable insights, or the professionally useful book over the scholarly one. Though individual ethnographers may have chosen such ideals, the community of ethnographers has not done so. Ethnography remains scientific to the degree that it still tries accurately to understand—and portray—the people it investigates.

Equality

Yet, truth is only one of the ideals that regulate post-colonial ethnography; there is a political ideal as well. This second regulative ideal is "equality": the presumption that ethnographers are not superior to those whose lives they view, and that their "advanced" societies are not superior to the less well-off. This ideal tells us that ethnographers and natives are in the same boat, metaphysically and epistemologically speaking. Metaphysically, "equality" claims that neither ethnographers nor natives have higher worth. Judging worth is a cultural matter, for which each social group has its own criteria; yet, all such criteria are themselves supported by group practices, so the judgments are circular.[5] Old-style ethnographers often absorbed the judgments of their time, which placed less-powerful "Others" lower on the evolutionary or economic scale. Post-colonial ethnographers show that such scales are cultural artifacts, designed to favor one's own side, and are thus not valid. In fact, no such ranking scale is valid, for all are products of limited value-systems. It is but a small step from this denial of differential worth to a presumption of social equality—though this step is an indemonstrable act of faith. Ethnography has long overtly claimed this faith, embodied in its taboo against ethnocentrism; post-colonial ethnographers aver merely to be more consistent than their predecessors, though this consistency also makes them more "right" in their tradition's eyes.

The epistemological argument is similar. Barring omniscience, no cultural group has a confirmably better knowledge of the universe than does any other—in the abstract. Though one group may legitimately claim to know more *for particular purposes* than another, it cannot claim these purposes to be intrinsically more important. To use an old comparison, science knows much about the empirical universe, because it equates "knowledge" with the empirically testable, while Christianity knows much about the soul, because it equates "knowledge" with what brings souls to salvation. Both stumble when they trespass on the other's domain, if only because each interprets the other's domain in its own terms. What any group counts as "knowledge" is thus as much a social product as are its judgments of worth, so deciding securely between rival claimants is not a human option.[6] Ethnographers cannot allege that they know more than natives, though they can claim to know differently. Here, too, equality is a matter of faith, for a proof would depend on an omniscience that cannot be. At most, we can say that all societies are equal in their not-knowing. All claims to valid knowledge are equally insecure.

What happens to the ethnographic method when ethnographers assume metaphysical and epistemological equality with their informants?

To begin, ethnographers can no longer take the role of educated outsiders, come to help natives sort out their conceptual affairs. No more can they speak with the imperial voice: "You think you are testing your faith with snakes, but actually you are displaying your manhood"; "You think you are honoring your ancestors, but actually you are reaffirming your kin ties." Post-colonial ethnography bans the missionary position and its presumption of native ignorance. More precisely, equality demands that native interpretations of *our* beliefs be given as much weight as our interpretations of theirs. This changes ethnographic practice. If we are no longer imposing interpretations, but trading them, we begin to converse with our informants. In fact, ethnographers have always done so, but they have traditionally seen these conversations as means to an end: Our capture of Their worldview. Presuming equality means that we can no longer present just one side of the conversation; we must present both. Our dialogues become the subject of ethnography, not its means, and ethnography becomes personal: a matter of a cross-cultural encounter rather than a one-way view.

In consequence, ethnographic reports have changed. Their old rhetorical form—"here are the people and this is their way of life"—hid both the natives' and the ethnographer's subjectivity. Now that form has shifted. Ethnographic writing has become personal, not because it has ceased trying to understand others, but because ethnographers have discovered that only personal writing can fully portray their encounters. What appears to be a retreat from science is actually a sign of increased commitment to it. Post-colonial ethnographers are no longer satisfied with their predecessors' shortcuts, as they seek a truer picture of their informants' lives.

Granted that post-colonial ethnographers value equality; and granted that this commitment has changed the way that they practice their craft. What makes "equality" a regulative ideal rather than just a sign of political allegiance? That is, what makes it scientific rather than partisan? For equality is not demonstrable: one cannot prove that people are equal any more than one can prove the existence of God. What makes this ideal universal rather than parochial?

The issue, at bottom, is the fear of bias. Ethnographers have long discouraged "going native," not just because doing so betrayed the discipline's imperial support, but also because they believed that only outsiders had the perspective to see things clearly. One should learn the natives' worldview, but not accept its values if one wants to get things right. Similarly, ethnographers (and others) sought to bar extraneous values from their investigations, believing that only "value-freedom" guarantees truth. (The *MAD Magazine* story in which the Marxist surgeon decides to "liberate" an infected appendix from its "oppression" by the intestine—by removing the intestine!—illustrates the supposed dangers that value-laden science poses.) Yet, the alternative to the long view is not the close view, and the alternative to "value-freedom" is not bias. Midway between long and close views is the dialogue—the core of the post-colonial encounter. Post-colonial ethnographers are committed to that dialogue because they believe that it presents a truer picture of their informants than do more "objective" measures. This picture remains ethnography's goal. But dialogue depends on values, among them a commitment to equality with former colonial subjects. Dialogue is hard enough anyway; if one does not enter it with the right attitude, it will not take place. Even to have a dialogue, one must be willing to encounter others, to listen and be listened to. One must bring oneself to that dialogue, values and all—for that is what one is asking of one's respondent. Above all, one must be willing to change: one's values, one's mind, one's life.

Not every discipline needs this engagement. Generalizing science does not, because it does not treat individual lives. But ethnography does because its prime task involves those lives' representation. Dialogue makes such representation possible, and it can only happen when ethnographers treat their subjects as equals. Post-colonial ethnography is dedicated to the proposition that the growth of knowledge is not just a matter of accumulating facts, though that helps. It is real dialogue with others that opens our society to their ways of seeing, which in turn change and enrich us.

The commitment to equality is not partisan precisely because it, alone, allows ethnography to fulfill its mission. Imagine, for a moment, an ethnographer committed to equality studying the American ruling class. Would she intentionally distort her informants' meanings in order to support her own views? Would he impose his own concepts on these informants' world, suppressing their own? To do so would be to violate her or his own ideals—as much in boardrooms as in the poorest barrios or the wildest forest. It would violate the principle of equality between ethnographer and informant and would undercut ethnography's chief intention: of presenting an honest portrayal of others' lives.

This is a rather specific human interest, in Habermas's (1968) sense of that term. It comes *from* a value-stance, for its faith is a radical faith in Western universalism: not the belief that the West *is* universal, but the faith that humans can approach the universal by transcending their limited visions through dialogue with everyone. But it is not limited *to* that value-stance, for its goal is the accurate representation of others' lives. Post-colonial ethnography claims that its predecessors' unwillingness to embrace equality blinded them to their own values and closed them to real dialogue; thus, they missed much of what they could have learned.

Ethnography's Hidden Politics

To this way of seeing, all ethnography is political—in both its colonial and its post-colonial versions. The former supports colonial power-relations; the latter undercuts them—and does so at the level of its regulative ideals. Post-colonial anthropological ethnographers once served the Empire, but they do so no longer. Sociological ethnographers, for the most part, still serve the middle class.

All such service is political, in the sense that its commitments contain an implicit vision of public life. The choice is not just between empire and democracy, for plebiscitary democracy can be as unequal as dictatorship, albeit with velvet gloves. A commitment to equality implies support for what Arnold Mindell (1995) calls "deep democracy"—a regime in which every voice is heard and valued. Is this not what post-colonial ethnographers do: give voice to those with few means to speak? Is it not their task to help us understand deeply their informants' lives? This intention, systematically and universally applied, would give everyone a voice, placing all on an equal footing—a revolutionary political vision. Though not explicit for most post-colonial ethnographers, some such vision is implicit in the ideals regulating their work.

The effect of reading (and doing) post-colonial ethnography is the realization that we are one human family, not divided into "masters" and "slaves." We are all human, with different blindnesses and strengths, but we live under a regime that arbitrarily crushes some people and arbitrarily elevates others. Ethnographies that presume that all people are equal undercut the legitimacy of this regime by undercutting the inequality on which it is based. Science thus supports a liberatory vision of social development.[7]

Like "truth," "equality" is a special kind of ideal: one that pushes its holders out of their complacence. Commitment to neither value adds to people's biases; quite the contrary, such commitments demand that they give them up. This, to be sure, is a very Western value. The West, for good or ill, has sought to understand the rest of the world—an activity that post-colonial ethnographers hope to salvage from its longtime intellectual companion: the wish to dominate it.

Yet, revolt against our own society's imperial intentions is only half the issue. Is not this push for equality, in itself, a form of Western imperialism? Does it not erode traditional Chinese authorities, for example, as much as Western ones (De Bary and Tu 1998)? Or undermine Pueblo Indian efforts to use secret knowledge to protect themselves against Western conquest (Fulbright 1994)? Why should ethnographers expect the members of other societies to value—or participate in—activities that change their ways? The honest answer is that we cannot. Post-colonial ethnography erodes all systems of rank, the Rest with the West. It is foolish to think that everyone will cooperate. The post-colonial commitment to equality may well limit ethnographers' access to ranked locales.

To this, one can only say, "So be it." Imperial ethnography tried to overcome native resistance by force and became part of the colonial enterprise. Post-colonial ethnographers have renounced force and so must accept that there are things that they will not learn. Dialogue can only reach those who are willing to talk, and that does not include everyone.

The truth, though, is that force would not open these mouths, anyway. And insisting that ethnographers live out their commitment to "equality" brings us a truer picture of those natives who will talk to them than we ever had before.

In fact, that is the beauty of regulative ideals. Though apparently limiting scientific inquiry, they actually deepen it. A commitment to "truth" enables science to understand the world more completely; a commitment to "equality" empowers ethnographers to take their subjects more seriously. Just as Kant's ideal of "God" steered him toward a universal, not a limited morality, so these ideals steer us toward a broader, not a limited science. It remains a particularizing science—one that seeks truth in the particulars of life and presumes human equality as the way to reach it. Value-laden it is, but science precisely because of it.

NOTES

1. Some of the ideas in this chapter appeared as "Disciplinary conflicts in the study of religions: Anthropology, sociology, and 'lines in the sand.'" *Method and Theory in the Study of Religion*, volume 13, issue 4, 2001. Reprinted by permission of Brill Academic Publishers.

2. See, inter alia: Clifford (1988); Fox (1991); C. Geertz (1998); Gupta and Ferguson (1997); Marcus and Fischer (1986); Rosaldo (1989).

3. Gavin Smith (1999) provides one model of such engagement. Though the bulk of his book is abstract, he provides a moving description of the events that led him to his political commitments.

4. Thomas Kuhn (1970) puts forth a compatible image of science, though without Peirce's residual positivist optimism. Kuhn's (1977) insistence that experience matters, however, aligns him with Peirce against those who treat scientific knowledge as a pure social construction.

5. This is even true of "reasoned" judgments, on two counts. First, only some societies defer to reason, so claims for its superiority presume those society's values—which they were supposed to prove. Second, even those who salute reason cannot agree about what they find "reasonable." Each social group constructs "reason" in its own image, beyond which none can appeal. Such are the consequences of human cognitive limitation (See, inter alia, Hollis and Lukes 1982; Horton and Finnegan 1973; S. Brown 1979).

6. This, too, is true of philosophers, who often forget that they are as much a society as any "primitive" tribe. They have their rules of evidence, argument, and proof, which they enforce with much the same techniques as do other groups. Given their premises, they are right to do so—but one does not have to grant

those premises! Peter Winch (1958) was surely right in noting that philosophy and Azande witchcraft are both equally suited to their aims, though those aims differ so much that neither can be aptly applied to the other's sphere.

7. Feminism has long acknowledged the legitimacy of politically engaged scholarship, though in a somewhat different mode. For some comments on feminist methodology, see Reinharz (1992) and Neitz (1993; 1995).

References

Abu-Lughod, Lila. 1988. *Veiled Sentiments: Honor and Poetry in a Bedouin Society*. Berkeley: University of California Press.

Adams, Barbara. 1994. "Running Out of Time: Global Crises and Human Engagement." Pp. 92–112 in *Social Theory and the Global Environment*, edited by Michael Redclift and Ted Benton. London and New York: Routledge.

Agar, Michael. 1980. "Hermeneutics in Anthropology: A Review Essay." *Ethos* 8(3): 253–72.

Aho, James A. 1990. *The Politics of Righteousness: Idaho Christian Patriotism*. Seattle: University of Washington Press.

———. 1994. *This Thing of Darkness: A Sociology of the Enemy*. Seattle: University of Washington Press.

———. 1997. "The Apocalypse of Modernity." Pp. 61–72 in *Millennium, Messiahs, and Mayhem: Contemporary Apocalyptic Movements*, edited by Thomas Robbins and Susan J. Palmer. New York: Routledge.

Albanese, Catherine L. 1990. *Nature Religion in America: From the Algonkian Indians to the New Age*. Chicago: University of Chicago Press.

Allen, Robert. 1987. "Reader-Oriented Criticism and Television." Pp. 74–112 in *Channels of Discourse: Television and Contemporary Criticism*, edited by Robert Allen. Chapel Hill: University of North Carolina Press.

Ammerman, Nancy Tatom. 1987. *Bible Believers: Fundamentalists in the Modern World*. New Brunswick, NJ: Rutgers University Press.

Anderson, Benedict. 1991. *Imagined Communities: Reflections on the Origins and Spread of Nationalism*. 2nd expanded ed. London: Verso.

Anderson, Kathryn, Susan Armitage, Dana Jack, and Judith G. Wittner 1987. "Beginning Where We Are: Feminist Methodology in Oral History." *Oral History Review* 15:103–27.

Ardener, Edwin. 1972. "Belief and the Problem of Women." Pp. 135–58 in *The Interpretation of Ritual: Essays in Honour of A.I. Richards*, edited by J. S. LaFontaine. London: Tavistock.

Asad, Talal, ed. 1973. *Anthropology and the Colonial Encounter*. London: Ithaca Press.

Asch, Patsy. 2000. "Enough Time to Wonder." Unpublished manuscript.

Balslev, Anindita Niyogi. 1991. *Cultural Otherness: Correspondence with Richard Rorty*. Shimla: Indian Institute of Advanced Study.

Bauer, Paul F. 1976. "The Homosexual Subculture at Worship: A Participant Observation Study." *Pastoral Psychology* 25(2): 115–27.

Beck, Ulrich. 1992. *Ecological Politics in an Age of Risk*. Cambridge: Polity Press.

Becker, Howard S. 1967. "Whose Side Are We on?" *Social Problems* 14:239–47.

———. 1986. *Writing for Social Scientists: How to Start and Finish Your Thesis, Book, or Article*. Chicago: University of Chicago Press.

Becker, Penny Edgell and Nancy L. Eiesland. 1997. *Contemporary American Religion: An Ethnographic Reader*. Walnut Creek, CA: AltaMira Press.

Behar, Ruth. 1996. *The Vulnerable Observer: Anthropology That Breaks Your Heart*. Boston: Beacon Press.

Behar, Ruth and Deborah Gordon, eds. 1995. *Women Writing Culture*. Berkeley: University of California Press.

Bellah, Robert N. 1970. "Religious Evolution." Pp. 20–50 in *Beyond Belief: Essays on Religion in a Post-Traditional World*. New York: Harper & Row.

Bendroth, Margaret Lamberts. 1993. *Fundamentalism and Gender, 1875 to the Present*. New Haven: Yale University Press.

Bennett, Susan. 1998. *Theatre Audiences: A Theory of Production and Reception*. New York and London: Routledge.

Berger, Helen. 1998. "The Earth is Sacred: Ecological Concerns in America Wicca." Pp. 213–20 in *Religion in a Changing World: Comparative Studies in Sociology*, edited by Madeline Cousineau. Westport, CT: Praeger.

Beyer, Peter. 1994. *Religion and Globalization*. London: Sage Publications.

Birckhead, Jim. 1976. "Toward the Creation of a Community of Saints." Ph.D. diss. University of Alberta, Canada.

———. 1993. "'Bizarre Snakehandlers'—Popular Media and a Southern Stereotype." Pp. 163–89 in *Images of the South: Constructing a Regional Stereotype on Film and Video*, edited by Karl G. Heider. Athens: University of Georgia Press.

———. 1996. "Snake Handlers—Heritage, Salvation, and Celebrity in the '90s." *Appalachian Journal* 23(3): 260–74.

———. 1997. "Reading 'Snake Handling': Critical Reflections." Pp. 19–84 in *Anthropology of Religion: A Handbook*, edited by Stephen D. Glazier. Westport, CT: Greenwood Press.

———. 2000. "'And I Can't Feel At Home in This World Anymore'—Experiencing Serpent Handling: From 'Snake Hollow' to Ruby Wax, and the 'X-Files'." Australian Anthropological Society Annual Conference. Perth, Australia, September 21–23.

———. 2001. "Monitored Lives: Writing Indigenous Land Management and the State (Part One)." *Practicing Anthropology* 23(1): 32–35.

Bissinger, Buzz. 1998. "Shattered Glass." *Vanity Fair*, September, 176–90.

Bloch, Jon P. 1998. "Alternative Spirituality and Environmentalism." *Review of Religious Research* 40(1): 55–73.

Bloch, Marc. 1953. *The Historian's Craft*. New York: Vintage Books.

Borofsky, Robert. 2000. "To Laugh or Cry?" *Anthropology News* 41(2): 9–10.

Bourdieu, Pierre. 1977. *Outline of a Theory of Practice*. London: Cambridge University Press.

Bowie, Fiona. 2000. *The Anthropology of Religion*. Oxford: Blackwell.

Brasher, Brenda. 1998. *Godly Women: Fundamentalism and Female Power*. New Brunswick, NJ: Rutgers University Press.

Briggs, Jean L. 1970. *Never in Anger: Portrait of an Eskimo Family*. Cambridge, MA: Harvard University Press.

Brown, David H. 1999. "Altared Spaces: Afro-Cuban Religions and the Urban Landscape in Cuba and the United States." Pp. 155–230 in *The Gods of the City*, edited by Robert Anthony Orsi. Bloomington: Indiana University Press.

Brown, Fred and Jeanne McDonald. 2000. *The Serpent Handlers: Three Families and Their Faith*. Winston-Salem, NC: John F. Blair.

Brown, Karen McCarthy. 1985. "On Feminist Methodology." *Journal of Feminist Studies in Religion* 1:76–79.

———. 1991. *Mama Lola: A Vodou Priestess in Brooklyn*. Berkeley: University of California Press.

———. 1998. "Religion Outside the Institutions." Conference on Religion Outside the Institutions. Center for the Study of American Religion, Princeton, NJ, June 6.

Brown, Michael F. 1997. *Channeling Zone: America Spirituality in an Anxious Age*. Cambridge: Harvard University Press.

Brown, S. C., ed. 1979. *Philosophical Disputes in the Social Sciences*. Sussex, UK: Harvester Press.

Burawoy, Michael, Joshua Gamson, and Alice Burton, eds. 1991. *Ethnography Unbound: Power and Resistance in the Modern Metropolis*. Los Angeles: University of California Press.

Burke, T. Patrick. 1984. "Must the Description of a Religion Be Acceptable to a Believer?" *Religious Studies* 20:631–36.

Butler, Judith. 1993. *Bodies That Matter: On the Discursive Limits of Sex*. New York: Routledge.

Buttel, Fredrick. 1987. "New Directions in Environmental Sociology." *Annual Review of Sociology* 13:465–88.

Canan, Penelope. 1996. "Bringing Nature Back In: The Challenge of Environmental Sociology." *Sociological Inquiry* 66(1): 29–37.

Cantero, Araceli. 2000. "Unidos en la Fé, la Virgen y el Dolor." *La Voz Católica*, September, 12–13.

Carter, Lewis F. 1990. *Charisma and Control in Rajneeshpuram: The Role of Shared Values in the Creation of a Community.* New York: Cambridge University Press.

Catton, W. 1992. "Separation Versus Unification in Sociological Human Ecology." In *Advances in Human Ecology*, vol. 1, edited by L. Freese. Greenwich, CT: JAI Press.

Chagnon, Napoleon. 1968. *Yanomamö: The Fierce People.* New York: Holt, Rinehart and Winston.

Chidester, David and Edward Linenthal. 1995. *American Sacred Space.* Bloomington: Indiana University Press.

Clastres, Pierre. 1998. *Chronicle of the Guayaki Indians.* New York: Zone Books.

Clemmer, Richard O. 1978. *Continuities of Hopi Cultural Change.* Ramona, CA: Acoma Books.

Clifford, James. 1986. "Introduction: Partial Truths." Pp. 1–26 in *Writing Culture: The Poetics and Politics of Ethnography*, edited by James Clifford and George E. Marcus. Berkeley: University of California Press.

———. 1988. *The Predicament of Culture: Twentieth Century Ethnography, Literature, and Art.* Cambridge: Harvard University Press.

———. 1989. "Reply to Roth." *Current Anthropology* 30(5): 561–63.

———. 1997a. "Spatial Practices: Fieldwork, Travel, and the Disciplining of Anthropology." Pp. 185–222 in *Anthropological Locations: Boundaries and Grounds of a Field Science*, edited by Akhil Gupta and James Ferguson. Berkeley: University of California Press.

———. 1997b. *Routes: Travel and Translation in the Late Twentieth Century.* Cambridge, MA: Harvard University Press.

Clifford, James and George E. Marcus, eds. 1986. *Writing Culture: The Poetics and Politics of Ethnography.* Berkeley: University of California Press.

Clough, Patricia. 1998. *End(s) of Ethnography.* rev. ed. New York: Peter Lang.

Coleman, Simon. 1989. "Controversy and the Social Order: Responses to the Religious Group in Sweden." Ph.D. diss. University of Cambridge.

———. 1991. *Livets Ord Och Det Svenska Samhället.* Uppsala: Tro och Tanke.

———. 1996. "Words as Things: Language, Aesthetics and Objectification of Protestant Evangelicalism." *Journal of Material Culture* 1(1): 107–28.

———. 2000. *The Globalization of Charismatic Christianity: Spreading the Gospel of Prosperity.* Cambridge: Cambridge University Press.

Coleman, Simon and Bob Simpson. 1999. "Unintended Consequences? Anthropology, Pedagogy and Personhood." *Anthropology Today* 15(6): 3–6.

Comer, James P. 1988. *Maggie's American Dream: The Life and Times of an American Family.* New York: New American Library.

Cooey, Paula. 1989. "Experience, Body, and Authority." *Harvard Theological Review* 82(3): 325–42.

Cook, Judith and Mary Fonow. 1990. "Knowledge and Women's Interests: Issues of Epistemology and Methodology in Feminist Sociological Research." Pp. 69–93 in *Feminist Research Methods: Exemplary Readings in the Social Sciences*, edited by Joyce M. Nielsen. Boulder, CO: Westview Press.

Cotera, Martha. 1977. *The Chicana Feminist*. Austin, TX: Information Systems Development.

Covington, Dennis. 1995. *Salvation on Sand Mountain: Snake Handling and Redemption in Southern Appalachia*. Reading, MA: Addison-Wesley.

Crapanzano, Vincent. 1992. *Hermes' Dilemma and Hamlet's Desire: On the Epistemology of Interpretation*. Cambridge, MA: Harvard University Press.

Crick, M. 1985. "'Tracing' the Anthropological Self: Quizzical Reflections on Fieldwork, Tourism and the Ludic." *Social Analysis* 17:71–92.

Csordas, Thomas J. 1993. "Somatic Modes of Attention." *Cultural Anthropology* 8:135–56.

———. 1994. *The Sacred Self: A Cultural Phenomenology of Charismatic Healing*. Berkeley: University of California Press.

———. 1997. *Language, Charisma, and Creativity: The Ritual Life of a Religious Movement*. Berkeley: University of California Press.

Cushing, Frank Hamilton. 1990. *Cushing at Zuni: The Correspondence and Journals of Frank Hamilton Cushing, 1879–1884*. Edited by Jesse Green. Albuquerque: University of New Mexico Press.

Dall, Christine. 1989. *Wild Women Don't Have the Blues*. California Newsreel. 58 min.

Daly, Herman E. and John B. Cobb. 1994. *For the Common God*. Boston: Beacon Press.

Daly, Mary. 1978. *Gyn/Ecology: The Metaethics of Radical Feminism*. Boston: Beacon Press.

Dash, Julie, with Toni Cade Bambara and bell hooks. 1992. *Daughters of the Dust: The Making of an African American Woman's Film*. New York: New Press.

Davidman, Lynn. 1991. *Tradition in a Rootless World: Women Turn to Orthodox Judaism*. Berkeley: University of California Press.

———. 2000a. *Motherloss*. Berkeley: University of California Press.

———. 2000b. "Studying Close to Home: The Intersection of Life and Work." *Sociology of Religion* 61(4): 425–32.

Davis, Elizabeth Lindsey. 1933. *Living as They Climb: A History of the National Association of Colored Women*. Washington, DC: Moorland Spingarn Research Center, Howard University.

Davis-Floyd, Robbie and P. S. Arvidson, eds. 1997. *Intuition: The Inside Story*. London: Routledge.

Davis-Floyd, Robbie and Elizabeth Davis. 1997. "Intuition as Authoritative Knowledge in Midwifery and Homebirth." Pp. 145–76 in *Intuition: The Inside Story*, edited by Robbie Davis-Floyd and P.S. Arvidson. London: Routledge.

De Bary, Wm. Theodore and Tu Wei-ming, eds. 1998. *Confucianism and Human Rights*. New York: Columbia University Press.

D'Emilio, John. 1983. *Sexual Politics, Sexual Communities: The Making of a Homosexual Minority in the United States 1940–1970*. Chicago: University of Chicago Press.

Denzin, Norman K. 1997. *Interpretive Ethnography: Ethnographic Practices for the 21st Century*. Thousand Oaks, CA: Sage Publications.

Denzin, Norman K. and Yvonne S. Lincoln, eds. 1994. *Handbook of Qualitative Research*. Thousand Oaks, CA: Sage Publications.

DeVault, Marjorie. 1999. *Liberating Method: Feminism and Social Research*. Philadelphia: Temple University Press.

Dilthey, Wilhelm. 1883. *Introduction to the Human Sciences: An Attempt to Lay a Foundation for the Study of Society and History*. Translated by Ramon J. Betanzos. Detroit: Wayne State University Press, 1988.

Dodson, Jualyne E. 1989. "Class Consciousness and Resistance of Southern African Methodist Episcopal Women." Unpublished manuscript.

Dodson, Jualyne E. and Cheryl Townsend Gilkes. 1986. "Something Within: Social Change and Collective Endurance in the Sacred World of Black Christian Women." *Women and Religion in America* 3:80–128.

Dollard, John. 1937. *Caste and Class in a Southern Town*. New York: Doubleday [1957].

Domhoff, G. William. 1974. *Bohemian Grove and Other Retreats: A Study in Ruling-Class Cohesiveness*. New York: Harper & Row.

Douglas, Mary. 1966. *Purity and Danger: An Analysis of Concepts of Pollution and Taboo*. New York: Praeger.

———. 1970. "Heathen Darkness, Modern Piety." *New Society*, March 12, 432–34.

———. 1975. *Implicit Meanings: Essays in Anthropology*. London: Routledge & Kegan Paul.

———. 1979. "Passive Voice Theories in Religious Sociology." *Review of Religious Research* 21(1): 51–61.

Du Bois, W. E. B. 1924. *The Gift of Black Folk: The Negroes in the Making of America*. Millwood, NY: Kraus-Thompson Organization [1975].

Dumont, Jean-Paul. 1978. *The Headman and I: Ambiguity and Ambivalence in the Fieldworking Experience*. Austin: University of Texas Press.

Dunlap, Riley and Angela Mertig, eds. 1992. *American Environmentalism: The U.S. Environmental Movements, 1970–1990*. New York: Taylor and Francis.

Dunne, Brenda J. 1997. "Subjectivity and Intuition in the Scientific Method." Pp. 121–28 in *Intuition: The Inside Story*, edited by Robbie Davis-Floyd and P. S. Arvidson. London: Routledge.

Dwyer, Kevin. 1982. *Moroccan Dialogues: Anthropology in Question*. Baltimore: Johns Hopkins University Press.

Dylan, Bob. 1965. "It's All Right, Ma (I'm Only Bleeding)." In *Bringing It All Back Home*. New York: Columbia Records.

Eckberg, Douglas Lee and T. Jean Blocker. 1989. "Varieties of Religious Involvement and Environmental Concern: Testing the Lynn White Thesis." *Journal for the Scientific Study of Religion* 28(4): 509–17.

Eckstein, Susan. 1999. "Globalization and Mobilization: Civil Society Resistance to the New World Order." Annual Meeting of the American Sociological Association, Chicago.

Eder, Klaus. 1996. *The Social Construction of Nature: A Sociology of Ecological Enlightenment*. Thousand Oaks, CA: Sage Publications.

Ekman, Ulf. 1985. *Tro Som Övervinner Världen*. Uppsala: Livets Ord.

El-Affendi, Abdelwahab. 1991. "Studying My Movement: Social Science Without Cynicism." *International Journal of Middle East Studies* 23:83–94.

Elkins, James. 1996. *The Object Stares Back: On the Nature of Seeing*. New York: Simon and Schuster.

Erikson, Kai T. 1995. *A New Species of Trouble: The Human Experience of Modern Disasters*. New York: Norton.

Errington, Fredrick and Deborah Gewertz. 1989. "Tourism and Anthropology in a Post-Modern World." *Oceania* 60:37–54.

Esler, Gavin. 1983. "Snakes in Church." *The Listener*, August 18, 2–4.

Evans-Pritchard, Edward E. 1940. *The Nuer*. New York: Oxford University Press, 1969.

———. 1956. *Nuer Religion*. New York: Oxford University Press.

Fabian, Johannes. 1983. *Time and the Other: How Anthropology Makes Its Object*. New York: Columbia University Press.

Feibelman, James K. 1969. *An Introduction to the Philosophy of Charles S. Peirce*. Cambridge: MIT Press.

Firth, Raymond Wilson. 1936. *We, the Tikopia; a Sociological Study of Kinship in Primitive Polynesia*. London: G. Allen & Unwin.

Fischer, Michael M. J. 1986. "Ethnicity and the Post-Modern Arts of Memory." Pp. 194–233 in *Writing Culture: The Poetics and Politics of Ethnography*, edited by James Clifford and George E. Marcus. Berkeley: University of California Press.

Fitzgerald, Frances. 1986. *Cities on a Hill: A Journey Through Contemporary American Cultures*. New York: Simon and Schuster.

Fonow, Mary Margaret and Judith A. Cook, eds. 1991. *Beyond Methodology: Feminist Scholarship as Lived Research*. Bloomington: Indiana University Press.

Fortunato, Frank. 1980. "Snake Handlers: Risking Death As a Test of Faith." *Hustler*, April, 50–54, 58, 123–24.

Foucault, Michel. 1980. *Power/Knowledge: Selected Interviews and Other Writings*. Edited by Colin Gordon. New York: Pantheon Books.

Fox, Richard G., ed. 1991. *Recapturing Anthropology: Working in the Present*. Santa Fe: School of American Research Press.

Frazer, James. 1890. *The Golden Bough: A Study in Comparative Religion.* London: Macmillan.

Freedberg, David. 1988. *The Power of Images: Studies in the History and Theory of Response.* Chicago: University of Chicago Press.

Freire, Paolo. 1970. *Pedagogy of the Oppressed.* New York: Herder and Herder.

Fulbright, John W. 1994. "'Dialogue' in the Context of Secrecy and War: A Reply to Geertz." *Religion* 24:12–14.

Gates, Henry L. 1988. *The Signifying Monkey: A Theory of Afro-American Literacy Criticism.* New York: Oxford University Press.

Gates, Henry L. and K. A. Appiah, eds. 1993. *Alice Walker: Critical Perspectives Past and Present.* New York: Amistad Press.

Geertz, Armin W. 1987a. *Hopi Indian Altar Iconography.* Leiden: E.J. Brill.

———. 1987b. *Children of Cottonwood: Piety and Ceremonialism in Hopi Indian Puppetry.* Assisted by Michael Lomatuway'ma. Lincoln: University of Nebraska Press.

———. 1989. "A Container of Ashes: Hopi Prophecy in History." *European Review of Native American Studies* 3(1): 1–6.

———. 1990a. "Hopi Hermeneutics: Ritual Person Among the Hopi Indians of Arizona." Pp. 309–35 in *Concepts of Person in Religion and Thought*, edited by Hans G. Kippenberg, Yme B. Kuiper, and Andy F. Sanders. Berlin: Mouton de Gruyter.

———. 1990b. "The Study of Indigenous Religions in the History of Religions." Pp. 31–43 in *Studies on Religions in the Context of Social Sciences: Methodological and Theoretical Relations*, edited by Witold Tyloch. Warsaw: Polish Society for the Science of Religions.

———. 1990c. "Reflections on the Study of Hopi Mythology." Pp. 119–35 in *Religion in Native North America*, edited by Christopher Vecsey. Moscow: University of Idaho Press.

———. 1991a. "Hopi Prophecies Revisited: A Critique of Rudolph Kaiser." *Anthropos* 86:199–204.

———. 1991b. "Native American Art and the Problem of the Other: An Introduction to the Issues." *European Review of Native American Studies* 5(2): 1–4.

———. 1992/94. *The Invention of Prophecy: Continuity and Meaning in Hopi Indian Religion.* 1st ed.: Knebel: Brunbakke Publications; 2nd ed.: Los Angeles: University of California Press.

———. 1994a. "On Dendrolatry and Definitions: Perspectives from the Study of Oral Traditions." Pp. 661–65 in *The Notion of "Religion" in Comparative Research*, edited by Ugo Bianchi. Rome: "L'Erma" di Bretschneider.

———. 1994b. "On Reciprocity and Mutual Reflection in the Study of Native American Religions." *Religion: An International Journal* 24(1): 1–7.

———. 1994c. "Critical Reflections on the Postmodern Study of Religion." *Religion: An International Journal* 24(1): 16–22.

————. 1996. "Contemporary Problems in the Study of Native North American Religions with Special Reference to the Hopi." Pp. 393–414 in "To Hear the Eagles Cry: Contemporary Themes in Native American Spirituality," edited by Lee Irwin, special issue of *The American Indian Quarterly* 20 (3 & 4). Lincoln: University of Nebraska Press, 1997.

————. 1997. "Hermeneutics in Ethnography: Lessons for the Study of Religion." Pp. 53–70 in *Vergleichen und Verstehen in der Religionswissenschaft: Vorträge der Jahrestagung der DVRG*, edited by Hans-Joachim Klimkeit. Wiesbaden: Harrassowitz Verlag.

————. 1999. "Ethnohermeneutics in a Postmodern World." Pp. 73–86 in *Approaching Religion, Part I: Based on Papers Read at the Symposium on Methodology in the Study of Religions Held at Åbo, Finland on the 4th–7th August 1997*, edited by Tore Ahlbäck. Åbo and Stockholm: The Donner Institute for Research in Religious and Cultural History and Almqvist & Wiksell International.

Geertz, Clifford. 1973a. *The Interpretation of Cultures: Selected Essays*. New York: Basic Books.

————. 1973b. "Thick Description: Towards an Interpretive Theory of Culture." Pp. 3–30 in *The Interpretation of Cultures: Selected Essays*, edited by Clifford Geertz. New York: Basic Books.

————. 1977. "Found in Translation: On the Social History of the Moral Imagination." *Georgia Review* 31(4): 788–810.

————. 1988. *Works and Lives: The Anthropologist as Author*. Stanford, CA: Stanford University Press.

————. 1998. "Deep Hanging Out." *New York Review of Books*, October 22, 69–72.

Gellner, Ernest. 1983. *Nations and Nationalism*. Ithaca: Cornell University Press.

————. 1995. *Anthropology and Politics: Revolution in the Sacred Grove*. Oxford: Blackwell.

George, Sheba. 1998. "Caroling with the Keralites: The Negotiation of Gendered Space in an Indian Immigrant Church." Pp. 265–94 in *Gatherings in Diaspora: Religious Communities and the New Immigration*, edited by R. Stephen Warner and Judith G. Wittner. Philadelphia: Temple University Press.

Gilkes, Cheryl Townsend. 1985. "Together and in Harness: Women's Traditions in the Sanctified Church." *Signs: Journal of Women in Culture and Society* 11(4): 678–99.

Gitlitz, David. 1996. *Secrecy and Deceit: The Religion of the Crypto-Jews*. Philadelphia: The Jewish Publication Society.

Goffman, Erving. 1963. *Stigma: Notes on the Management of Spoiled Identity*. Englewood Cliffs, NJ: Prentice-Hall.

Goldman, Anne. 1996. *Take My Word: Autobiographical Innovations of Ethnic American Working Women*. Berkeley: University of California Press.

Goldman, Marion S. 1999. *Passionate Journeys: Why Successful Women Joined a Cult*. Ann Arbor: University of Michigan Press.

Good, Kenneth. 1996. *Into the Heart: One Man's Pursuit of Love and Knowledge Among the Yanomami*. Reading, MA: Addison-Wesley.

Gordon, Avery. 1997. *Ghostly Matters: Haunting and the Sociological Imagination*. Minneapolis: University of Minnesota Press.

Gould, Rebecca. 1997. "Getting (Not Too) Close to Nature: Modern Home-steading as Lived Religion in America." Pp. 217–42 in *Lived Religion in America: Toward a History of Practice in American Religious History*, edited by David D. Hall. Princeton, NJ: Princeton University Press.

Graves, Robert. 1948. *The White Goddess*. New York: Farrar, Straus, and Giroux.

Griffith, R. Marie. 1997. *God's Daughters: Evangelical Women and the Power of Submission*. Berkeley: University of California Press.

Groothius, Rebecca Merrill. 1994. *Women Caught in the Conflict*. Grand Rapids: Baker Books.

Gubkin, J. Liora. 2000. "Friday Night Live: It's not Your Parents' Shabbat." Pp. 199–210 in *GenX Religion*, edited by Richard W. Flory and Donald E. Miller. New York: Routledge.

Gupta, Akhil and James Ferguson, eds. 1997. *Culture, Power, Place: Explorations in Critical Anthropology*. Chapel Hill: Duke University Press.

Guth, James, John C. Green, and Corwin E. Smidt. 1995. "Faith and the Environment: Religious Beliefs and Attitudes on Environmental Policy." *American Journal of Political Science* 39:364–82.

Haan, Norma, Robert N. Bellah, Paul Rabinow, and William M. Sullivan, eds. 1983. *Social Science as Moral Inquiry*. New York: Columbia University Press.

Habermas, Jürgen. 1968. *Knowledge and Human Interests*. 1971. Boston: Beacon Press.

Hall, David D., ed. 1997. *Lived Religion in America: Toward a History of Practice in American Religious History*. Princeton: Princeton University Press.

Hall, John R. 1987. *Gone from the Promised Land: Jonestown in American Culture History*. New Brunswick, NJ: Transaction Publishers.

Hannigan, John. 1995. *Environmental Sociology: A Social Constructionist Perspective*. London and New York: Routledge.

Haraway, Donna. 1991. *Simians, Cyborgs and Women: The Reinvention of Nature*. New York: Routledge.

Harding, Susan Friend. 1987. "Convicted by the Holy Spirit: The Rhetoric of Fundamental Baptist Conversion." *American Ethnologist* 14(1): 167–81.

———. 2000. *The Book of Jerry Falwell: Fundamentalist Language and Politics*. Princeton, NJ: Princeton University Press.

Hardy-Fanta, Carol. 1993. *Latina Politics: Gender, Culture and Political Participation in Boston*. Philadelphia: Temple University Press.

Harris, Marvin. 1968. *The Rise of Anthropological Theory: A History of Theories of Culture.* New York: Thomas Y. Crowell.

Harrison, Daphne Duval. 1988. *Black Pearls: Blues Queens of the 1920s.* New Brunswick: Rutgers University Press.

Hearn, Virginia. 1979. *Our Struggle to Serve.* Waco, TX: Word Books.

Hernandez, Frances. 1993. "The Secret Jews of the Southwest." Pp. 411–54 in *Sephardim in the Americas: Studies in Culture and History,* edited by Martin A. Cohen and Abraham J. Peck. Tuscaloosa: University of Alabama Press.

Herzfeld, Michael. 1998. *Portrait of a Greek Imagination: An Ethnographic Biography of Andreas Nenedakis.* Chicago: University of Chicago Press.

Higginbotham, Evelyn Brooks. 1993. *Righteous Discontent: The Women's Movement in the Black Baptist Church, 1880–1920.* Cambridge: Harvard University Press.

Hollis, Martin and Steven Lukes, eds. 1982. *Rationality and Relativism.* Cambridge, MA: MIT Press.

Holmström, Krister. 1986. *Biblisk Framgångsteologi.* Uppsala: Livets Ord.

Holub, Robert C. 1992. *Crossing Borders: Reception Theory, Poststructuralism and Deconstruction.* Madison: University of Wisconsin Press.

Hood, Ralph W., Jr. 1998. "When the Spirit Maims and Kills: Social Psychological Considerations of the History of Serpent Handling Sects and the Narrative of Handlers." *International Journal for the Psychology of Religion* 8(2): 71–96.

Horowitz, Irving Louis, ed. 1974. *The Rise and Fall of Project Camelot, Studies in the Relationship Between Social Science and Practical Politics.* rev. ed. Cambridge, MA: MIT Press.

Horton, Robin and Ruth Finnegan, eds. 1973. *Modes of Thought: Essays on Thinking in Western and Non-Western Societies.* London: Faber & Faber.

Humphreys, Laud. 1970. *Tearoom Trade: Impersonal Sex in Public Places.* Chicago: Aldine.

Hunter, James Davidson. 1987. *Evangelicalism: The Coming Generation.* Chicago: University of Chicago Press.

Hymes, Dell. 1962. "The Ethnography of Speaking." In *Anthropology and Human Behavior,* edited by Thomas Gladwin and W. C. Sturtevant. Washington, D.C.: Anthropological Society.

———, ed. 1969. *Reinventing Anthropology.* New York: Random House.

Immergut, Matthew. 2000. "Religion and the Environment in the Ironbound." Working paper. Drew University.

Isasi-Díaz, Ana María. 1993. *En la Lucha/In the Struggle: Elaborating a Mujerista Theology.* Minneapolis: Fortress Press.

Iser, Wolfgang. 1989. *Prospecting From Reader Response to Literary Anthropology.* Baltimore: Johns Hopkins University Press.

Jackson, Michael. 1987. "On Ethnographic Truth." *Canberra Anthropology* 10(2): 1–31.

Jacobs, Sylvia M. 1982. *Black Americans and the Missionary Movement in Africa.* Westport, CT: Greenwood Press.

Jade. 9997. *Cella Training Program Workbook.* [1997]. Madison, WI: Reformed Congregation of the Goddess.

Jaggar, Alison M. 1989. "Love and Knowledge: Emotion in Feminist Epistemology." Pp. 145–71 in *Gender/Body/Knowledge: Feminist Reconstructions of Being and Knowing,* edited by Alison M. Jaggar and S. Bordo. New Brunswick, NJ: Rutgers University Press.

James, Allison, Jenny Hockey, and Andrew Dawson, eds. 1997. *After Writing Culture: Epistemology and Praxis in Contemporary Anthropology.* New York: Routledge.

Jarman, Neil. 1997. *Material Conflicts: Parades and Visual Displays in Northern Ireland.* Oxford: Berg Publications.

Jensen, Jeppe Sinding and Luther Martin, eds. 1997. *Rationality and the Study of Religion.* Aarhus: Aarhus University Press.

Kant, Immanuel. 1781. *Critique of Pure Reason.* New York: St. Martin's Press [1965].

Katz, Jonathan Ned. 1992. *Gay American History: Lesbians and Gay Men in the U.S.A.* rev. ed. New York: Meridian.

Kaufman, Debra. 1991. *Rachel's Daughters.* New Brunswick, NJ: Rutgers University Press.

Kearns, Laurel. 1996. "Saving the Creation: Christian Environmentalism in the United States." *Sociology of Religion* 57(1): 55–70.

———. 1997. "Noah's Ark Goes to Washington." *Social Compass* 44:349–66.

———. 1999a. "Is It Eco-Justice or Environmental Justice? The Role of Religion in the Environmental Justice Movement." Annual Meeting of the Association for the Sociology of Religion. Chicago, August.

———. 1999b. "Justice for All: Environmental Racism and Environmental Justice." Annual Meeting of the American Academy of Religion. Boston, November.

Keller, Evelyn Fox. 1985. *Reflections on Gender and Science.* New Haven: Yale University Press.

King, Deborah E. 1988. "The Context of a Black Feminist Ideology." *Signs: Journal of Women in Culture and Society* 14(1): 265–95.

Kleinman, Arthur and Joan Kleinman. 1991. "Suffering and Its Potential Transformation: Towards an Ethnography of Interpersonal Experience." *Culture, Medicine, and Psychiatry* 15(3): 275–301.

Kleinman, Sherryl and Martha A. Copp. 1993. *Emotions and Fieldwork.* Qualitative Research Methods Series, vol. 28. Newbury Park, CA: Sage.

Kotlowitz, Alex. 1991. *There Are No Children Here: The Story of Two Boys Growing Up in the Other America.* New York: Doubleday.

Kozol, Jonathan. 1988. *Rachel and Her Children: Homeless Families in America.* New York: Crown.

Krieger, Susan. 1983. *The Mirror Dance: Identity in a Women's Community.* Philadelphia: Temple University Press.

———. 1988. *Social Science and the Self: Personal Essays as an Art Form.* Philadelphia: Temple University Press.

Kroeber, Alfred L. 1952. *The Nature of Culture.* Chicago: University of Chicago Press.

Kuhn, Thomas S. 1970. *The Structure of Scientific Revolutions.* 2nd ed., enlarged. Chicago: University of Chicago Press.

———. 1977. *The Essential Tension: Selected Studies in Scientific Tradition and Change.* Chicago: University of Chicago Press.

Lavie, Smadar. 1990. *The Poetics of Military Occupation: Mzeina Allegories of Bedouin Identity Under Israeli and Egyptian Rule.* Berkeley: University of California Press.

Layton, Robert. 1994. *Who Needs the Past? Indigenous Values and Archaeology.* London: Routledge.

Lemann, Nicholas. 1992. *The Promised Land: The Great Black Migration and How It Changed America.* New York: Vintage.

LeVine, Robert A. 1970. "Outsiders' Judgements: An Ethnographic Approach to Group Differences in Personality." Pp. 388–97 in *A Handbook of Method in Cultural Anthropology*, edited by Raoul Naroll and Ronald Cohen. New York: Columbia University Press.

Lewis, Oscar. 1951. *Life in a Mexican Village: Tepoztlán Restudied.* Urbana: University of Illinois Press.

Liebman, Seymour. 1970. *The Jews in New Spain.* Coral Gables: University of Miami Press.

Liebow, Elliot. 1967. *Tally's Corner: A Study of Negro Streetcorner Men.* Boston: Little, Brown & Company.

Little, Paul E. 1999. "Environments and Environmentalism in Anthropological Research: Facing a New Millennium." *Annual Review of Anthropology* 28:253–84.

Lloyd, G.E.R. 1990. *Demystifying Mentalities.* Cambridge: Cambridge University Press.

Luhrmann, Tanya. 1989. *Persuasions of the Witch's Craft: Ritual Magic and Witchcraft in Present-Day England.* Oxford: Blackwell.

Lyotard, Jean François. 1984. *The Post-Modern Condition: A Report on Knowledge.* Minneapolis: University of Minnesota Press.

MacHor, James L. and Phillip Goldstein. 2000. *Reception Study: From Literary Theory to Cultural Studies.* New York and London: Routledge Press.

MacNaughten, Phil and John Urry. 1995. "Towards a Sociology of Nature." *Sociology* 29:203–20.

Malcolm, Kari Torjesen. 1982. *Women at the Crossroads.* Downers Grove, IL: InterVarsity Press.

266   References

Manning, Christel. 1999. *God Gave Us the Right*. New Brunswick, NJ: Rutgers University Press.
Marcus, George E. 1998. *Ethnography Through Thick and Thin*. Princeton, NJ: Princeton University Press.
Marcus, George E. and Michael J. Fischer. 1986. *Anthropology as Cultural Critique: An Experimental Moment in the Human Sciences*. Chicago: University of Chicago Press.
Marty, Martin. 1997. "The Public Place and All the Other Publics." Annual Meeting of the Society for the Scientific Study of Religion, November.
Masnerus, Laura. 1998. "Newark's Toxic Tomb." *The New York Times*, November 8, sec 14, p 1.
Mays, Benjamin E. 1971. *Born to Rebel: An Autobiography*. New York: Charles Scribner and Sons.
McCutcheon, Russell T. 1999. *The Insider/Outsider Problem in the Study of Religion*. London: Cassell.
McDannell, Colleen. 1995. *Material Christianity*. New Haven: Yale University Press.
McGuire, Meredith B. 1982. *Pentecostal Catholics: Power, Charisma, and Order in a Religious Movement*. Philadelphia: Temple University Press.
———. 1988. *Ritual Healing in Suburban America*. New Brunswick, NJ: Rutgers University Press.
———. 1990. "Religion and the Body: Rematerializing the Human Body in the Social Sciences of Religion." *Journal for the Scientific Study of Religion* 29(3): 283–96.
———. 1996. "Religion and Healing the Mind/Body/Self." *Social Compass* 43(1): 101–16.
McNally, Michael. 1997. "The Uses of Ojibwa Hymn Singing at the White Earth: Toward a History of Practice." Pp. 133–59 in *Lived Religion in America: Toward a History of Practice in American Religious History*, edited by David D. Hall. Princeton, NJ: Princeton University Press.
Mead, Margaret. 1953. *New Lives for Old: Cultural Transformation—Manus 1928–1953*. New York: Morrow.
Melucci, Alberto. 1995. "The Process of Collective Identity." Pp. 41–63 in *Social Movements and Culture*, edited by Hank Johnston and Bert Klandermans. Minneapolis: University of Minnesota Press.
Merchant, Carolyn. 1990. *The Death of Nature: Women, Ecology and the Scientific Revolution*. San Francisco: Harper.
Milton, Kay. 1993. *Environmentalism: The View from Anthropology*. London: Routledge.
Mindell, Arnold. 1995. *Sitting in the Fire: Large Group Transformation Using Conflict and Diversity*. Portland, OR: Lao Tse Press.
Monsay, Evelyn H. 1997. "Intuition in the Development of Scientific Theory and

Practice." Pp. 103–20 in *Intuition: The Inside Story*, edited by Robbie Davis-Floyd and P. S. Arvidson. London: Routledge.

Mooney, James. 1965. *The Ghost Dance Religion and the Sioux Outbreak of 1890*. Chicago: University of Chicago Press.

Morgan, David. 1996. "Would Jesus Have Sat for a Portrait?: The Likeness of Christ in Popular Reception of Sallman's Art." Pp. 181–206 in *Icons of American Protestantism: The Art of Warner Sallman*, edited by David Morgan. New Haven: Yale University Press.

Morgan, Robin. 1970. *Sisterhood is Powerful*. New York: Random House.

Mudimbe, V. Y. 1988. *The Invention of Africa: Gnosis, Philosophy and the Order of Knowledge*. Bloomington: Indiana University Press.

Murphy, Raymond. 1997. *Sociology and Nature: Social Action and Context*. Boulder, CO: Westview Press.

Murray, Harry. 1943. *Thematic Apperception Test*. Cambridge, MA: Harvard University Press.

Narayan, Uma. 1989. "The Project of Feminist Epistemology: Perspectives from a Non-Western Feminist." Pp. 256–69 in *Gender/Body/Knowledge: Feminist Reconstructions of Being and Knowing*, edited by Alison M. Jaggar and S. Bordo. New Brunswick, NJ: Rutgers University Press.

Nason-Clark, Nancy. 1997. *The Battered Wife: How Christians Confront Family Violence*. Louisville, KY: Westminster/John Knox Press.

Neitz, Mary Jo. 1985. "Antinomianism Versus Authoritarianism: Women's Spiritual Power and Patriarchal Norms." Annual Meeting of the Association for the Sociology of Religion. San Antonio, August.

———. 1987. *Charisma and Community: A Study of Religious Commitment Within the Charismatic Renewal*. New Brunswick, NJ: Transaction Books.

———. 1993. "Inequality and Difference: Feminist Perspectives in the Sociology of Religion." Pp. 165–185 in *Future for Religion? New Paradigms for Social Analysis*, edited by William H. Swatos, Jr. Newbury Park, CA: Sage Publications.

———. 1994. "Quasi-Religions and Cultural Movements: Contemporary Witchcraft as a Churchless Religion." *Religion and the Social Order* 4(12): 127–49.

———. 1995. "Feminist Theory and Religious Experience." Pp. 520–34 in *Handbook of Religious Experience*, edited by Ralph W. Hood, Jr. Birmingham, AL: Religious Education Press.

———. 2000. "Queering the Dragonfest: Changing Sexualities in a Post-Patriarchal Religion." *Sociology of Religion* 61(4): 369–91.

Nidel, David. 1984. "Modern Descendants of *Conversos* in New Mexico." *Western States Jewish History* 16(3): 249–63.

Numrich, Paul David. 1996. *Old Wisdom in the New World: Americanization in Two Immigrant Theravada Buddhist Temples*. Knoxville: University of Tennessee Press.

Olesen, Virginia. 1994. "Feminisms and Models of Qualitative Research." Pp. 158–74 in *The Handbook of Qualitative Research*, edited by Norman K. Denzin and Yvonne S. Lincoln. Thousand Oaks, CA: Sage.

Olwig, Karen and Kirsten Hastrup. 1997. *Siting Culture: The Shifting Anthropological Object*. London: Routledge.

Omi, Michael and Howard Winant. 1994. *Racial Formation in the United States From the 1960's to the 1990's*. New York: Routledge.

Ong, Walter J. 1982. *Orality and Literacy: The Technologizing of the Word*. London: Methuen.

Orsi, Robert Anthony. 1985. *The Madonna of 115th Street: Faith and Community in Italian Harlem 1880–1950*. New Haven: Yale University Press.

———. 1996. *Thank You, St. Jude: Women's Devotion to the Patron Saint of Hopeless Causes*. New Haven: Yale University Press.

———. 1998. "Snakes Alive: Resituating the Moral in the Study of Religion." Pp. 201–226 in *In Face of the Facts: Moral Inquiry in American Scholarship*, edited by Richard Wightman Fox and Robert B. Westbrook. Cambridge: Cambridge University Press.

———, ed. 1999. *Gods of the City*. Bloomington: Indiana University Press.

Overing, Joanna, ed. 1985. *Reason and Morality*. London: Tavistock.

Parkin, Frank. 1988. *Krippendorf's Tribe*. 1998. Bantam Books.

Passerini, Luisa. 1993. "Women's Personal Narratives: Myths, Experiences, and Emotions." Pp. 189–97 in *Interpreting Women's Lives: Feminist Theory and Personal Narratives*, edited by The Personal Narratives Group. Bloomington: Indiana University Press.

Patterson, Beverly Bush. 1995. *The Sound of the Dove: Singing in Appalachian Primitive Baptist Churches*. Urbana: Illinois University Press.

Peacock, James L. 1986. *The Anthropological Lens: Harsh Light, Soft Focus*. Cambridge: Cambridge University Press.

Peirce, Charles Sanders. 1877. "The Fixation of Belief." *Popular Science Monthly* 12:1–15.

———. 1955. *Philosophical Writings of Peirce*. Edited by Justus Buchler. New York: Dover Publications.

Peña, Milagros. 1995. *Theologies and Liberation in Peru: The Role of Ideas in Social Movements*. Philadelphia: Temple University Press.

Piaget, Jean. 1929. *The Child's Conception of the World*. Totowa, NJ: Littlefield, Adams, and Co. [1972].

Piper, John and Wayne Grudem. 1991. *Recovering Biblical Manhood and Womanhood: A Reponse to Biblical Feminism*. Wheaton, IL: Crossway Books.

Poloma, Margaret. 1982. *The Charismatic Movement: Is There a New Pentecost?* Boston: Twayne.

Popper, Karl Raimund, Sir. 1932. *The Logic of Scientific Discovery*. New York: Basic Books [1959].

Primiano, Leonard Norman. 1993. "Intrinsically Catholic: Vernacular Religion and Philadelphia's 'Dignity.'" Ph.D. diss. University of Pennsylvania.

Radway, Janice A. 1991. *Reading the Romance: Women, Patriarchy, and Popular Literature.* Chapel Hill: University of North Carolina Press.

Ransom, Roger L. and Richard Sutch. 1977. *One Kind of Freedom: The Economic Consequences of Emancipation.* New York: Cambridge University Press.

Rappaport, Roy. 1979. *Ecology, Meaning and Religion.* Richmond, CA: North Atlantic Books.

Reagon, Bernice Johnson. 1982. "My Black Mothers and Sisters, or On Beginning a Culture Autobiography." *Feminist Studies* 8(1): 81–96.

Redclift, Michael and Ted Benton, eds. 1994. *Social Theory and the Global Environment.* London and New York: Routledge.

Redfield, Robert. 1930. *Tepoztlán, a Mexican Village: A Study of Folk Life.* Chicago: University of Chicago Press.

Reinharz, Shulamit, with Lynn Davidman. 1992. *Feminist Methods in Social Research.* New York: Oxford University Press.

Richardson, James T., Mary W. Stewart, and Robert B. Simmonds. 1978. "Researching a Fundamentalist Commune." Pp. 235–251 in *Understanding New Religions*, edited by Jacob Needleman and George Baker. New York: Seabury Press.

Riggs, Marcia Y. 1994. *Awake, Arise, and Act! A Womanist Call for Black Liberation.* Cleveland: Pilgrim Press.

Rosaldo, Michelle and Louise Lamphere, eds. 1974. *Woman, Culture, and Society.* Stanford, CA: Stanford University Press.

Rosaldo, Renato. 1989. *Culture and Truth: The Remaking of Social Analysis.* Boston: Beacon Press.

Rose, Wendy. 1984. "Just What's All This Fuss About Whiteshamanism Anyway?" Pp. 13–24 in *Coyote Was Here: Essays on Contemporary Native American Literary and Political Mobilization*, edited by Bo Schöler. Aarhus: University of Aarhus Press.

Roth, Paul A. 1989. "Ethnography Without Tears." *Current Anthropology* 30(5): 555–69.

Runyan, William McKinley. 1982. *Life Histories and Psychobiography.* New York: Oxford University Press.

Said, Edward W. 1978. *Orientalism.* New York: Pantheon.

———. 1985. "Orientalism Reconsidered." Pp. I: 14–27 in *Europe and Its Others*, edited by Francis Barker et al. Colchester: University of Essex.

Sangren, P. Steven. 1988. "Rhetoric and the Authority of Ethnography: 'Postmodernism' and the Social Reproduction of Texts." *Current Anthropology* 29(3): 405–35.

Santmire, Paul H. 1985. *The Travail of Nature: The Ambiguous Ecological Promise of Christian Theology.* Philadelphia: Fortress Press.

Santos, Richard. 1983. "Chicanos of Jewish Descent in Texas." *Western States Jewish Historical Quarterly* 15:289–333.

Sarsby, Jacquie. 1984. "Special Problems of Fieldwork in Familiar Settings." P. 132 in *Ethnographic Research: A Guide to General Conduct*, edited by R. F. Ellen. London: Academic Press.

Scanzoni, Letha Dawson, and Nancy A. Hardesty. 1992. *All We're Meant to Be.* Grand Rapids: William B. Eerdman's.

Schuvaks, Daniela. 1996. "Esther Seligson and Angelina Munoz-Huberman: Jewish Mexican Memory and the Exile to the Darkest Tunnels of the Past." Pp. 75–100 in *The Jewish Diaspora in Latin America: New Studies in History and Literature*, edited by David Sheinin and Lois Baer Barr. New York: Garland.

Schwartz, Scott. 1999. *Faith, Serpents, and Fire: Images of Kentucky Holiness Believers.* Jackson: University Press of Mississippi.

Seidman, Steven. 1997. "The 'Closet' in the U.S. Today." Cultural Studies Colloquium. University of California at Santa Barbara, February.

———. 1998. "Are We Still in the Closet? Notes Towards a Sociological and Cultural Turn in Queer Theory." *European Journal of Cultural Studies* 1(2): 177–92.

Seligson, Esther. 1991. "De la Memoria y la Identidad." *Noaj* 6:34–36.

Sennett, Richard and Jonathan Cobb. 1972. *The Hidden Injuries of Class.* New York: Alfred Knopf.

Shaffir, William B. 1991. "Managing a Convincing Self-Presentation: Some Personal Reflections on Entering the Field." Pp. 72–81 in *Experiencing Fieldwork: An Inside View of Qualitative Research*, edited by William B. Shaffir and Robert A. Stebbins. Newbury Park, CA: Sage Publications.

Shaw, Stephanie. 1995. "Black Club Women and the Creation of the National Association of Colored Women." Pp. 433–77 in *"We Specialize in the Wholly Impossible": A Reader in Black Women's History*, edited by Darlene Clark Hine, Wilma King and Linda Reed. Brooklyn: Carlson Publications.

———. 1996. *What a Woman Ought to Be and to Do: Black Professional Workers During the Jim Crow Era.* Chicago: University of Chicago Press.

Shay, Roshani and Ted Shay. 1995. "Better Dead Than Red: Local Letters and the Rajneesh Movement." Pp. 131–54 in *Sex, Lies, and Sanctity: Religion and Deviance in Contemporary North America*, edited by Mary Jo Neitz and Marion S. Goldman. Greenwich, CT: JAI Press.

Sherkat, Darren E. and Christopher G. Ellison. 1999. "Recent Developments and Current Controversies in the Sociology of Religion." *Annual Review of Sociology* 25:363–94.

Shibley, Mark A. and Jonathon L. Wiggins. 1997. "Greening Mainline and American Religion." *Social Compass* 44(3): 330–48.

Shokeid, Moshe. 1995. *A Gay Synagogue in New York.* New York: Columbia University Press.

Smith, Christian. 1996. *Disruptive Religion: The Force of Faith in Social Movement Activism*. New York: Routledge.

Smith, Dorothy E. 1987. *The Everyday World as Problematic: A Feminist Sociology*. Boston: Northwestern University Press.

———. 1990. *The Conceptual Practices of Power: A Feminist Sociology of Knowledge*. Boston: Northwestern University Press.

Smith, Gavin. 1999. *Confronting the Present: Towards a Politically Engaged Anthropology*. Oxford: Berg Publications.

Spickard, James V. 1991a. "Spiritual Healing Among the American Followers of a Japanese New Religion: Experience as a Factor in Religious Motivation." *Research in the Social Scientific Study of Religion* 3:135–56.

———. 1991b. "Experiencing Religious Rituals: A Schutzian Analysis of Navajo Ceremonies." *Sociological Analysis* 52(2): 191–204.

Stacey, Judith and Susan Elizabeth Gerard. 1990. "We Are not Doormats: The Influence of Feminism on Contemporary Evangelicals in the United States." Pp. 98–117 in *Uncertain Terms: Negotiating Gender in American Culture*, edited by Faye Ginsberg and Anna Lowenhaupt Tsing. Boston: Beacon Press.

Stanczak, Gregory C. 2000. "The Tradition as Alternative: The GenX Appeal of the International Church of Christ." Pp. 113–35 in *GenX Religion*, edited by Richard W. Flory and Donald E. Miller. New York: Routledge.

Starhawk. 1982. *Dreaming the Dark: Magic, Sex, and Politics*. Boston: Beacon Press.

Stewart, Kathleen. 1996. *A Space on the Side of the Road: Cultural Poetics in an 'Other' America*. Princeton, NJ: Princeton University Press.

Stocking, George. 1992. *The Ethnographer's Magic and Other Essays in the History of Anthropology*. Madison: University of Wisconsin Press.

Stoller, Paul and Cheryl Olkes. 1987. *In Sorcery's Shadow: A Memoir of Apprenticeship Among the Songhay of Niger*. Chicago: University of Chicago Press.

Strathern, Andrew. 1979. *Ongka: A Self-Account by a New Guinea Big-Man*. London: Duckworth.

Sundberg, Norman, Marion S. Goldman, Nathan Rotter, and Douglas Smythe. 1992. "Personality and Spirituality: Comparative TAT's of High-Achieving Rajneesheees." *Journal of Personality Assessment* 59:326–39.

Sundquist, Eric. 1992. *The Hammers of Creation: Folk Culture in Modern African-American Fiction*. Athens, GA: Mercer University Press.

Swimme, Brian and Thomas Berry. 1994. *The Universe Story: From the Primordial Flaring Forth to the Ecozoic Era—A Celebration of the Unfolding of the Cosmos*. San Francisco: HarperSanFrancisco.

Tambiah, Stanley J. 1990. *Magic, Science, Religion and the Scope of Rationality*. Cambridge: Cambridge University Press.

Taussig, Michael. 1993. *Mimesis and Alterity: A Particular History of the Senses*. New York: Routledge.

Thornton, Robert J. 1988. "The Rhetoric of Ethnographic Holism." *Cultural Anthropology* 3(3): 285–303.

Tidball, Keith and Christopher P. Toumey. 2000. "Signifying Serpents: Hermeneutic Change in Appalachian Pentecostal Serpent Handling." Unpublished paper.

Trinh, T. Minh-ha. 1989. *Woman, Native, Other: Writing Postcoloniality and Feminism.* Bloomington: Indiana University Press.

Turner, Edith. 1987. *The Spirit and the Drum: A Memoir of Africa.* Tucson: University of Arizona Press.

Tweed, Thomas A. 1997a. *Our Lady of the Exile: Diasporic Religion at a Cuban Catholic Shrine in Miami.* New York: Oxford University Press.

———. 1997b. "Introduction." Pp. 8–9 in *Retelling U.S. Religious History,* edited by Thomas A. Tweed. Berkeley: University of California Press.

———. 2000. "Proclaiming Catholic Inclusiveness: Ethnic Diversity and Ecclesiastical Unity at the National Shrine of the Immaculate Conception." *U.S. Catholic Historian* 18:1–18.

Tyler, Stephen A. 1978. *The Said and the Unsaid: Mind, Meaning and Culture.* New York: Academic Press.

———. 1987. *The Unspeakable: Discourse, Dialogue and Rhetoric in the Postmodern World.* Madison: University of Wisconsin Press.

———. 1989. "Reply to Roth." *Current Anthropology* 30(5): 556.

Tyson, Ruel W., Jr., James L. Peacock, and Daniel W. Patterson. 1988. *Diversities of Gifts: Field Studies in Southern Religion.* Urbana: University of Illinois Press.

United Church of Christ (UCC) Commission for Racial Justice. 1987. *Toxic Wastes and Race in the United States.* New York: United Church of Christ.

van den Berghe, Pierre L. 1980. "Tourism as Ethnic Relations." *Ethnic and Racial Studies* 3:375–92.

Van Maanen, John. 1988. *Tales of the Field: On Writing Ethnography.* Chicago: University of Chicago Press.

Vayda, Andrew P. and Bonnie McKay. 1975. "New Directions in Ecology and Ecological Anthropology." *Annual Review of Anthropology* 4:181–97.

Vonnegut, Kurt, Jr. 1969. *Slaughterhouse Five.* New York: Dell Books.

Wagner, Melinda Bollar. 1997. "The Study of Religion in American Society." Pp. 85–101 in *The Anthropology of Religion: A Handbook,* edited by Stephen D. Glazier. Westport, CT: Greenwood Press.

Walker, Alice. 1982. *The Color Purple.* 10th anniversary ed. [1992]. New York: Harcourt Brace Jovanovich.

———. 1998. *By the Light of My Father's Smile.* London: Women's Press.

Warner, R. Stephen. 1988. *New Wine in Old Wineskins: Evangelicals and Liberals in a Small Town Church.* Berkeley: University of California Press.

Warner, R. Stephen and Judith G. Wittner, eds. 1998. *Gatherings in Diaspora: Religious Communities and the New Immigration.* Philadelphia: Temple University Press.

Warner, W. Lloyd, et al. 1963. *Yankee City.* New Haven: Yale University Press.

Wax, Ruby. 2000. *Ruby's American Pie.* ABC Australia. Screened July 23.

Weaver, Jace. 1996. *Defending Mother Earth: Native American Perspectives on Environmental Justice.* Maryknoll, NY: Orbis Books.

Wells-Barnett, Ida B. 1997. *Southern Horrors and Other Writings: The Anti-Lynching Campaign of Ida B. Wells, 1892–1900.* Edited by Jacqueline Jones Royster. Boston: Bedford Books.

Whitehead, Tony Larry and Mary Ellen Conaway, eds. 1986. *Self, Sex, and Gender in Cross-Cultural Fieldwork.* Urbana: University of Illinois Press.

Whittier, Nancy. 1995. *Feminist Generations: The Persistence of the Radical Women's Movement.* Philadelphia: Temple University Press.

Whyte, William Foote. 1943. *Street Corner Society: The Social Structure of an Italian Slum.* Chicago: University of Chicago Press.

Wilcox, Melissa M. 2000. "Two Roads Converged: Religion and Identity Among Lesbian, Gay, Bisexual, and Transgendered Christians." Ph.D. diss. University of California at Santa Barbara.

Williams, Patricia. 1991. *Alchemy of Race and Rights: Diary of a Law Professor.* Boston: Harvard University Press.

Williamson, William Paul. 1999. "The Experience of Religious Serpent Handling: A Phenomenological Study." Ph.D. diss. University of Tennessee at Knoxville.

Wilson, Bryan R. 1970. *Religious Sects.* New York: McGraw-Hill.

Winch, Peter. 1958. *The Idea of a Social Science, and Its Relation to Philosophy.* London: Routledge & Kegan Paul.

Wittner, Judith G. 1998a. "A Reader Among Fieldworkers." Pp. 365–83 in *Gatherings in Diaspora: Religious Communities and the New Immigration,* edited by R. Stephen Warner and Judith G. Wittner. Philadelphia: Temple University Press.

———. 1998b. "Rounds of Collaboration." Our Texts, Our Selves: Writers, Research, and Audiences. University of Missouri, Columbia, Missouri, October.

Wolf, Eric R. 1982. *Europe and the People Without History.* Berkeley: University of California Press.

Wolf, Margery. 1992. *A Thrice-Told Tale: Feminism, Postmodernism, and Ethnographic Responsibility.* Stanford, CA: Stanford University Press.

Worsley, Peter. 1968. *The Trumpet Shall Sound: A Study of "Cargo" Cults in Melanesia.* 2nd ed. New York: Schocken Books.

Yu, Pei-Lin. 1997. *Hungry Lightning: Notes of a Woman Anthropologist in Venezuela.* Albuquerque: University of New Mexico Press.

Contributors

JIM BIRCKHEAD (Ph.D. University of Alberta) teaches anthropology at Charles Sturt University, Australia, where he conducts research on the cultural and spiritual connection of indigenous people to their customary "country" in Australia and in Papua, New Guinea. He also works as a native title consultant for the United Githabul Tribal Nation, and is a co-author of *Culture, Conservation and Biodiversity* (John Wiley). He has done field research on serpent-handling religion in Southern "Appalachia" since 1970.

KAREN MCCARTHY BROWN (Ph.D. Temple University) is Professor of Anthropology of Religion at the Drew University Graduate and Theological Schools. Her most famous book is *Mama Lola: A Vodou Priestess in Brooklyn* (Berkeley). She is currently directing the Newark Project, a Ford Foundation-sponsored ethnographic mapping of religions in Newark, New Jersey.

SIMON COLEMAN (Ph.D. Cambridge) teaches anthropology at the University of Durham, England. His main research interest has been the spread of Christian evangelicalism and religious fundamentalism around the world, with a special focus on Scandinavia. His books include *The Globalisation of Charismatic Christianity: Spreading the Gospel of Prosperity* (Cambridge) and *Pilgrimage, Past and Present in the World Religions* (with J. Elsner, Harvard).

LYNN DAVIDMAN (Ph.D. Brandeis University) is Associate Professor of American Civilization, Judaic Studies, and Women's Studies at Brown University. She wrote the award-winning *Tradition in a Rootless World: Women Turn to Orthodox Judaism* (California), and has published widely on feminism and religious studies. Her chapter is based on her latest book, *Motherloss* (California). She is currently studying American Jews who do not attend synagogue.

ARMIN W. GEERTZ (D.Phil. University of Aarhus) is Professor of the History of Religions at the University of Aarhus, Denmark. He is the author of several books on the Hopi Indians of Arizona, most importantly *The Invention of Prophecy* (California). He is the past Chair of the Danish Association for the History of Religions, and has served as officer for other international professional organizations. He has edited the *Renner Studies on New Religions.*

CHERYL TOWNSEND GILKES (Ph.D. Northeastern) is Associate Professor of Sociology at Colby College and Assistant Pastor of the Union Baptist Church in Cambridge, Massachusetts. She has published a wide range of articles in social science, women's studies, religious studies, and African American studies, along with *If It Wasn't for the Women . . . : Women's Experience and Womanist Culture in the Black Church and Community* (Orbis). She is currently working on a book about the contemporary Black Church.

MARION S. GOLDMAN (Ph.D. University of Chicago) is Professor of Sociology and Religious Studies at the University of Oregon. She is the author of numerous scholarly articles on such topics as the far Right, the Jesus People Movement, and Rajneesh sannyasins. Her most recent book is *Passionate Journeys: Why Successful Women Joined a Cult* (Michigan). Her new work focuses on Esalen Institute and its impact on American spirituality.

JULIE INGERSOLL (Ph.D. University of California at Santa Barbara) is Assistant Professor of Religion, Culture, and Society at the University of North Florida. Her research, publication, and teaching have focused on religion and politics, women and religion, and religion and culture. Her chapter is based on her forthcoming book *Engendered Conflict: Constructing Masculinity and Femininity in Conservative Protestantism.*

JANET L. JACOBS (Ph.D. University of Colorado) is Professor of Women's Studies at the University of Colorado at Boulder. She is the author of several books and edited collections, including *Divine Disen-*

chantment: Deconverting from New Religions (Indiana) and *Victimized Daughters: Incest and the Development of the Female* (Routledge). She has spent the last several years studying modern descendants of the Spanish Crypto-Jews and her book on the subject is forthcoming from the University of California Press.

LAUREL KEARNS (Ph.D. Emory University) is Associate Professor of Sociology of Religion at the Drew University Graduate and Theological Schools, with a special focus on religions and ecology. She has published several articles on Christian-related ecological activism, and is working on a book on the subject: *Saving the Creation: Christian Environmentalism in the U.S.* Her current research, on the emerging environmental justice movement, pays particular attention to issues of ecological degradation in communities of color.

J. SHAWN LANDRES (MA, C.Phil., University of California, Santa Barbara; M. St, University of Oxford) is a doctoral candidate in Religious Studies at the University of California, Santa Barbara, and a research student in Social Anthropology at Lincoln College, Oxford. Most recently he was a member of the faculty of the Institute of Social and Cultural Studies, Matej Bel University, Banská Bystrica, Slovakia. He has published several articles on Generation X and religion, as well as sociological and anthropological studies in ritual, identity, and civil society in East-Central Europe and the United States. He has done fieldwork in the Slovak Republic and the United States.

MEREDITH B. McGUIRE (Ph.D. New School for Social Research) is Professor of Sociology and Anthropology at Trinity University. She is past-President of both the Society for the Scientific Study of Religion and the Association for the Sociology of Religion. She is the author of *Religion: The Social Context* (Wadsworth), *Ritual Healing in Suburban America* (Rutgers), and *Pentecostal Catholics* (Temple), among other works. Her fieldwork sites include rural Ireland, suburban New Jersey, and San Antonio, Texas. Her current research examines U.S. popular religion and spirituality in a historical and cross-cultural context.

NANCY NASON-CLARK (Ph.D. London School of Economics) is Professor of Sociology at the University of New Brunswick in Canada and the coordinator of the Religion and Violence Research Team of the Muriel

McQueen Fergusson Centre for Family Violence Research. She is past-President of the Association for the Sociology of Religion. She has most recently authored *The Battered Wife: How Christians Confront Family Violence* (Westminster/John Knox Press) and numerous articles and book chapters exploring the link between religion, violence, and gender. She is currently completing a book entitled *Congregations and Family Crisis*.

MARY JO NEITZ (Ph.D. University of Chicago) is Professor of Sociology at the University of Missouri at Columbia. She is past-Chair of the Sociology of Religion section of the American Sociological Association, and author of *Charisma and Community: A Study of Religious Commitment Within the Charismatic Renewal* (Transaction). She is completing a second fieldwork-based book, *Crafting Tradition: Wicca, Community, and Cultural Change*, on her study of feminist and neopagan witches in North America.

MILAGROS PEÑA (Ph.D. State University of New York at Stony Brook) is Associate Professor of Sociology and Women's Studies at the University of Florida. She is the author of *Theologies and Liberation in Peru: The Role of Ideas in Social Movements* (Temple), and several articles on Latinas and religion. She is currently working on a book manuscript comparing non-governmental women's organizations in Michoacán with those in the greater El Paso, Texas, region of the United States.

JAMES V. SPICKARD (Ph.D. Graduate Theological Union) is Associate Professor of Sociology and Anthropology at the University of Redlands and Research Consulting Professor at the Fielding Institute. He has published extensively on sociological and anthropological approaches to religion, and is the co-editor of *World History from the World's Historians* (McGraw-Hill). His fieldwork includes studies of a new Japanese religion, a liberal Episcopal congregation, and Catholic social activists. His recent work examines the logic of universal human rights in a multicultural world.

THOMAS A. TWEED (Ph.D. Stanford) teaches Religious Studies and American Studies at the University of North Carolina and serves as associate dean for undergraduate curricula. He has authored or edited four books, including the award-winning *Our Lady of the Exile: Diasporic Religion at a Cuban Catholic Shrine in Miami* (Oxford). Most of his historical and ethnographic research has focused on religions in the United States, especially Roman Catholicism and Asian religions.

MELISSA M. WILCOX (Ph.D. University of California at Santa Barbara) is a faculty fellow in Religious Studies at the University of California, Santa Barbara. Her research focuses on the role of religion in individual and communal identity within lesbian, gay, bisexual, and transgender communities.

Index

Academy/academic life, 25, 27–33, 34, 39, 48–49, 56–57, 78–80, 83–86, 133, 144, 233, 240
activism, 27–32, 58–59, 113–124, 189, 212–216, 221, 224, 226
African Americans, 127–133, 175–191, 213–214
"anglas," 117–118
anointing power, 135, 143
anthropology, 3, 4–5, 42, 64, 75–87, 100, 109–110, 131–133, 227; critiques of traditional ethnography, 8–9, 12, 131–132, 143, 199, 228–229, 232, 239, 241–244; vs. sociology, 7, 100, 218, 237–239
Appalachia, 134–145
artifacts, 21–22, 66–68
Australia, 138, 140, 141, 144
authenticity, 26, 59, 129–131, 146–147, 159–160, 198, 232–233
authority, 227, 230–231, 233, 237

belief, 77, 87, 100
Bhagwan Shree Rajneesh (Osho), 146–150, 157
bisexual, 47–50. *See also* LGBT
blues singer, 185–188, 191
body, 204–206, 208–210, 211, 217
boundaries, borders, 6, 30–31, 33–46, 47–51, 78–80, 82, 89, 95, 111–112, 117–119, 131–133, 156–157, 208, 213, 222, 242; U.S./Mexico border, 113–124. *See also* insider/outsider; Self/Other

California. *See* Metropolitan Community Church; New Song Church
Catholics, 21–22, 34, 66–74, 90, 92, 94, 199–200, 206–207, 210

Chicanas, Chicana, Chicano, 114–122
children, 28
Christianity: African American, African, 67, 175, 184–187, 190, 191, 213–214; Base Christian groups, 118–119; charismatic/pentecostal, 34, 77–83, 134–143, 199–200, 206–207, 210; conservative/evangelical, 32, 77–83, 102, 107, 110, 162–174, 213; Cuban Catholicism, 66–72; gender roles, 27; and homosexuals, 50–59
class, social, 176–182, 183–184, 186–187, 188–189, 213, 238–239, 248
clergy, 28, 39, 67, 71, 135–138, 139–140, 142, 186, 215
colonialism, 7, 127–128, 176, 188, 208, 229, 237, 239, 241, 245–246, 247, 249–251
Color Purple, The, 175–191
composites, 162–174
confidentiality, 52–53, 146–147, 149, 154, 157–159
conversion, 63, 72–73, 79, 82, 90–95, 102, 108–109, 200
cross-cultural encounter, 75–87, 132, 234, 239–240, 248, 250–251
crypto-Judaism. *See* Judaism
culture, 132; anthropological approaches to, 8, 65, 131, 229, 231–232, 239; and nature, 217–218, 221, 223; writing about, 8–9, 11–12, 25, 131–133, 134–135

dialogical approach, 231–235, 240, 248, 250–251
diaspora, 66–67
discourse, 82, 85–86, 87, 98, 227, 239
dreams, 23

El Paso/Ciudad Juarez, 113–114, 116–124
emotion, 11, 18–20, 25, 27–32, 74, 96, 207–209
environment, 212–224
epistemology, 5, 9, 12, 18, 49, 63, 68, 73, 84,
    103, 211, 231, 244–251
ethics, 9, 54–56, 130, 133
ethnicity. *See* identity, ethnic
ethnography: anthropological vs. sociological,
    7, 100, 199, 237–239; as construct,
    146–161, 244; critical, 38, 175–177, 190,
    191; criticizing traditional forms, 4–8, 44,
    85–86, 88, 103, 142–145, 146, 159–160,
    199, 216, 218, 232, 239, 241–244, 246,
    247–248; and death, 144–145; as "deep
    hanging out," 142–143, 244; and emotion,
    19–20, 74, 207, 240; and the environment,
    212–224; gendered, 207; "going native,"
    42–43, 49, 70–71, 77, 129–130, 157,
    237–238; and literature, 175–191; as mu-
    tual reflection, 132, 233–235; as partial, 19,
    176–177; postmodern, 9, 88, 127, 244,
    245–246; reading, 162–174, 175–191; as
    representation, 100–112, 130–133, 134–145,
    248; and self-discovery, 18–20, 24–25,
    95–99, 156–157; as transformation, 25–26,
    27–32, 70–71, 95–99, 214; writing, 8–9,
    11–12, 25, 33, 43–44, 127, 130–133,
    134–145, 146–147, 150–152, 155–156,
    159–160, 242–244. *See also* identity, of
    ethnographer; reflexivity
ethnohermeneutics, 233–235
eurocentrism, 231
experience, 195–198, 204–210
"experience-distant"/"experience-near,"
    195–198

family, 30–32
feminism, 4, 38, 99, 113–114, 120–121, 124,
    163, 166, 169–171, 156–157, 217–218, 224;
    feminist research methods, 43, 45, 115; fem-
    inist theory, 89, 191, 231
field, the, 78–80, 83–84, 85, 102–105
fieldwork, 4–8, 44, 63–65, 66, 75–77, 78–84,
    90–92, 95–98, 101–102, 105–110, 114–119,
    128–129, 132, 135–142, 152–154, 199–200,
    201–205, 214, 216, 239–240; as magic,
    75–77, 83, 87. *See also* ethnography

gay. *See* LGBT
gaze, anthropological, 80–81, 111

gender, 23, 27, 31–32, 44, 98, 119–120,
    162–164, 173, 178, 201–203, 208
generalizing inquiry, 1–2, 248
globalization, 77–78, 101

healing, 205–206, 210, 216
hermeneutics, 227–228, 233–234
history, historians, 63, 65, 73, 210–211, 232
Holiness Church, 134–139, 142
homosexual. *See* LGBT
Hopi Indians, 225–226, 230, 232

identity, 33–46; construction, 19, 25–26, 51,
    92–95, 146–147; ethnic, 70, 92–95, 98–99,
    106; of ethnographer, 6–7, 24–25, 35–43,
    50–51, 52–53, 57, 68–71, 89, 95–99,
    101–102, 106–107, 108–109, 111, 200–204,
    241; of informant, 25–26, 40–41, 47–49, 66,
    92–93, 95–96; postmodern, 92–95; sexual,
    48, 57, 60; social, 6–7; stigmatized, 51–52.
    See also self-presentation
immigrants, 66–74, 115–118, 132
imperialism. *See* colonialism
Inquisition, 90, 93–95, 97, 99
insider/outsider, 6, 33–46, 48–51, 57, 68–71,
    73, 115–116, 157, 163, 172, 229–230. *See
    also* Self/Other
intercultural understanding. *See* cross-cultural
    encounter
interpreter's position, 68–75, 100, 241–242
Ireland, 201–205

Judaism, 104–105, 108–109; crypto-Judaism,
    89–99; Orthodox, 21, 24–25; Sephardic, 90,
    92, 97, 99

kashrut 108

Latinas/Latinos, 113–124, 215
lesbian, 34–35. *See also* LGBT
LGBT, 47–60
Livets Ord ("Word of Life Foundation"),
    77–83, 86

Ma Anand Sheela (Sheela Silverman),
    146–147, 153–154, 157
Mama Lola, 127–133, 160
meaning, 2, 19–20, 24, 26, 35, 39, 50, 55, 65,
    66–68, 85, 95–99, 123, 144–145, 187,
    195–198, 200, 210, 216, 227, 233, 243

memory, 17–19, 66, 93–95, 97, 204–205
Metropolitan Community Church, 50–53
Mexico, 91–93, 95–96. *See also* El Paso/Ciudad
   Juarez; U.S./Mexico border
Miami, 66–70
millenialism, 225–226
mimesis, 75–77, 83, 85, 87
mind/body/self, 204–205, 209
ministers. *See* clergy
mothers, 17–19, 21–23, 28, 201–205, 207

narrative, 9, 12, 17–19, 23, 25–26, 43–44, 45,
   81, 82, 92–95, 97–98, 115–116, 160,
   162–163, 165–166, 170, 206, 239
Native Americans, 67, 219, 220, 228. *See also*
   Hopi Indians
nature, 212–224
Newark, N.J., 214–216, 222
New Song Church, 102, 107, 110
non-government organizations (NGOs),
   115–122
non-institutional religion. *See* religion, non-
   institutional

objectivity, 5, 10, 20, 27, 42, 49, 54, 57, 89,
   92–93, 195–196, 199, 207, 218, 227, 239,
   244. *See also* subjectivity
oppression, 93–95, 98, 113–114, 121, 124,
   176–185, 186–187, 188–190
orientalism/occidentalism, 226, 228–229,
   231–233, 239, 241
Other, 8, 42, 75, 82–83, 85, 99, 102–103,
   106–110, 142, 213, 218, 226, 228–231,
   238–239, 246. *See also* Self

particularizing inquiry, 2–4, 44
passion, 29, 31
patriarchy, 8, 38, 40, 41, 59, 162–163, 166, 169,
   207
phenomenology, 197–198, 209–210
pilgrims, 66–67, 69–70
politics, 7, 9, 57, 70–71, 84, 101, 108, 116–124,
   179, 185–186, 189, 212–215, 225–226, 233,
   237–238, 240–241, 249–250
postmodern, 92–95, 162–163, 232–233. *See
   also* ethnography, postmodern
power, 233, 234; organizational, 164, 166,
   167–168, 171–172, 191; political, 7, 79,
   120–121, 179, 214, 249; social, 7–8, 10, 42,
   26, 59, 80, 84, 85–86, 127, 132, 176–191,

207; spiritual, 134–135; in submission,
   163–166, 167, 172–173
presentation. *See* self-presentation
prophecy, 225–226
Protestants, 77, 78–83, 102, 107, 110, 134–135,
   162–173, 185–186, 213, 216

race, racism, 116, 175–191. *See also* identity,
   ethnic
Rajneeshpuram, 146–149, 154, 157
reading. *See* ethnography, reading
reflexivity, 20, 21, 25, 73, 82, 83, 98, 100,
   102–105, 107, 108–110, 127–129, 210,
   239
regulative ideals, 244–251
religion (*see also specific religions*): conflict
   in, 164–172, 179; general study of, 10,
   13–14, 218–220, 226, 234–235; indigenous, 225–226, 238–239; and nature,
   218–219, 220–222, 224; non-institutional,
   21–22, 26, 127–129, 219; and violence,
   28–32. *See also* women, religion and spirituality of
representation, 8–9, 19, 24–25, 43–44, 53–54,
   65–66, 75–77, 81–82, 85–86, 103, 106–112,
   130–133, 143–145, 229, 232. *See also*
   ethnography
resistance, 176–177, 179, 181, 183–184, 187,
   189
rituals, 21–22, 35–36, 39–40, 65, 66, 72, 73, 74,
   76, 79, 80, 95, 96–98, 128–129, 134–136,
   137–138
Rotary Club, 101, 107

sannyasin, 147–159
Self, 76, 89, 95–99, 140–142, 144–145, 233. *See
   also* Other
Self/Other, 49, 76, 82, 144–145, 240
self-presentation 51–54, 81–82, 101–102,
   106–107
self-reflection, 8, 18, 21, 25, 227–231. *See also*
   reflexivity
serpent handling, 134–145
shrines, 21–22, 66–67, 71–72
Slovakia, 101, 104, 106, 108, 109, 111
social class, 176–182, 183–184, 186–187,
   188–189, 213, 238–239, 248
social movements, 116–122, 212–215
South, the, 175–191
Southwest, the, 90–91, 95–96, 97, 113–124

subjectivity, 5, 25, 27, 45, 59, 76–77, 198, 201,
    205, 207, 209, 247–248. *See also* objectivity
Sweden. *See* Livets Ord ("Word of Life Organi-
    zation")

talented tenth, 184; the female, 177
texts, 227, 229, 232, 233, 239
theology, theologians, 84–85
therapy, 21, 22, 24–25
transgender. *See* LGBT

universalism, 231–232, 249
univocality, 162–174
U.S./Mexico border, 113–124

violence, 28–32, 178–182, 188–189
Vodou, 127–129, 216

voyeurism, 143–144
vulnerability, 26, 129, 210–203

"watched watcher," 107–108, 111
Wicca, witches, 33–35, 37–38, 40–41, 44, 45
women, 24–25, 33–46, 131, 146–147, 150–152,
    162–174, 175–191, 201–204, 214; intuition,
    206–208, 211; violence against, 11, 27–32,
    120; women, religion and spirituality of, 34,
    41, 43, 90–92, 94–96, 118–120, 162–174;
    women's movement, 113–114, 116–124,
    179
Word of Life. *See* Livets Ord ("Word of Life
    Foundation")
writing, 8–9, 11–12, 35, 33, 43–44, 103, 127,
    130–133, 134–145, 146–147, 150–152,
    155–156, 159–160, 227–228, 232